The Power of Urban _____ _____ Places

The Power of Urban Ethnic Places discusses the growing visibility of ethnic heritage places in American society. The book examines a spectrum of case studies of Chinese, Latino and African American communities in the U.S. It disagrees with the perception the rise of ethnic enclaves and heritage places are signs of separatism or balkanization. The author argues instead for an understanding of how they generate new businesses and jobs, address racial injustice, and create a framework for multicultural inclusion in American public history, education, and the arts. By understanding urban ethnic places, the text discusses how we can be better prepared to harness the changes related to globalization rather than be hurt or divided by forces of economic restructuring and social change.

Jan Lin immigrated to the U.S. from Taiwan in 1966. He has been teaching sociology at Occidental College since 1998. He is the author of *Reconstructing Chinatown: Ethnic Enclave, Global Change* (Minneapolis: University of Minnesota Press, 1998), and *The Urban Sociology Reader* (London: Routledge, 2005).

Metropolis and Modern Life
A Routledge Series
Edited by Anthony Orum, University of Illinois, Chicago and
Zachary Neal, Michigan State University

This series brings original perspectives on key topics in urban research to today's students in a series of short accessible texts, guided readers, and practical handbooks. Each volume examines how longstanding urban phenomena continue to be relevant in an increasingly urban and global world, and in doing so, connects the best new scholarship with the wider concerns of students seeking to understand life in the twenty-first-century metropolis.

Available
The Gentrification Debates by Japonica Brown-Saracino
Common Ground? by Anthony Orum and Zachary Neal

Forthcoming
The Connected City by Zachary Neal
World of Suburbs by Richard Harris
Urban Tourism and 21st Century Cities by Costas Spirou

The Power of Urban Ethnic Places

Cultural Heritage and Community Life

Jan Lin

Routledge
Taylor & Francis Group

NEW YORK AND LONDON

First published 2011
by Routledge
270 Madison Ave, New York, NY 10016

Simultaneously published in the UK
by Routledge
2 Park Square, Milton Park, Abingdon, Oxon OX14 4RN

Routledge is an imprint of the Taylor & Francis Group, an informa business

© 2011 Taylor & Francis

Typeset in Adobe Caslon and Copperplate Gothic by
Florence Production Ltd, Stoodleigh, Devon
Printed and bound in the United States of America on acid-free paper by
Walsworth Publishing Company, Marceline, MO

Library of Congress Cataloging in Publication Data
Lin, Jan.
    The power of urban ethnic places: cultural heritage and
community life/Jan Lin—1st ed.
        p. cm.—(Metropolis and modern life)
    Includes bibliographical references and index.
    1. Sociology, Urban—United States.   2. Ethnic neighborhoods—
United States—History.   3. Minorities—United States—Politics
and government.   I. Title.
HT123.L466 2011
307.76089′00973—dc22   2010015831

ISBN13: 978–0–415–87982–8 (hbk)
ISBN13: 978–0–415–87983–5 (pbk)
ISBN13: 978–0–203–84301–7 (ebk)

CONTENTS

ILLUSTRATIONS

Figures

Tables

SERIES FOREWORD
ANTHONY ORUM AND ZACHARY NEAL

This series brings original perspectives on key topics in urban research to today's students in a series of short accessible texts, guided readers, and practical handbooks. Each volume examines how longstanding urban phenomena continue to be relevant in an increasingly urban and global world, and in doing so, connects the best new scholarship with the wider concerns of students seeking to understand life in the twenty-first-century metropolis.

In this addition to the series, Jan Lin shows how the modern metropolis is being remade by efforts to preserve the ethnic heritage and culture in several major American cities. Lin devoted many years and a great deal of time to a detailed study of different ethnic sites in four major American cities: Houston, Los Angeles, Miami and New York City. In each city he examined how ethnic groups had entered the city, how they were treated by the indigenous population and institutions, and the ultimate result of their efforts to make new settlements in the city. As a careful social historian, Lin argues that only in recent times have the efforts by ethnic groups and institutions actually promoted the development of new ethnic centers, museums, and other sites in the city, the result of which has been to help establish a new metropolis as the older one has disappeared. He shows, for example, how the efforts to develop Chinatowns in Los Angeles and

New York City have varied, and how the ethnic preservation efforts in Houston have differed from those in Miami. Through this comprehensive and insightful treatment of many sites, his work discloses the importance of ethnic culture and ethnic cultural movements in recent times. Lin also considers some key dilemmas, among them the one that exists between the efforts to preserve an authentic ethnic culture in the form of new memorials and sites, on the one hand, and the interest of local leaders and officials to use such sites to promote tourism and bring new monies into the city, on the other. This book, in the end, is a powerful, indeed memorable, demonstration of the changing nature of the contemporary metropolis, and of how the thousands of new immigrants are helping to remake it in vital and significant ways.

PREFACE

This book is a tool for educators to spark student discovery of the multicultural heritage of American cities. I wish to expose teachers and students to cultural heritage outreach, documentary, and field research opportunities in urban minority communities. The book will be of interest to those promoting community-based learning and civic engagement in the academy. Educators and students are key constituencies in the public history sector as researchers, volunteers, and audiences. As both producers and consumers of historical knowledge, they play an important role in preserving ethnic history and making heritage relevant to the continuing life of ethnic communities and their relation to broader public life in America.

The emergence of a multicultural heritage sector represents the new power of minority communities to fight racism and discriminatory stereotypes, portray historical struggles against injustice, and create more cohesive cultural identities to address continuing challenges. Through their contributions to public history, ethnic heritage places enrich our broader collective imagination as our cities are experiencing the shocks of global economic and cultural transition. Cultural heritage work can promote trust, reciprocity, and social capital in ethnic communities confronted by urban decline, disinvestment, and poverty.

I was inspired to write this book through people I met while volunteering and doing field research at ethnic history museums and heritage centers in Chinese, Latino, and African American neighborhoods in four U.S. cities, namely New York, Miami, Houston, and Los Angeles. I assess the economic challenges and political variables they contend with through case study comparisons, and identify some demonstration projects and best practices that emerged in the course of my field research. I give suggestions for sustaining the future of ethnic heritage work through enhancing partnerships with the educational sector as well as the arts.

This book takes an interdisciplinary point of view, and is most relevant to courses in sociology, history, and urban planning. It also suits interdisciplinary programs such as American studies and ethnic studies. I offer a comparative cross-ethnic perspective where prevailing studies usually focus on single ethnic minority groups. I address the micro-dynamics of urban street and neighborhood life as well as the macro-dynamics of immigration, urban investment, and transnational capitalism in our contemporary cities. My book addresses the interaction between local and global dynamics, of community change in global context, in a way not commonly addressed in the existing literature. I also explore the role of cultural heritage in strategies of economic and community recovery from disaster in the case of New York's Chinatown after the 9/11 disaster.

ACKNOWLEDGMENTS

The publication of this book owes much to the commitment of Stephen Rutter of Routledge and book series editor, Anthony Orum, who showed sustained interest and gave ongoing encouragement as the manuscript was being reviewed and underwent the revision process. I thank them and the anonymous reviewers for their thoughtful criticisms on the structure and argument, and suggestions on broadening the book's appeal for general readers such as enhancing the quality of personal narrative.

A shorter version of Chapter 6 was published previously as "Los Angeles Chinatown: Tourism, Gentrification, and the Rise of an Ethnic Growth Machine," *Amerasia Journal* 34, 3 (2008): 110–25. I thank editor Russell Leong and Kyeyoung Park for their comments.

I wish to acknowledge all the participants in the Los Angeles Chinatown Oral History Project in spring 2006. I thank all the Occidental College students in my two Freshman Cultural Studies Program seminars on Los Angeles, "From Pueblo to World City," and project assistant Elizabeth Chang. Special recognition goes to Philip Arsenis, Kristen Bonilla, Claudia Castillo, Jason Ellinwood, Colin Englesberg, Cristina Franco, Peter Ringold, and Amy Unger for conducting the interviews that were excerpted in Chapter 1. Thanks to the oral history informants quoted, including Suellen Chang, Ella Yee

Quan, Munson Kwok and Don Toy. Eugene Moy of the Chinese Historical Society of Southern California and Pauline Wong of the Museum of the Chinese in the Americas helped organize the project and identify informants for students to interview.

The Center for Community-Based Learning at Occidental College and its director Maria Avila were also helpful in sending me to the "Arts and Community Development" conference sponsored by Florida Learn and Serve, held in Coral Gables, Florida in spring 2006. The research in Chapter 5 was supported by a Faculty Enrichment Grant from Occidental College that funded a research trip to Miami in summer 2007. The Faculty Enrichment Grant also funded some production costs for the book.

The U.S. Department of Housing and Urban Development grant that I directed for Occidental College from 1999 to 2002 funded by the Office of University Partnerships for a Community Outreach Partnership Center was helpful for stimulating my practical involvements and research. Among the community partners I recognize are Kathy Mas-Gallegos of Avenue 50 Studio, Linda Allen (artist, gallery owner, and a leader of the Eagle Rock Community Preservation and Revitalization Organization), and Nicole Possert of the Highland Park Heritage Trust, and Suzanne Siegel of the Arroyo Arts Collective, the L.A. Bridges After-School Program that partners Luther-Burbank Middle School and the Hathaway (Sycamores) Family Resource Center in Highland Park, and the Arroyo Seco Academy of Franklin High School.

The research in Chapter 2 was supported by a Miner D. Crary Summer Fellowship from Amherst College in 1996 that funded research trips to Miami and Los Angeles. An earlier version of the chapter was published as "Globalization and the Revalorizing of Ethnic Places in Immigration Gateway Cities," *Urban Affairs Review* 34, 2 (November 1998): 313–39. I thank Leland Saito, Sharon Zukin, editor Dennis Judd, and anonymous reviewers for their suggestions and criticisms.

The research in Chapter 4 was supported by a Research Initiation Grant from the University of Houston in the summer of 1994.

Jacqueline Hagan, Nestor Rodriguez, and Gary Dworkin were helpful in familiarizing me with Houston's ethnic communities. An earlier version of the chapter was published as an article, "Ethnic Places, Postmodernism, and Urban Change in Houston," in *Sociological Quarterly* 36, 4 (1995): 629–47. I thank Bill Simon, Lynn Randolph, Sharon Zukin, Ron Lembo, editor Norman Denzin, and anonymous reviewers for their helpful comments during the writing of that article.

I thank other intellectual colleagues and friends who have given me their critical and constructive feedback over the years, including Karin Aguilar-San Juan, Warren Goldstein, Joel Stillerman, Perry Chang, Susan Pearce, Juulia Kauste, Phil Kasinitz, and Lily Hoffman. I signal Andy Carroll for his camaraderie and regularly asking about my research. He provoked dialogue and reflection that helped clarify my thinking. I recall especially a discussion we had while walking on the National Mall in Washington, DC during the Smithsonian Folklife Festival in the summer of 2006 that precipitated a particularly memorable instance of intellectual epiphany.

I give thanks also to people who gave me special help in the field, including Charlie Lai, Cynthia Lee, Frank Lang, Thomas Yu, Amy Chin, John Leo, Lenwood Johnson, Dan Nip, William Estrada, Bruce Kaji, Cook Sunoo, Dorothy Fields, Kris Smith, Philip Bacon, Irby McKnight, Leslie Pantin, Tony Wagner, Tanya Bravo, and Corinne Moebius.

I acknowledge also family members, Fu-Yun Lin, Ben Lin, Dorothy Patterson Lin, Fiona Lin, Sam Lin, Qian Zhang, Sofia Lin and Kenneth Lin for their support and encouragement. My wife Nina Froeschle has been a dear companion and sweet source of inspiration during the years of research and writing of my book.

ABBREVIATIONS

AAFE	Asian Americans for Equality
AAFEE	Asian Americans for Equal Employment
AAFNY	Asian American Federation of New York
AFSCME	American Federation of State, County, and Municipal Employees
APV	Allen Parkway Village
ASA	American Sociological Association
BAME Church	Bethel African Methodist Church
BID	business improvement district
CACA	Chinese American Citizens Alliance
CAMLA	Chinese American Museum of Los Angeles
CBD	central business district
CCBA	Consolidated Chinese Benevolent Association
CDC	community development corporation
CHSSC	Chinese Historical Society of Southern California
CIA	Central Intelligence Agency
COPC	Community Outreach Partnership Center
CPC	Chinatown Planning Council
CPDC	Civic Partnership and Design Center
CRA	Community Redevelopment Agency

CREATE	Committee to Revitalize and Enrich the Arts in Tomorrow's Economy in Chinatown
CSWA	Chinatown Staff and Workers Association
DOT	Department of Transportation
DPZ	Duany Plater-Zyberk and Company, Architects and Town Planners
FEMA	Federal Emergency Management Agency
HACH	Housing Authority of the City of Houston
HUD	Department of Housing and Urban Development
LISC	Local Initiatives Support Corporation
M&M	Merchants and Manufacturers Association
MDPL	Miami Design Preservation League
MOCA	Museum of Contemporary Art
MoCA	Museum of the Chinese in the Americas
MTA	Metropolitan Transportation Authority
NAACP	National Association for Advancement of Colored People
NAFTA	North American Free Trade Agreement
NASA	National Aeronautic and Space Administration
NET	Neighborhood Enhancement Team
NYCHP	New York Chinatown History Project
PRC	People's Republic of China
PTSD	post-traumatic stress disorder
RCI	Rebuild Chinatown Initiative
RLI	Request for Letter of Intent
SEIU	Service Employees International Union
WTC	World Trade Center
YMRP	Young Mother's Residential Program

1

DOING ETHNIC HISTORY FROM COAST TO COAST

East Coast Memories

I came to the United States at the age of five from Taiwan and grew up in the suburbs of Washington, D.C. While I culturally assimilated to the English language and American ways of life and did well in high school, I never quite fitted into the social mainstream and had a tight group of off-center friends, some with anti-establishment views. At college in the early 1980s, I gravitated to campus student movements organizing around such issues as opposition to South African apartheid through divestment and a renewed peace movement for nuclear arms control. There was the growth of identity politics connecting to social movements for women, racial–ethnic minorities and gays/lesbians. After college I worked as a management analyst in public service with the unemployment office in Boston, Massachusetts and volunteered as a tenant organizer on the weekends. I had learned to work on a professional level within the governmental establishment but I continued to do my rabble-raising in the Somerville neighborhood where I lived.

I entered graduate school in the late 1980s at the New School for Social Research in New York City, a compact university located in Greenwich Village that was a historical fount of dissidence and critical thinking. Faculty and students were actively engaged in agendas of academic research as well as social movement politics. My mentor, Janet Abu-Lughod, was a world-renowned scholar in urban and globalization research with experience also in planning and community studies. She encouraged me to do action research in the field and sparked my understanding of how social change in local and neighborhood contexts are affected by world-level forces. After doing participatory action research as an organizer and recording secretary with the Joint Planning Council of the Lower East Side, I turned to Manhattan's Chinatown as my focus for research and action. Around this time, I learned of the work of the New York Chinatown History Project, established by founders such as John Kuo Wei Tchen and Charlie Lai, to preserve and document the history of Chinese immigration through the gateway of New York City. I volunteered as an intern as part of the team documenting research and an exhibition on the history of garment workers. I also worked on the board of It's Time, a Chinatown housing and community development organization.

On the West Coast, Chinese American historians were already broadening public understanding of the legacy of Chinese immigration into the mining and railroad industries and their subjection to terrible collective racial violence and immigrant exclusion from the late nineteenth century to the mid-twentieth centuries.[1] The East Coast was somewhat a backdrop to the West Coast story until the 1960s, when dynamics of "globalization" brought new flows of Chinese labor and capital and Manhattan's Chinatown emerged to become America's largest Chinese enclave.[2] While there was less of a history of "ethnic cleansing" episodes on the East Coast, the historians of the New York Chinatown History Project brought attention to the history of immigrant struggle and adjustment in the tenement neighborhoods and sweatshops of the manufacturing and service sector. The laundry workers and garment workers of the East Coast were heroes of Chinese American history like the miners and railroad workers of the West Coast.

I was drawn to the work of the New York Chinatown History Project through a sense of personal epiphany and self-discovery. I was already intrigued by the history of the Lower East Side as a portal of immigration to the United States. The adjacent ethnic enclave of Chinatown gave me an opportunity to examine the ancestors to my own Chinese American odyssey, immigrants who didn't have as comfortable a middle-class upbringing as I did and had to struggle over greater barriers of economic hardship and racial prejudice. Other projects were emerging like the Eldridge Street Synagogue and the Tenement Museum established by Ruth Abrams, to preserve the ethnic heritage of Little Italy and the Jewish Lower East Side. Going to Chinatown for me became a cultural pilgrimage of personal discovery as well as a being in a field site for ethnographic and participant action research. Chinatown was for me not a religious site, but a spiritual and educational destination. My pilgrimage was a search for ethnic heritage.

I make a comparison between my local and urban exploration of roots and racial–ethnic heritage in the immigrant gateway of Chinatown and the Lower East Side, to international pilgrimages to ancestral homelands or cultural heritage sites such as the phenomenon of Chinese Americans going to China. Jewish Americans make quite comparable journeys when they visit the Tenement Museum or Holocaust museums, tour the concentration camps of Eastern Europe, or travel to Israel to work on a kibbutz. Ethnic heritage sites offer explorations of ethnic collective memory that may be locally rooted or dispersed in a global diaspora. In the U.S. context, they pluralize our understanding of public history and collective memory while charting the way to a more internationalist understanding of America's place in the still changing global order.

A decade earlier, Alex Haley had documented his own pilgrimage of cultural heritage discovery in Africa with the story of his ancestor, Kunta Kinte, who was kidnapped in Gambia and brought to the province of Maryland in 1767 to be a slave. His 1976 documentary novel, *Roots: The Saga of an American Family*, was subsequently developed into a popular television mini-series and won the Pulitzer Prize. Alex Haley ultimately took some legal challenges related to authorship but his cumulative efforts did a lot to spur interest in family genealogy and ethnic heritage work in America.[3] President Barack Obama made a similar pilgrimage to Kenya in his journey to see his father and meet the African side of his family, in the final section of his book, *Dreams from My Father: A Story of Race and Inheritance.*

West Coast Oral Histories

In spring 2006, in my current role as sociology professor at Occidental College in Los Angeles, California, I taught two sections of a freshman undergraduate seminar called "Los Angeles: From Pueblo to World City." A significant part of the work for the semester was a community-based learning project in Los Angeles Chinatown that put the students to work in teams to conduct oral histories of leaders in the community. We all read Lisa See's colorful and well-researched family history, *On Gold Mountain: The One-Hundred-Year-Old Odyssey of My Chinese-American Family*, and made field orientation trips to Chinatown. We partnered with the Chinese American Museum of Los Angeles and the Chinese Historical Society of Southern California to identify dozens of leaders representing different sectors of business and community life, including restaurants, art galleries, journalistic media, community organizing, education, the historical societies, and also a former Miss Chinatown. We tried to create a sample that was mix-gendered and included a variety of adult age groups.[4]

This Los Angeles oral history project was different from my earlier work in New York City that exposed the quiet struggles of the Chinese proletariat, laundry workers, and garment workers who toiled unseen but contributed to the classic iconography of immigrant labor and adjustment to America. The Los Angeles Chinatown oral histories were more representative of the middle-class business and community leadership. Our students posed general open-ended questions about personal memories of family life and growing up, vocational and voluntary accomplishments, and reflections on history and social change in Los Angeles Chinatown.

The Los Angeles Chinatown oral history project was a significant experience of intergenerational and intercultural encounter, since the college students were mainly white and Latino and decades younger than the informants. I was about a decade younger than many of the informants, but I feel very much a part of the same social movement, commonly described as the Asian American movement.[5] I wanted the students to experience education through active real-world involvement with people and a community beyond the textbook. Oral history work offers great opportunities for transformative intercultural experience in the interaction between interviewers, interviewees, and audiences. I feature particularly excerpts from the founders and leaders of Chinese American historical societies and community organizing groups. Their voices resonate with the wisdom and energy of decades of professional and voluntary work documenting the oral history and heritage of Chinese Americans and promoting the value of social activism and educational volunteerism to the community.

Suellen Cheng is a curator at the El Pueblo de Los Angeles Cultural Monument and founding president of the Chinese American Museum of Los Angeles and speaks of overcoming personal shame over humble beginnings and promoting the history of immigrant struggle in Los Angeles Chinatown:

> I think being a historian, I have the responsibility of sharing the experiences and stories of all individuals and not just the select stories of the elites. I grew up learning the history of important people's stories, and often felt ashamed of sharing my story, because everybody would say, "Oh what did your father do?" . . . I was ashamed of even talking about my mother, because my mother was not fortunate to actually even have a day of formal education. In Fujian province, where they were born, they were poor and they were in the remote countryside.[6]

Suellen has directed, trained, and mentored many students and professional staff over the years in the business of researching, curating, and exhibiting ethnic artifacts and heritage, fundraising, staff development, and building management. The day she spoke with Occidental College students, there was the sound of marchers from a passing demonstration protesting for immigrant rights, and she stressed that "history is actually repeating itself" as she reflected on the earlier struggle of immigrant ancestors. It was May Day, May 1, the international day of labor protest, which has drawn new support in recent years in U.S. cities from the immigrant rights movement.

Ella Yee Quan, a founder of the Chinese Historical Society of Southern California, reflects with humor and aplomb on the personal as well as the public side of oral history work. Her challenge to promote the oral history of Chinese American women continues to resonate. Ella Yee is one of four Chinese American women honored on a temporary mural (1994–2000) at a Chinatown Metro plaza on Cesar Chavez Boulevard done by the artist Carolyn Nye.

> It was fun because we started something and we kept pushing it into people's faces, like this is the historical society and we interviewed people and we were able to publish some books with the history and some of the history surprised us. We are American born and from there I went on to looking up my own family history. I was going to write it up but I didn't, but all the materials of us [are] there and we have gotten a lot of people interested. And we worked on the World War II war book about the Chinese that were in the war because everybody mentions one group of people and ignores everyone else so we had our book. And we interviewed three, four hundred veterans and I think we found only two women but anyways, it was put into a book form, but many of the families, the young ones, sons, grandsons, great grandsons were particularly interested to see what their ancestors and grandparents did in the war. But when the book came out they all became interested and more and more people went and studied it up and researched their history. That was very satisfying.[7]

Munson Kwok came to Los Angeles Chinatown from San Francisco, descended from a Chinese American family that arrived by ship at the northern Californian coast in the early 1860s. He says that the Chinese Historical Society of Southern California was founded from social agitation from a diverse social leadership to create a social movement that would foster a more coherent community self-identity. In his account, the promoting of heritage and community self-identity becomes defensive weaponry against community threat or degradation:

> We got into the history side of things at the time, which was around the early 1970s. The community's identity was something that was being questioned, especially by the government establishment here. A place like Chinatown had a lot of impoverished people—immigrants who were of Chinese extraction, given over either as refugees during the time of the Vietnam War, or after 1955, as poor immigrants. They were not getting their fair share of city, or community, services. The reason that they were not is that they didn't have a cohesive identity which government could recognize as a serviceable group. So several Chinatown activists of that era, including labor leaders, school teachers, ministers and intellectuals, decided this was not acceptable. So they began to get together in different groups and organize different forums by which this could be corrected. And one of them that came out of that was the Chinese American Historical Society of Southern California in 1975. That's when I got involved, because of my interest in history.[8]

Munson Kwok works professionally as an aerospace engineer, so he engages in activist and volunteer work in Los Angeles Chinatown during his off-hours. He is also national president of the Chinese American Citizens Alliance, founded in Los Angeles in 1912 to advocate for civil rights and immigration rights for Chinese Americans.

In his oral history, Don Toy reflects on the pursuit of learning through volunteerism and social movement activism, which included working while he was in college in the Delano grape fields of California's central valley. The Delano grape strikes gave birth to the United Farm Workers movement led by Cesar Chavez in the mid-1960s.

> I always tell young people, you can get education in different ways. School is only one of the ways, life experience another, travel another, working with organizations, whether you're interested or not, another.

Some of the jobs you hear about immigrants working in restaurants and farms for low wages and how you have no energy after work is true. Well when I was in college, I took a summer to go up to the grape fields in Delano, and basically picked grapes. If you experience it, then you understand it. I don't know what the hardest work you ever did was, but nothing's going to compare to ten to twelve hours and more of work in the hot sun picking grapes or lettuce. Then you have an understanding of what people go through, to make a living, to sacrifice and survive and this is in the United States, not in a third world country.

But picking grapes and other similar experiences . . . puts things in perspective, it makes you more aware. What I do with that awareness is that I have an understanding—and hopefully I can share that awareness, so that when people don't understand, and say, "these people, immigrants are all bad," I can help them understand that that's not how it is. And hopefully with this type of awareness you can kill and break down a lot of stereotypes, and you look at a lot of commonalities, the things that, bottom line, as humans, we need. Hopefully with awareness, when there are injustices, people will stand up and speak. I'm under no illusion that I'm so great, and can change everything. But I'm hoping that, in our own little way and through our own little messages, I truly believe if we can influence another person, and they another one, that's what is going to help us. In the long run, what I'd like to do with all of these injustices, conditions, stereotypes, problems, situations, misunderstandings, etc.—are happening, the bottom line, is that we realize and recognize "yes, you know, it really does exist and we can do something to change for the better." So hopefully, we'll have better understanding and won't be afraid of each other.[9]

Don Toy has spent most of his career as director of the Chinatown Teen Post, which offers recreational activities, counseling and social services for at-risk youth. Over the years, they have expanded their work to include senior programs, legal aid and civil rights assistance for families.

Ethnic Heritage, Art, and Community Development

Over the past 15 years, I carried on my field research on ethnic enclaves and ethnic history as I moved from New York City to Los Angeles. Along the way, I also did field research in Houston (where I also taught for three years) and Miami, cities small enough for me to comprehend entirely and compare multiple enclaves (including Latino and black). I limited my focus to Chinese enclaves in New York and L.A., which are larger metropolitan centers that are harder to understand completely with the greater diversity of ethnic groups. While my first book, *Reconstructing Chinatown*, concentrated on economic and political functions of a single ethnic enclave, this book compares the culture and heritage sector in several Asian, Latino, and African American enclaves in four immigration gateway cities.

I believe the growth of the ethnic historic preservation movements and cultural heritage organizations are important avenues to fight racial–ethnic prejudice and discrimination and contribute to local economic and community development. The ethnic heritage sector preserves and displays the cultural legacy of racial–ethnic ancestry so that new generations can look back and comprehend with better insight the trajectory of their posterity. When history workers and other community activists fight to save and restore important vernacular buildings and historic homes and establish heritage museums, they foster places of communal sentiment and symbolism that can better resist the slum clearance bulldozer and the redevelopmental marketplace. These ethnic places acquire a kind of sacred quality that can draw visitors in a way similar to how holy destinations attract religious pilgrims. Ethnic heritage places may be charged with moral worth like religious places, giving people a sense of spiritual belonging. Like religious sites, they may become the fountainhead of festivals and other celebrations of ethnocultural life, wellsprings of group solidarity that percolate to the surface, a contemporary updating of what the French anthropologist Emile Durkheim called "collective effervescence" in totemic rituals ([1912] 2008).

I also believe that preservation of ethnic cultural heritage can be a tool in promoting neighborhood stability and sustainability through fostering community solidarity and self-identity. This often takes the form of preserving original downtown neighborhoods that become focal points for organizing, fundraising, and reinvestment by latter-generation ethnic populations that have residentially dispersed into the suburbs. The preservation of vernacular buildings, historic homes, parks, and monuments become spatial touchstones for the recuperation of trust, reciprocity, and social capital in the ethnic community. Ethnic heritage organizations have strong educational missions that can help bridge generational divides within their communities. They may also act as incubators for other community-based organizations. The New York Chinatown History Project, for instance, was founded in a tenement building that was saved from demolition and also housed the offices for a senior center, a manpower training project, and a Chinese dance school.

My personal interest in forging ties between heritage work and community development practice was born in my initial work in New York's Chinatown, but I continued this work while I was teaching in Houston, Texas in the early 1990s. I more intensively delved into community development work from 1999 to 2003, when I was principal investigator on an Office of University Partnerships grant from the U.S. Department of Housing and Urban Development (HUD) awarded to Occidental College to work in the communities of Northeast Los Angeles that surrounded the college. While this grant funded multi-dimensional work in several areas including U.S. census research and local asset mapping, small business development surveys, tenant organizing, a job/housing fair, community website development and technology training, nutrition programs, and environmental fair, I have found persisting public interest in the community heritage work of our Northeast Los Angeles Community Outreach Partnership Center. We produced two community history reports on Eagle Rock and Highland Park that were conducted by Occidental College student Jean Won and me. Local archives and field interviews were important research sources in these reports that charted the urban and environmental history of the two neighborhoods through successive phases of Native American, Euro-American, Latino, and Asian immigrant settlement in the region.[10]

Community arts became a focus as we supported community mural work in Chinatown and in the largely Latino community of Highland Park. At the time, a regional arts scene had emerged in Northeast Los Angeles with the opening of dozens of art galleries and a burgeoning community-based mural movement. Art gallery owners were well represented in the local business leadership and active participants in our survey and outreach work. Some such as Rock Rose Cafe and Avenue 50 Studio strongly associated themselves with the Latino arts scene and other subcultural art genres. The arts scene extended to Chinatown, which experienced even more explosive growth buoyed by white investors (some local and some European) opening galleries in antique and curio shops formerly owned by Chinese Americans. While the galleries in Northeast Los Angeles represented a more equal mix of white and Latino artists with many having roots in the community, the scene in Chinatown showed greater signs of gentrification accompanied by interethnic and socioeconomic class transition.

I grew intrigued to understand more fully the transformative potential of the arts sector in the contemporary city. I believe the arts can contribute vitally to community development. I have seen how the arts can be a factor in mobilizing public trust, reciprocity, and community social capital through promoting youth involvement in community murals, artistic gardens, and public art projects. The Latino community mural movement in Los Angeles has helped to sustain a cultural heritage that reaches back to the Mexican muralists of the early twentieth century such as Diego Rivera and David Alfaro Siqueiros who championed proletarian and indigenous values with their iconography. The contemporary mural movement draws on more recent iconography such as Cesar Chavez and other Chicano social movement leaders of the 1960s. A leader in the movement is Judith Baca who is the creator of "The Great Wall of Los Angeles," a series of mural pieces that celebrate racial–ethnic history and social change, painted on the concrete wall of the Los Angeles River. She has trained hundreds of muralists and is founder of the Social and Public Art Resource Center (SPARC), currently housed at the University of California at Los Angeles. Her Cesar Chavez Digital Mural Lab uses state-of-the-art computer

Figure 1.1 Avenue 50 Studio. Photo by Jan Lin.

technology to create an online repository of existing murals as well as in designing new murals for communities throughout the region.[11]

The connection I draw between Asian American history projects and Latino murals is that ethnic heritage can be constructed through history as well as art. These phenomena suggest the past can be preserved and made useful to invigorate the present while helping to imagine and sustain the future. Museums and murals both act as repositories of collective sentiment and representations of ethnic heritage. They may be silent sites in the daily sense but are focal centers for educating, volunteering, commemorating and for festival life. While museums are effective edifices for the preservation of cultural artifacts, murals and other forms of public art are more susceptible to deterioration, and the mural movement is highly sensitive to the need for effective conservation and restoration.

I think there is a growing arts and heritage sector that racial–ethnic minorities can promote while stimulating education, social change, and community development in their communities. The continued conservation of murals and other heritage arts, and historic preservation of important buildings can be sustained through effective fundraising, staff development, and the growth of community-based organizations. The success of this ethnic nonprofit sector stems largely from its association with entrepreneurs within the "enclave economy" and leaders in the community. Much of its impetus is local in nature but some communities can appeal to the transnational or diasporic community. Chinese American history projects can appeal to overseas Chinese visitors. The Japanese American National Museum in Los Angeles' Little Tokyo achieved much of its fundraising success through overseas Japanese corporate support. The Chicano mural movement in Los Angeles can appeal to its international origins in Mexican muralism. Cuban Americans promote the hemispheric nature of Latin American culture in the "Little Havana" district of Miami. Ethnic heritage places can help us understand local–global dynamics in the process of economic and cultural change in American life.

Ethnic Community or Ethnic Theme Park?

The future of the ethnic community will be impacted by how the heritage and arts interests work with the entrepreneurs of the ethnic enclave economy as well as the public sector. Cultural leaders and community activists of the ethnic enclave can become established in the urban public sector as curators, cultural affairs programmers, and museum directors to work in the interests of the ethnic community. As cultural heritage is increasingly viable as an urban tourism and redevelopment strategy, public officials and redevelopment agencies can utilize ethnic neighborhoods as hip or edgy sites for tourism, destination shopping, residential and commercial gentrification. Ethnic entrepreneurs and business leaders may become interpenetrated with the local urban "growth machine" through the work of ethnic chambers of commerce and through the fostering of ethnic business improvement districts. In my research I questioned many public and community leaders on the balance between community and cultural preservation interests, and the dynamics of growth, redevelopment, and gentrification that could be engendered by promoting the ethnic neighborhood as an urban destination. I also asked questions about how growth affected the existing low-income residential and middle-class commercial sector. Cultural heritage work is a legitimate device for education, public affairs, and community development, but ethnic destinations can resemble "ethnic theme parks" as they are commercialized for popular consumption by tourism and convention interests.

The concept of the ethnic theme park was initially coined by Jerome Krase (1999) in his studies of New York's Little Italy, which is replete with cultural attractions such as restaurants, cafes, gelaterias, markets, and street processions for Roman Catholic patron saints, such as the popular Feast of San Gennaro Festival. Since Little Italy is no longer much of a residential enclave and Italian Americans are widely dispersed in the suburbs, the caricaturing moniker is rather strangely fitting. I find similar trends occurring in the adjacent neighborhood of Chinatown, however, which is still a dense residential community for Chinese immigrants, although congestion and the lack of affordable housing are also sending Chinese from Manhattan to the outer boroughs and the suburbs. A case in point is the erection of a tourist kiosk in December

2004 at a crossroads adjacent to Canal Street in Chinatown, which identifies the neighborhood as a tourist location and orients visitors to restaurants, curio shops, markets, parks, cultural monuments, and historical sites. The kiosk staff promote parades and celebrations on such holidays as the Chinese New Year and the Autumn Moon Festival.

Ethnic cultural tourism is also taking place in Harlem, where local entrepreneurs and preservationists have worked to capitalize on the legacy of the Harlem Renaissance as well as the neighborhood's status as a prominent representation of the music and entertainment traditions of Black America in projects such as the Apollo Theater restoration and Harlem USA, a retail and entertainment mega-complex on the main commercial artery, 125th Street. The phenomenon of racial–ethnic "cultural branding" is even stronger in Harlem, where corporations such as Disney, Magic Johnson Theaters, Sony, and AOL Time Warner have made major investments, lured by such efforts as the Abyssinian Development Corporation and the Upper Manhattan Empowerment Zone (UMEZ), which is federally funded (Hoffman 2003). African immigrant street vendors selling jewelry, African-origin arts and crafts, and other products have thronged to the district to capitalize on the surge in tourist traffic and given the district a growing pan-African transnational air (Stoller 2002).

There is a growing "ethnic circuit" of tourism and heritage sites in U.S. cities, especially in immigrant gateway cities like New York, Miami, Houston, and Los Angeles. These cities are nodal "world cities" in a global economy increasingly marked by cross-border flows of labor, capital, and trade in goods and services. In Miami, Cuban and other Latin American immigrant and investment interests have sought to preserve important heritage sites and ethnic retail businesses along Southwest 8th Street, dubbed Calle Ocho, site of the festive Carnival Miami every spring. In Overtown, sites of African American heritage interest are being preserved, restored, and assembled into an Overtown Folklife Village that recreates some of the dynamism of segregated Colored Town in its early twentieth-century heyday, when the Lyric Theater was the focus of an entertainment area dubbed "Little Broadway" and "The Great Black Way." In Houston, an annual International Festival touts its metropolitan image as a world city and heritage preservation and cultural tourism projects are under way in Chinatown, the Mexican American neighborhoods, and the African American Third Ward. In Los Angeles, ethnic heritage preservation and tourism efforts are focused downtown at the original downtown plaza, and Mexican American Olvera Street, with significant activity in adjacent Chinatown and Little Tokyo, as well as in the mid-Wilshire corridor in Koreatown. In black Los Angeles, there are two significant efforts under way, one surrounding the Dunbar Hotel along the old Central Avenue entertainment district near downtown and the other an ensemble of African American heritage, musical and cultural sites and festival events surrounding Leimert Park in West Los Angeles.

My interest in ethnic places is thus also aimed at contributing to a broader understanding of the growing place of culture as an instrument of urban planning and policy. Cultural heritage strategies can foster a sense of place and help to sustain local communities and cultures, but cultural heritage can also be easily appropriated by global capitalism for promoting urban redevelopment. Questions of authenticity, ownership, and local autonomy may be raised. Cultural heritage may be used as an organizing weapon or an educational and social asset, but cultural heritage can become an image bank to be appropriated by the governmental establishment and capitalist system to stimulate investment and tourism.

Outline of Chapters

This book comprises eight chapters, and explores the growth of ethnic landmarks, museums, and other cultural heritage sites and their connection to dynamics of economic and cultural change in America. I look also to past history to better contextualize the present. Chapter 1 gives a personal overview over 15 years of work doing oral history, research, teaching, and community development work in a variety of ethnic communities. I introduce the major themes of my book and describe my research methods.

Chapter 2 gives a conceptual overview of the sociological and theoretical dimensions behind the growing power of ethnic enclaves and ethnic heritage places in American society. I discuss the classic urban sociology literature on the changing view of ethnicity and ethnic places over the course of the twentieth century. I introduce the four immigration gateway cities that I did research in, namely New York, Miami, Houston, and Los Angeles. I highlight how ethnic enclaves have counterbalanced much of the urban decline associated with suburbanization and deindustrialization. I explore and compare the growth of ethnic heritage sites across the four case study cities. I discuss the relevance of the case studies to globalization theory and global–local dynamics. I discuss the relevance of ethnic heritage work to the arts, education, and the promoting of social capital in the community.

In Chapter 3, I go back in urban history to the imperialist era of U.S. capitalism, when urban expositions and world's fairs were common and ethnic cultures were popular attractions in an environment of expansionary Manifest Destiny, economic liberalism, and free trade. I conceptually outline three historical phases in city building and the development of U.S. capitalism, including the imperialist, fordist and postfordist periods. I move on to consider more specifically the economic and social milieu surrounding the world's fairs of the imperialist era. I make a historical note on the Statue of Liberty, one of the greatest landmarks of the City Beautiful period of urban growth. I describe the characteristics of fordism and its relationship to slum clearance and urban renewal episodes in U.S. history.

Chapters 4 and 5 both comprise comparative case studies of ethnic enclaves in two immigration gateway cities, Houston and Miami. Chapter 4 addresses the new economic and cultural power of ethnic economies and heritage places in Houston. This is compared with earlier historical episodes when city managers and the general public viewed ethnic places as undesirable areas of overcrowding and social pathology, and subjected them to slum clearance and urban renewal. Preservation and renewal are now the order in Houston's ethnic places in connection with the rise of "postmodern" architectural and planning practices. I outline three historical stages of city building and ethnic place development in Houston, corresponding with successive architectural genres of early modernism, high modernism, and postmodernism. I compare three different racial–ethnic case study sites in the

Latino East End, Chinatown, and the African American Fourth Ward. I include the latest developments in the black Third Ward.

Chapter 5 offers a comparison of economic and local culture projects in the black enclave of Overtown and the Cuban enclave of Little Havana in Miami. The chapter begins with a historical analysis of the rise of Miami through phases of fordist development and urban renewal (when Overtown was subjected to slum clearance), and then postfordist development, tied to the emergence of ethnic enclaves such as Little Havana and the rise of Miami as a global city. I go on to depict the growth of a booming high-rise property market in Miami and the transition of the Art Deco preservation process in South Beach to a speculative property market driven by transnational capital and gentrification. South Beach presents a set of lessons for preservation efforts in Overtown and Little Havana. I offer a detailed comparison of preservation and ethnic arts activities in Overtown and Little Havana through the voices of community stakeholders.

The next two chapters examine the Chinatowns of Los Angeles and New York. Chapter 6 includes a historical perspective on Los Angeles Chinatown from the nineteenth to the twenty-first centuries. I outline three discrete historical stages in the development of Los Angeles Chinatown, through the drive-to-maturity, fordist, and postfordist periods of U.S. capitalism. I identify important national and local historical events as well as changes in immigration policy in depicting successive historical experiences of segregation, removal, and renewal of Los Angeles Chinatown. I chart the economic renewal of Chinatown since the 1960s, the influx of the Vietnamese and the growth of an ethnic "growth machine." Community leaders give their views on the impact of a new Chinatown arts scene comprising dozens of galleries, the arrival of the Gold Line Metro, and impending redevelopment and gentrification on community life.

Chapter 7 considers the recent history of heritage preservation movements in New York's Chinatown and the Lower East Side, with attention to the Museum of the Chinese in the Americas and the Tenement Museum of the Lower East Side. I go on to examine the impact and community response to the 9/11 disaster. I review work of the Rebuild Chinatown Initiative, a comprehensive planning process led by Asian Americans for Equality. I discuss how the erection of a Chinatown tourist kiosk promotes the image of a theme park of ethnic cultural attractions. I compare this to Weber's "iron cage" of bureaucratic rationality. I examine the phenomenon of deflected immigration and the suburban residential dispersal of Chinese Americans. I identify efforts to build a world-class Chinatown cultural center which supporters hope will draw suburban Chinese Americans. I address authenticity and cultural ownership issues. I discuss useful synergies between the preservation of affordable housing and cultural heritage in residential tenement buildings.

I start the conclusion in Chapter 8 by invoking the work of Jane Jacobs and her relevance to this book. I move on to compare the case studies by urban history and politics. I make a basic distinction between disinvested ghettos and reinvesting ethnic enclaves. I compare the cases by community power structure and I determine that a nonprofit–public partnership offers the best opportunities for heritage preservation while controlling the dynamics of redevelopmental growth. I identify some model demonstration projects and best practices from the case studies. I consider the links between ethnic heritage preservation and the New Urbanist design and planning movement. I conclude with a discussion of issues of authenticity and folk revival.

Research Methods

I deployed the methods of comparative and historical sociology in my research, conducting case studies among Chinese, African American, and Latino communities in four different immigration gateway cities, namely New York, Miami, Houston, and Los Angeles. I compared case studies both within and across these cities that increasingly have acquired a "world" or "global" character. I conducted ethnographic observation and interviews at each location in an effort to capture the complex ethnographic nuances of local neighborhoods like the classic community studies of urban anthropology and sociology, while also exploring the dynamics of economic and cultural change in greater comparative and global context. I also reach back in urban history to the nineteenth- and early twentieth-century "world's fairs" to better interpret the impact of cultural heritage sites and "ethnic theme parks" in the contemporary era.

I pursued classic participant observation as well as participatory action research methods in the course of my research. I did neutral participant observation in New York, Miami, Houston, and Los Angeles Chinatown by walking through the neighborhoods and attending public events. The oral history work in New York and Los Angeles can be classified as participatory action research insofar as we had the sense of empowering people that were previously unrecognized or marginalized through documenting their experiences. Oral history also privileges the voices of the research subjects as the generators of knowledge, thus neutralizing the status of the scientist/researcher as a technical expert (Park et al. 1993). My contract with the U.S. Department of Housing and Urban Development through its Office of University Partnerships for a Community Outreach Partnership Center (COPC) impacted my Los Angeles research. This government-funded outreach and research work was conducted with the mission of serving the low-income neighborhood and promoting asset-based community development. The HUD work influenced my awareness of the links between cultural heritage, the arts, and local development. Through all these efforts I have engaged in a public sociology that links educational research with public action through the creating of academic–community partnerships.

The kind of "public sociology" that I pursue has its precedents in urban sociology and planning in the work of figures such as Jane Jacobs and Herbert Gans, who through scholarship as well as civic engagement sought to promote and defend the integrity of low-income urban neighborhoods that were stigmatized and devalued by the capitalist and governmental establishment in favor of slum clearance and modernization through urban renewal. Michael Burawoy has more recently promoted public sociology during his tenure as president of the American Sociological Association (ASA) in 2004, through his presidential address and the creating of a Task Force on Institutionalizing Public Sociology, and numerous lectures, symposia, and public debates. Burawoy distinguishes public sociology from a professional sociology that speaks largely to its own audience. He sees public sociology as reaching to diverse publics, beyond the scope of the university, to enter into public dialogues on fundamental values. The audiences are local, national, and global. Teaching is a central mission because students are the first public and they carry sociology into other walks of life. These principles resonate well with those espoused by C. Wright Mills in his classic book on sociology, *The Sociological Imagination* ([1959] 2000). Here he calls for sociology that sparks the ability of individuals to comprehend how their personal biographies are embedded in larger historical and societal structures, and help connect their experience of private troubles with larger social dialogues and public issues.

Over the past 15 years, I also did interview research in a variety of ethnic communities where I resided, or through field research trips. These sites included the Chinese enclave of New York, the Chinese, Mexican, and African American areas of Houston, Texas, the Little Havana district and African American community of Overtown in Miami, and the Chinatown, Little Tokyo, and Mexican American districts of Los Angeles. Among my informants were dozens of ethnic community activists and leaders, historians and curators, artists, restaurant owners, art gallery owners, business leaders, urban planners, and public officials. Each one of these cities has been a focal point of Latin American and Asian immigration to the U.S. over the last 50 years. I was interested in examining the local historical and political dynamics that led to the preservation of ethnic landmarks and cultural districts, and the linking of these efforts to neighborhood revitalization, urban planning, and globalization dynamics in urban economies.

Finally, I also did archival historical research work examining photographs, news stories, and other archival documents at the Museum of the Chinese in the Americas, the Black Archives of Miami, the Historical Museum of South Florida, the archives of the Chinese Historical Society of Southern California, the Huntington Library, the California Historical Collection at the University of Southern California, and the archives of the Los Angeles Public Library.

2

ETHNIC COMMUNITIES AND CULTURAL HERITAGE

Cities are accumulation points for economic and political power in our society, and principal prisms of our cultural heritage. Here the forces of the marketplace and the polity build the iconic buildings, monuments, and public spaces that represent our great national achievements and collective memories. These edifices of stone, brick, and steel transform the transitory cycles of human experience into durable landmarks for posterity. Museums, theaters, and cultural centers play similar landmark functions, but these places play an even more significant role in the active transmission of culture and heritage through serving as spaces for exhibition, artistic expression, and story telling. While cultural heritage places have been historically linked to the national imagination and the ideology of nation building, my book considers the growing visibility of ethnic heritage places in our society. I believe the growing participation of ethnic communities in the preservation and imagination of heritage amounts to a multicultural transformation of our public history and community life. Cultural heritage museums do outreach to schools and artists and stimulate ethnic social capital in the service of community development. They are commonly located in ethnic enclaves in immigration gateway cities that are nexus points in the global economy. I disagree with any popular perceptions that the rise of ethnic enclaves and heritage places are harbingers of separatism or balkanization. By better understanding the power and dynamics of ethnic enclaves and heritage places in our society, I think we will be better prepared to harness the economic and cultural changes related to globalization rather than be hurt or divided by these same forces of economic and cultural restructuring.

Ethnic Place Preservation and Public History

Ethnic communities engage in preservation of historical buildings, monuments, and theaters to commemorate their heroes, family ancestors, and culture in the process of adaptation to life in America. Advancing this work are family genealogists and oral history projects, ethnic history museums, ethnic writers, historians, and academics. Their efforts sustain the ongoing importance of ethnic places of the city and representations of ethnic culture in the minds of the people and the collective memory of America. The growth of an ethnic heritage and culture sector is especially prominent in the immigrant gateway cities of the U.S., such as New York, Miami, Houston, and Los Angeles, which have experienced new flows of labor and capital from Latin America, the Caribbean, and Asia. African Americans and white ethnic Americans have also established heritage projects exploring their African and European roots.

Ethnic memorials and public history museums have a distinct impact on our collective life and heritage. They mediate the memory of ethnic collective traumas and racial injustice through exhibitions and educational work on such experiences as immigrant struggles in tenement housing, Chinese immigrant exclusion, Japanese American wartime internment, slum clearance of black communities, and the displacement of Cuban exiles to the U.S. Through their cumulative impact, they contribute to a gradual transformation in our collective understanding of American history. They are a part of a growing "social history" movement that explores and makes visible the histories of minority, subcultural, and vernacular groups marginalized or ignored in the annals of official history and public commemoration. They are vehicles of a new pluralism in the landscape of U.S. public memory. They are connected to the political and intellectual work of ethnic studies movements in our universities and to the creative work of ethnic genre writers and artists.

The saving of historic buildings since the mid-nineteenth century had acted frequently as a unifying focus for national pride or as landmarks of stylistic excellence. Public history in America has traditionally been a landscape of great buildings, museums, memorials, and other sites commemorating the exploits of founding fathers, great statesmen, and local heroes especially from the white middle- to upper-class elite. The preservation of their legacy is apparent in the landscape of national monuments and the Smithsonian museum complex in Washington, D.C., as well as the central business districts and prime elite neighborhoods in many U.S. cities. Across the landscapes of America can be seen the great cultural monuments and landmarks of the colonial and imperialist periods of U.S. history, such as Plymouth Rock, George Washington's birthplace at Mount Vernon, the Jamestown colony, and Mount Rushmore. Historic battlefields like that in Manassas, Virginia, and memorials such as the Tomb of the Unknown Soldier at Arlington Cemetery, celebrate stories of war, heroism, and sacrifice in the context of colonization and nation building.

Over the last few decades, however, historic preservation has become increasingly democratized in America. In her book *The Power of Place* (1995), Dolores Hayden declares that the new social history has informed diverse projects of architectural preservation and museumization, especially building types associated with the habitation and everyday working lives of the poor and racial–ethnic minorities, such as tenements, factories, union halls, or churches. While chiefly examining sites in downtown Los Angeles such as El Pueblo Historical Monument, Little Tokyo, and the Biddy Mason Homestead, she also identifies dozens of seminal locations throughout the nation such as Ellis Island, the Lower East Side Tenement Museum in New York, the Black Heritage Trail in Boston, and the Women's Rights National Historical Park at Seneca Falls, New York. Through historic and archival preservation, building and walking tours, oral histories and multimedia documentaries, these projects give visibility and voice to previously marginalized cultural groups such as women, racial–ethnic minorities, and immigrants. Where many minority groups lack access to cultural capital to document their own history, oral history has become an increasingly legitimate method of reconstructing the past and raising minority authority in historical circles.

Sociological Terminology

I generally use the terminology "ethnic" rather than "racial" because ethnicity relates more to ancestral heritage and the ongoing transmission of culture, whereas race is a more biological and genetic terminology with a historical relation to ideologies of European colonialism and rule over non-European peoples. We must not forget, however, that injustices of prejudice and discrimination also relate to ethnic experience through phenomena such as ethnocentrism, ethnoviolence and "ethnic cleansing." In the field of sociology, there has been recent interest in ethnic enclave economies that are seen as a protected sector created by newcomer immigrants who are initially marginalized as outsiders by the host society. There are many positive social benefits and economic multipliers accruing from ethnic solidarity in the enclave economy, but there is also co-ethnic exploitation of labor in the sweatshop enterprises of this sector. The growth of the ethnic heritage and arts sector also presents a double-edged sword. Ethnic heritage and arts development offers opportunities for education and community development within ethnic neighborhoods, but the growing consumption of ethnic heritage and culture by outsiders can also threaten the ongoing stability of the ethnic residential and small business sector.

I use the terms "ethnic enclaves," "communities," and "places" somewhat interchangeably, but there are subtle differences in meaning associated with each terminology. "Ethnic enclave" is a sociological term that refers especially to the economic dimension of ethnic subeconomies and their role in immigrant adaptation and social mobility in America. "Ethnic community" is a broader term relating to the social life of the people, in the context of arenas like family, neighborhood, and church. "Ethnic place" is a geographic term referring to the spatial territory of the community in terms of buildings, landmarks, and cultural sites. The concept of "place" in geographic thought includes an exploration of cultural values. While ethnic places were historically often denigrated as "slums," ethnic communities have acquired new power to advance their self-definition to protect themselves and counter racial and ethnic prejudice. While preservation of museums, theaters, and landmarks are important avenues in representing a cultural heritage, history is also made usable to the present through exchanges with the arts and education sectors.

I have done research in the African American communities of Houston and Miami. While black neighborhoods are often described as racial enclaves, in order to highlight the incidence of segregation, oppression, and poverty, I would also describe them as African American communities with a rich ethnocultural life and history. I include them in my discussion of ethnic enclaves, communities, and places because they are experiencing similar transformations.

The Removal and Renewal of Ethnic Communities through Urban History

The recent renewal of ethnic places is a notable contrast with the nineteenth and early twentieth centuries, when ethnic places were subjected to slum clearance and removal by governing urban elites. The massive immigrations of the industrial era (1840–1920) drew primarily from the "new stock" non-White Anglo-Saxon Protestant (non-WASP) European immigration (Catholic, Jewish). Industrial core cities of the Northeast and Midwest (NE–MW) drew the bulk of the foreign immigration to the United States (Ward 1971). The Chicago School of Sociology viewed urban ethnic places (such as the Jewish "ghetto" Kleindeutschland, Little Italy, and Greektown) as "decompression chambers" for newly arrived immigrants, which aided their economic adaptation and cultural assimilation into American life (Ward 1989: 170). Burgess ([1925] 1967) codified the human ecological view that immigrant colonies were located in a zone-in-transition surrounding the central business district (CBD), and would wither away with upward mobility of later-generation ethnics and movement into outer residential suburbs.

The invasion–succession paradigm of the human ecologists privileged the invisible hand of the free market in determining urban land patterns and neglected political variables, including racial–ethnic discrimination and the interventions of the WASP-dominated state. Immigrant minorities were effectively relegated to the zone-in-transition by the formal and de facto restrictions, exclusions, and covenants of Anglo powerbrokers as much as by the market barriers presented by high rents in the CBD. The restrictions experienced by nonwhite minorities (e.g., Asians, Latinos, African Americans) were even greater than those experienced by white ethnic immigrants (e.g., Irish, Italians, Jews), especially in the cities outside of the NE–MW core region. African Americans and Latinos were thus faced with Jim Crow segregation laws and restrictive covenants, while Asian Americans were confronted with restrictive covenants and Alien Land Acts. Thus, in turn-of-the-century Los Angeles, Mexicans, African Americans, and Chinese occupied fallow real estate around the Olvera Street Plaza north of the Anglo-controlled CBD centered on Broadway. The Mexican barrio became known as the Sonora or "Dogtown." The Chinese mixed with African Americans on a corridor known as "Calle de los Negros" or "Nigger Alley" (Pearlstone 1990: 72). A Japanese colony appeared nearby at the intersection of East First and San Pedro Street. In Houston, Mexicans and African Americans formed an approximate ring around the Anglo CBD. A Chinese merchant colony arose on the eastern periphery of the CBD, serving primarily African Americans.

While ethnic settlements were shunned and segregated during the industrial period of American urban growth, city managers and the federal government actively began bulldozing and removing ethnic places under slum clearance policies of the interwar period, and more actively under urban renewal in the postwar period, to make room for expressway arterials, middle-class housing, or expansion of the CBD and government office buildings. Ethnic places were deemed unsanitary public health hazards, congested visual eyesores, and contagious mediums of vice and other social pathologies to middle-class urbanites. Chinatowns, Little Italies, and Mexican barrios were regarded as obstacles to modernization and cultural assimilation. In Manhattan's

Lower East Side, riverfront tenements were cleared to make way for the East River Drive and public housing. The Cross-Bronx Expressway severed a huge Jewish tenement community. Houston's Chinatown was relocated to facilitate expansion of the CBD, and in Los Angeles, Chinatown was relocated to facilitate the construction of the Union Railway Station. These are some prominent cases in immigrant neighborhoods, but many observers have noted that the predominant victims of urban renewal programs were African American communities.

Gans's (1962) seminal study, *The Urban Villagers*, heralded the emergence of a new academic and policy perspective that challenged the public stigma associated with Boston's West End as an "ethnic slum" by portraying the affirmative, social organizational functions of the Italian American "peer group society" in resolving everyday problems of urban poverty. The book is also memorable for its forceful critique of federal slum clearance policies on a number of counts, including:

1   lack of community input in the renewal process
2   lack of financial compensation to minority property owners in the eminent domain process
3   the absence of or inadequate relocation assistance to displaced families, and
4   the evaluative, rather than analytic, utility of terms such as "slum" in labeling ethnic places as undesirable and dysfunctional.

The Hart–Celler Immigration and Nationality Act of 1965, passed during the liberal political environment of the civil rights era, over-turned decades-long restrictive immigration quotas, auguring the arrival of a new wave of Latin American, Caribbean, and Asian immigration. The demographic, political, and cultural changes accompanying the civil rights movement and the Hart–Celler Act marked the passing of assimilation discourse as a battery of new conceptual paradigms emerged, which interpret ethnicity as an adaptable phenomenon that accompanies social change, rather than being a static, primordial status of premodernity; these include ethnic plural politics (Glazer and Moynihan 1963), emergent ethnicity (Yancey, Ericksen, and Juliani

1976), symbolic ethnicity (Gans 1979), ethnic enclave economies (Portes and Manning 1986, Zhou 1992), and panethnicity (Espiritu 1992). More recently, fertile new research has grown around concepts of globalization and transnationalism.

Studies of ethnic transnational communities draw attention to the binational cultural and economic networks in which new immigrants interact. These frequent interactions between home and host societies are enabled by innovations in communications and transportation technologies, which have shrunk the barriers of geography, economy, and culture between constituent nations of the global system of states. There is a reciprocal circuitry in the transnational practices of immigrants that include phenomena such as monetary remittances, seasonal labor migrations, and circular migrations through the life cycle, as well as dual residence, and binational investment practices (Rouse 1991, Rodriguez 1995). Dominican immigrants to the U.S., finds Peggy Levitt (2001), are like "transnational villagers" conducting exchanges that connect home and host society in the economic, political, and religious spheres of life. Chinese cosmopolitans from Hong Kong and Taiwan send their children (*xiao liuxuesheng*, "little foreign students," or more popularly "parachute kids") to study in U.S. schools and prospectively gain permanent residency while their parents (*kongzhong feiren*, "trapeze artists," or *taikongren*, "astronauts") frequently shuttle the transoceanic distances (Wong 2005: 7). Lessinger (1995) describes how the Indian government encouraged binational economic activity among South Asian Indian Americans by offering them continuing status as nonresident Indians. Portes (1996) deploys McLuhan's concept of the electronic "global village" to express the cosmopolitan affiliations of the new transnational citizens in charting a brave new world of diminishing cultural and geographic borders.

A more critical view on the growth of transnational identity is that of Arjun Appadurai (1990), who posits that revolutions in travel, satellite and mass media communication technologies have created a world of deterritorialization and social disjuncture with increasingly abrupt collisions between different social classes, races, and cultures. He offers a more alarming perspective on globalization through the lens of transnational ethnic conflict and violence, ethnic separatism, and fundamentalist movements that seek to censor and repatriate the modernist culture of the West and its mass media. But the black markets offering Hollywood films, recorded music, and other emblems of modernist Western culture can permeate even the most restricted fundamentalist or socialist states. Appadurai perceives ethnic identity as increasingly malleable and fragmented through the mass-mediated world of "ethnoscapes," which he believes have liberated ethnicity like "a genie [previously] contained in the bottle of some sort of locality" (1990: 15). Appadurai brings notes of contradiction and conflict to the analysis of ethnic identity in the era of transnationalism and globalization.

Appadurai brings attention to the loss of "place" and "community" with the growth of alternative cartographies of rootless, diasporic networks of nomads, refugees, expatriates, tourists, and economic and artistic cosmopolitans. I prefer not to throw the baby out with the bathwater; I think that time and space have been increasingly compressed in the "global village" but not finally exploded or thrown into a state of permanent disjuncture. Ethnic global villagers may be nearly freed from place-bounded restraints in their commercial and cultural pursuits, but ethnic places of the city are still highly significant as focal points of the economy, culture, and heritage. There is a new visibility to the ethnic locality within the emerging city of global capitalism.

Thus, in the postindustrial environment of the world cities, American ethnic places as global villages are now more ethnically polyglot with nonwhite immigrants, who interact in sustained transnational networks of association, rather than provincial urban villages resistant to and marginalized by the pressures of cultural assimilation. Through the combined window of opportunity created by a domestic social upheaval in civil rights and external developments in global capitalism, ethnicity has a greater resilience and gravity in arenas of economic, political, and cultural interaction. But globalization may be as pernicious as it is auspicious, and the merchants, place entrepreneurs, and cultural practitioners have encountered risks as well as advantages.

Globalization and Renewal of Ethnic Places in Immigration Gateway Cities

Globalization brings many economic and cultural benefits as well as costs. Financial deregulation and free trade have led to "runaway shops," deindustrialization, and urban decline in many "postindustrial" regions of the U.S. We have also seen how global capital, world trade, and immigration have promoted the growth of "world cities,"[1] which represent a vaunted road out of deindustrialization and urban decline. The dark side of world cities can be described with reference to class polarization, segregation and policing of neighborhoods, and interracial conflict (Friedmann and Wolff 1982, Davis 1987, Sassen 1988). Immigration gateway cities such as New York, Houston, Miami, and Los Angeles may be alternately identified as multicultural "gorgeous mosaics" or Malthusian "Noah's arks." Globalization conveys the fundamental and self-expanding power of global capitalism, but also the contradictions of socioeconomic class differences and racial–ethnic conflict.

As these transformations have progressed, the Chinatowns, Koreatowns, and Little Havanas of the postindustrial city have rejuvenated warehouse districts, retail corridors, and residential quarters of the zone-in-transition, reversing the obsolescence threatened with the decentralization of jobs and people to the urban periphery. Associated with the economic recovery of ethnic merchants and place entrepreneurs are the cultural reclamation efforts of a range of community-based artists, historians, and activists in undertakings such as public arts projects, cultural festivals, heritage preservation of certain symbolic or sacred cultural sites, and ethnic history museums, initiated often through acts of political contestation or community insurgency. These combined maneuvers mark the repossession of central urban economic and cultural spaces from which these ethnic actors were historically restricted, evicted, or displaced.

The new central-city ethnic places are primary purveyors of transnational commerce as well as culture, articulating closely with the world trade functions characteristic of world cities; furthermore, they may be employed by local state actors to project an image of the multiethnic city as an investment environment conducive to transnational corporate capital. Local state actors have found it advantageous to link ethnic commercial and cultural districts with economic devices such as world trade centers, convention center promotion, sports franchise expansions, arts promotion, and urban tourism.

Globalization is a salubrious as well as slippery terrain of new opportunities and potential risks for ethnic entrepreneurs and culture producers, which I comparatively examine through a number of cases in the emergent world cities. Among the complications that emerge are intergroup conflicts among ethnic communities. Intragroup conflicts also may occur, especially between local and overseas factions within groups, such as among Chinese and Japanese immigrants. More broadly, the repossession of ethnic commercial and cultural spaces may be critically conceptualized as a form of economic and symbolic revalorization that leads to redevelopment and gentrification that can threaten small-scale, local ethnic actors.[2] Ethnic places may authenticate "difference" while reinforcing class distinctions, serving as arenas for the investment and further accumulation of transnational capital.

Since the 1960s, the onset of globalization processes has been differentially constituted in the various immigration gateway cities. Community insurgency has accompanied the reclamation of ethnic places in some cities, while renewal efforts in other cities have involved greater cooperation between ethnic contenders and the local state. These contrasts reflect such factors as contingencies and variations in regional economies, the preceding history of local race and ethnic relations, traditions of community activism, and relations between local ethnics and overseas counterparts.

I chose New York, Miami, Houston, and Los Angeles as my case study cities because they have been among the top ten immigration gateway cities in the U.S. over the last 20 years. I refer to Miami and Houston as "world cities" that are more secondary in the international hierarchy of cities, while I refer to New York and Los Angeles as "global cities" with a more first-order position as command centers for international capitalism.

I conceptualize immigration gateway cities as a subset of world cities, which serve not only as command centers in the cross-border movement of capital and labor but also as critical nodes in processing flows of commodities and cultural products. The trade and transport firms concentrated in these cities facilitate the import and export of goods between the U.S. hinterlands and other global trading regions. Following this logic, we may observe that:

1   New York and Boston are gateways to Atlantic Rim trade
2   Miami, Dallas, and Houston are gateways to Latin American and Caribbean Rim trade, and
3   San Francisco and Los Angeles are gateways to Pacific Rim trade.

The notion of globalization and ethnic commerce as leading edges of postindustrial urban growth revises an argument struck among urbanists in the 1970s that the real consequence of deindustrialization was an interregional job and population shift from northeastern (Frostbelt) to southwestern (Sunbelt) cities as manufacturing firms were lured by lower wages, lower land costs, and anti-union "good business" climates in the Sunbelt. My argument counterbalances the incidence of decline and deindustrialization with the dynamism of globalization and immigration to explain the continued economic vigor of some older centers (e.g., New York City, Boston, and Chicago) in the 1990s (Waldinger 1989).

Ethnic enclaves and their ethnic enterprises have played a key role in reviving industrial, warehousing, and retailing districts of the central city, which were declining with the departure of manufacturing and commercial activities to peripheral locations. Macy's and Bloomingdale's abandoned their downtown locations to anchor the new shopping malls and "gallerias" of the suburban cloverleaves. Kresge's retooled and entered the suburban periphery to become Kmart, but the once ubiquitous Woolworth five-and-dime stores clung persistently to their downtown locales, finally closing their last 400 stores in July 1997. Pakistani immigrants have filled some of this niche in the demand for low-end retail with the opening of 99-cent and dollar discount stores in New York City (Kershaw 1997). But the new immigrant impacts on urban economies can be seen much more clearly across the geography of urban space.

New York City's midtown wholesaling district (from 14th to 34th Street) is a case in point. Previously dominated by white ethnic entrepreneurs (including Jewish and Italian immigrants), the district steadily lost economic vitality from the 1920s to the 1960s with the decentralization of manufacturing and retailing functions to the suburban and exurban periphery. Since the 1960s, however, new Asian, Latin American, and Caribbean entrants have filtered into the same built environment, renewing the economic dynamism of the district and giving it a more transnational atmosphere (a similar ethnic succession has occurred in the proximate Garment District). The New York Chinese Businessmen's Association purports to represent some 2,500 enterprises, mainly engaged in import–export wholesaling in the midtown area. A Korean business district of wholesalers, restaurants, and banks can be found in a rectangular area from 24th to 34th Street between Fifth and Sixth Avenues. In October 1995, it was officially recognized by the city of New York with the posting of "Koreatown" signage at the intersection of 32nd Street and Broadway (Min 1996: 39). Underneath the Broadway street sign can be found an accompanying sign designating the corridor as "Korea Way."

New York's Chinatown has grown expansively since the 1960s from its location in lower Manhattan, succeeding Jewish and Italian outmovers in nearby blocks of the Lower East Side. Dominicans have established a commercial and residential presence in the Washington Heights district of upper Manhattan. South Asian Indians, though residentially decentralized, retain a commercial and cultural district in the Jackson Heights area of Queens, which serves as the "symbolic heart" of the dispersed community (Lessinger 1995). Chinese, Koreans, and other immigrant groups have succeeded white ethnic outmovers, establishing a multiethnic "Asiantown" in the Flushing area of Queens.

In Houston, Chinese and Mexican merchants have given new life to the deteriorating near-city warehousing and industrial districts to the east of the CBD. The downtown Chinatown wholesalers import food and restaurant products through the port of Houston for distribution in the metropolitan area as well as throughout the South and Midwest. A "Little Saigon" of Indochinese merchants has emerged in the disused midtown area to the immediate south of the CBD. New Asian and Latino commercial activity also has emerged in the suburban west and southwest economic corridors of the metropolis. Mexican activity can be found in Houston Heights, Chinese along Bellaire Boulevard, South Asians along Hillcroft, and Koreans in the Harwin wholesaling corridor as well as in retailing and restaurants on Long Point Road. The entrance of new ethnic merchants was expedited largely by the availability of low commercial rents and high vacancy rates during the 1980s, when Houston experienced a severe regional recession because of the tumble in petroleum prices associated with the oil glut on the world market. Ethnic enclaves have helped to stabilize the local economy.

In Los Angeles, the nation's largest Koreatown has emerged in an approximately 20-square-mile area west of downtown, which was formerly more than 90 percent white. Businesses in the area are primarily Korean, but Koreans make up less than 15 percent of the residents, who are primarily Hispanic (mainly Mexican) (Min 1996: 35). The old Chinatown north of downtown has been enhanced with the emergence of Indochinese merchants along the north Broadway corridor. Latino merchants now burgeon along south Broadway. East of the CBD, Little Tokyo has experienced revival in the decades following the internment debacle. A suburban Chinatown that developed in Monterey Park in the 1970s has spread to become an expansive "ethnoburb" occupying many other cities in the San Gabriel Valley. Southward in Orange County, a "Little Saigon" of Vietnamese businesses and residents has sprouted in the city of Westminster.

In Miami, Cubans settled initially in the old Riverside–Shenandoah section of Miami (between Flagler Street and the Tamiami Trail), a historically Jewish residential enclave. The Tamiami (Tampa–Miami) Trail, otherwise known as Highway 41 or SW 8th Street, was from the 1930s to the 1950s the major commercial spine for the Jewish community. Postwar prosperity led to residential outmovement of upwardly mobile Jewish Americans into the Dade County suburbs, and the scene was set for the entrance of the Cubans in the 1960s, who redubbed SW 8th Street "Calle Ocho" (Eighth Street) as the surrounding district became known as Little Havana. Like the Jewish

American merchants who preceded them, the Cuban arrivals experienced discriminatory exclusions from the Anglo merchant establishment of Flagler Street, the main downtown commercial corridor. By the 1980s, Cubans themselves began filtering into the suburbs of Dade County, as Nicaraguans followed in their wake into the commercial and residential space of Little Havana. Though increasingly integrated residentially, the Cuban cultural and commercial presence remains conspicuous throughout the metropolis.

Although the new ethnic commercial enclaves are not exclusively located in central-city or near-city zones of the city—particularly in newer Sunbelt automobile-centered cities such as Miami, Houston, and Los Angeles, where immigrant enterprises have penetrated the suburban commercial corridors of feeder roads and strip malls—some of the more prominent (Chinatowns, Koreatowns, and Little Havanas) still occupy central locations. In my research, I focus on the transformations of the ethnic spaces of the zone-in-transition and city center.

Ethnic Preservation Movements

The linked civil rights and ethnic power movements of the 1950s and 1960s helped to initiate parallel projects of community action and heritage reclamation in American race and ethnic places. Cultural renewal efforts in ethnic communities were given further impetus during the years surrounding the American bicentennial activities of 1976, a period of cultural restoration during the nadir of the post-Watergate recessionary 1970s, which boosted the significance and respectability of ethnic history. Manhattan's Lower East Side now contains a number of ethnic museums and preserved heritage sites, including the Chinatown History Museum, the Eldridge Street Synagogue, and the Lower East Side Tenement Museum. Cultural and community insurgency were often linked. Activists with the Chinatown Basement Workshop assembled a trove of artistic and material cultural artifacts that was later transferred to the Chinatown History Project. This museum became a reality after protests for preservation surrounding the proposed auction of a public school building that had become tax-delinquent and fallen into city possession. The Little Italy

Restoration Association unsuccessfully fought to acquire an abandoned police headquarters for an Italian cultural center; the spectacular Beaux-Arts-style edifice instead was converted to a luxury condominium complex (Conforti 1996).

In Los Angeles, opposition to a police center expansion and a municipal plan to demolish some historical sites in the process of widening East First Street in Little Tokyo spurred an activist movement in Little Tokyo, which eventually gained National Historic Landmark status for a city block that holds 13 buildings of particular merit, including a number of historic storefronts.[3] The Hompa Hongwangi Buddhist Temple (built in 1925) was converted to the Japanese American National Museum. An "artistic sidewalk" wraps around the block, a multihued walkway of rose, white, and gray concrete afloat with images of *tsutsumi*, a Japanese custom of "wrappings" such as baskets, folded cloths, and suitcases. Quotes are also inscribed—warm memories of early neighborhood life in brass and harsh memories of internment in stainless steel. Sheila Levrant de Brettville, the designer of the Omoide no Shotokyo (Remembering Old Little Tokyo) walkway, said, "Buildings are like people. A portion of the story of the proprietors in each building is depicted . . . To evoke their personal narrative is to evoke the larger community in which they lived."[4] An antiquated housing barrack and watchtower (preserved and transferred from their original location at a Los Angeles processing center for Japanese Americans awaiting relocation to wartime internment camps in the desert) sit starkly across the street surrounded by barbed wire.

Also in Los Angeles, historians and community activists have been seeking to repossess ethnic history at the Olvera Street Plaza. The Plaza was the nucleus of El Pueblo de la Reina de Los Angeles (sobre el Rio de la Porciúncula), the original agricultural settlement built by an interracial assembly of laborers from Sonora and Sinaloa under the aegis of the Spanish crown in 1781. It passed into Mexican rule in 1822 until being conquered by the United States in 1847. The site faded from significance as Anglo attentions were fixed on shifting CBD growth to Pershing Square south of the old center. Chinatown was razed to make way for the Union Railway Station in the 1930s, however, and other portions of the district were cleared to make way for highways and government building expansions in the post-World War II era. El Pueblo de Los Angeles Historical Monument was finally completed by the California Recreation and Parks Commission in the late 1980s. There were a number of Chicano, Chinese, and Euro-American interests represented in the negotiations, and an agreement was brokered to establish a "prime historical period" of 1818–1932 that recognizes the sequence of Mexican, Chinese, and Euro-American settlers through the district. The appointment of a diverse slate of board members representing all ethnic communities by Mayor Riordan helped to broker intergroup differences.[5]

In Miami, Cuban American heritage reclamation efforts center on the "Freedom Tower" and the Tower Theater intersection on Calle Ocho in Little Havana. The so-called Freedom Tower, located on Biscayne Boulevard near harbor tourist amenities, was built in 1925 in the Spanish Renaissance architectural style, modeled after the Giralda Tower in Sevilla, Spain. For its first 32 years, it housed the offices of the *Miami Herald*. It later became the processing point for some 150,000 Cuban refugees airlifted to Miami on more than 3,000 "freedom flights" from 1965 to 1973. In the collective memory of Cuban émigrés, the Freedom Tower occupies an urban iconographic position similar to the fusion of New York City's Ellis Island and Statue of Liberty. The vacant building was held for a while by Saudi investors, but the Miami Office of Community Development and local preservationists won historic designation for the site while they prepared proposals for its future disposition.

At a more advanced level of restoration is the Tower Theater site at the intersection of SW 8th Street (Calle Ocho) and SW 15th Avenue, the "heart" of the Little Havana commercial corridor. The theater is notable among Cuban Americans as the first to begin screening American films dubbed in Spanish, giving many immigrants their most durable introduction to American culture. It is slated for conversion into a Latino film and performing arts center, with an interpretive museum of Cuban American culture, and associated restaurants and retail shops. Also on the intersection is Maximo Gomez Park, a favorite spot for domino tournaments, where elderly Cubans are especially known to congregate, smoking cigars and engaging in political discourse and reminiscing about Cuba. Star-shaped plaques on the sidewalk commemorate renowned celebrities such as Gloria Estefan and the "Queen of Salsa," actress/singer Celia Cruz. City planners now refer to Little Havana as the "Latin Quarter" to recognize the greater diversity of members of the Latino diaspora, such as Central Americans, who now occupy the district. The SW 8th Street corridor is also the site of the Calle Ocho street festival; drawing up to a million people every year in March, the event is vaunted by its promoters as the "world's largest block party."[6]

In Houston, Mexican merchant interests affiliated with the East End Chamber of Commerce have sought to promote the development of a promenade/bike trail and urban historical park along the length of the Buffalo Bayou from Allens Landing to the ship Turning Basin, to be marked at intervals with sites of natural, historical, and ethnic significance. Although the plan seems somewhat incongruous within the industrial environment of Houston's east side, proponents are quite serious about their proposal, brandishing the model of San Antonio's highly successful Riverwalk. Near the Our Lady of Guadalupe Church (the major spiritual and community center of the original Mexican settlement of the second ward of Houston) are a cluster of newer sites, including the palm-lined Guadalupe Plaza for civic gatherings and the partially constructed Mercado del Sol, intended as a Latino festival marketplace in an abandoned mattress factory.

The renewal of ethnic place culture in Houston and Miami takes place through the affirmation of ethnic pride and patriotism to America with less of the air of cultural insurgency and anger at past oppressions displayed in Los Angeles and New York. These differences extend from variations in the character of the preceding history experienced by each group in their respective locales, and in the legacy of historians and community activists. To illustrate, the strongly anti-communist Cubans, who are largely refugees/immigrants of the more liberal postwar civil rights period, were the beneficiaries of significant U.S. government assistance during their relocation and settlement, and they embrace the rhetoric of anti-communism. In Houston, the legacy of conquest and segregation has given way to a city where ethnic minority groups have new power as place entrepreneurs. By contrast, Los Angeles efforts document the atrocities of Anglo conquest and the stark historical experiences of ethnic exclusion, repatriation, and internment. In New York City, heritage activities have centered on the salvaging of quotidian artifacts of tenement life and documenting the quiet but noble struggles of immigrant progenitors as pushcart peddlers, laundry workers, and garment workers in the promising but punishing crucible of the Lower East Side. The Chinatown History Museum recently changed its name to the Museum of the Chinese in the Americas in an attempt to move its scope and operations beyond local provincialities to encompass and promote new transnational, diasporic approaches to the study and dissemination of migration history.

The Japanese and Chinese American places of New York and Los Angeles also have been the arena of contentious struggles between local and overseas interests. Overseas interests gradually have made investment inroads into Little Tokyo in Los Angeles as the commercial and cultural reclamation of the district has proceeded in the past three decades, a trend that has been encouraged by the L.A. Community Redevelopment Agency (CRA). Little Tokyo community activists, fearing displacement of elderly residents and mom-and-pop businesses, launched an unsuccessful effort to block construction of a hotel (the New Otani) and shopping center (Weller Court) financed by overseas Japanese capital in the early 1970s.[7] The "anti-eviction task force" decried public subsidies granted by the CRA to large investors via "tax increment financing" schemes, which reduced short-term land acquisitions costs through the expected guarantee of long-term incremental increases in tax liability (opponents viewed the short-run subsidies as a "land grab" on the part of overseas capital). Local interests were placated in the ensuing years by long-awaited CRA projects supporting smaller merchants (Japanese Village Plaza) and senior housing needs (Little Tokyo Towers and Miyako Gardens Apartments). The board of the Japanese American National Museum in its capital campaign, to finance a brand new pavilion across the street, in fact, aggressively courted overseas Japanese capital. Akio Morita, founder and chairman of the Sony Corporation, dedicated one of his executives to raising an initial nest egg of some \$9 million from the *Keidenren* of Japan (the major Japanese business federation). In revealing hyperbole, Morita has triumphantly saluted local Japanese American communities for the "inroads" they have made for Japanese corporate investments in the United States.[8]

New York's Chinatown has been the site of similar conflicts between local ethnics and their overseas counterparts. Encouraged by commercial dynamism in the district, the city in 1981 introduced revised zoning rules permitting high-density development near the entrance ramps of two bridges where there was a surplus of abandoned city-owned property (the Special Manhattan Bridge District). Community opposition quickly materialized, however, with the announcement of two major high-rise condominium projects to be financed by overseas Chinese capital. Protracted legal battles led to the revoking of one building permit, and the other project eventually was found culpable (with reference to the Mount Laurel doctrine) of inadequate "environmental impact review," where environment was given a wide latitude of meaning, including potential displacement of local residents and business and a negative impact on the community (Lin 1998c: 151–56).

There has not been such opposition between local and overseas Chinese interests in downtown Houston, where the Houston China-town Council has actively sought backing of overseas investors in their efforts to market Chinatown as a tourist amenity for delegates at the nearby George R. Brown Convention Center. A six-block mixed-use development is envisioned with restaurants offering world cuisines (including Chinese, Vietnamese, Korean, Thai, Mexican, Italian, and Texas-style barbecue), a farmer's market, community center, theater for Chinese opera and other performances, and housing. Representatives of Shenzhen, China (Houston's sister city), donated a gigantic Chinese gate with guardian lions.[9]

Transnational Capitalism and Postindustrial Growth Machines

The promoters of growth in postindustrial cities have had to contend with a variety of economic and fiscal crises associated with postwar deindustrialization and suburbanization, dual trends that have deprived central cities of employment, residents, and a vital tax base. The fiscal impoverishments accompanying these structural transformations were further deepened with the curtailment of federal revenue-sharing programs under the Reagan administration. Increasingly left to their own devices, the localities responded in part by working in greater partnership with the private corporate sector to foster economic growth (Fainstein et al. 1986, Judd and Swanstrom 1994). In a number of cities, international capital has been a critical component of this new growth. Local planners and city managers have been active agents in promoting the globalization of metropolitan economies (Smith and Feagin 1987), facilitated through devices restructuring the central-city built environment, such as the erection of world trade centers and the enlargement of port and airport facilities, convention centers, and tourist complexes.

In Miami, a Downtown Action Committee began a publicity project in 1975 for a "New World Center," which envisioned Miami as center of the hemispheric past and future. One of the resulting projects, the Omni International Complex (containing a luxury hotel, shopping mall, theaters, and restaurants), helped spur Biscayne Boulevard's emergence as the "Fifth Avenue of the South" (Parks 1991: 168). Biscayne Bay became not only an exclusive resort for the leisure classes but also a vital hub for the transshipment of tourists and commodities in the Latin American and Caribbean Rim. The port of Miami became the largest cruise ship port in the world. A free trade zone was created near Miami International Airport. Fortune 500 companies began making Coral Cables the site of their Latin American headquarters. There was a massive metropolitan building boom beginning in the 1980s.

In New York City, Chase Manhattan Bank President David Rockefeller formed a Downtown–Lower Manhattan Association in 1956, which commissioned studies recommending the razing and restructuring of the preindustrial built environment for global capital through the construction of a World Trade Center (WTC). The Port Authority of New York–New Jersey (which operates New York's port, airports, and major bridges and tunnels) assumed the WTC project in 1964, which, when completed between 1975 and 1980, became the world's largest office complex, helping to spur New York's recovery from the fiscal crisis of 1975. Now the material edifice and symbolic landmark for New York City's position as a command center and headquarters complex for global capitalism, the WTC has helped to offset losses in Fortune 500 corporation headquarters from the regional economy and has stimulated redevelopment in Lower Manhattan, including the World Financial Center and high-income residential projects at Battery Park City.

These shifts have been paralleled in Houston with the fading power of a local Anglo power elite, the "8F crowd" (so named because of the Lamar Hotel suite at which they traditionally met), in the wake of the entrance of transnational oil and gas industry firms into the regional economy. The George R. Brown Convention Center, designed like a postmodern ocean liner to recognize Houston's importance as a port city, was built in 1987. The city's global aspirations were touted with the Bush administration's choice of Houston as the site for the 1990 Economic Summit of the advanced industrialized Group of Seven (G-7) nations.

In Los Angeles, the steady entrance of a transnational corporate presence into its central business district was encouraged by long-time mayor Tom Bradley in the 1970s and 1980s. The metropolis promoted its growing visibility on the international stage when it hosted the Summer Olympics in 1984. As discussed by Mike Davis in his book, *City of Quartz* (1990), the CRA was a major player in transforming Bunker Hill and other downtown neighborhoods into a civic center for the elites as well as an advanced corporate headquarters and management complex for transnational capitalism. The First Interstate Bank World Center (also known as the Library Tower and now the U.S. Bank Tower) was completed in 1989 and is still the tallest skyscraper west of the Mississippi River. Japanese investors were greatly vested in the downtown building boom in the 1980s.

Urban growth machines, constituted of coalitions of place entrepreneurs (rentier capitalists) and public officials committed to local economic development, have been endemic to American cities since the era of westward expansion, but as Logan and Molotch (1987: 57–85) observe, growth machines of the modern era are alliances of a more "multifaceted matrix" of interests that include the local media, utility companies, universities, arts institutions, professional sports, organized labor, and small retailers. Judd and Swanstrom (1994) describe corporate center strategies, tourism, and sports franchise expansion as the centerpieces of contemporary urban redevelopment schemes. Urban tourism efforts are predicated upon the strategy of assembling clusters of attractions near restored railroad termini and hotel and convention center complexes, providing urban tourists, conventioneers, and business visitors with easy walking or transportation access (Law 1993: 128).

The spread of ethnic enterprise enclaves in U.S. cities, along with the new tendency in urban policy to create local "enterprise zones" and "empowerment zones" in public redevelopment areas, are symptoms of an emerging neoliberal city where the state grants tax concessions to attract private investment capital. These enterprise and empowerment zones depend on private–public partnerships in lieu of publicly financed community development strategies (Dávila 2004: 9). Neoliberalism is another way of describing globalization processes, but with more attention to policies touting the removal of political barriers to free trade. The neoliberal city in the U.S. tends to restructure government, deregulate business environments, and privatize collective assets, unlike the earlier period before the 1960s, when federal and local governments were more committed to spending on programs of collective consumption such as urban renewal, highway construction, public education, and public housing or government-subsidized mortgage programs. The retreat from urban public spending has done much to impoverish and marginalize such constituencies as the homeless, the elderly, and inner-city underclass. At the same time, entrepreneurial values are touted in the neoliberal project and a lively competitive spirit among localities ensues in the rush to marketize the city and attract private capital for economic restructuring and downtown redevelopment. Global competition has created pressure for the restructuring of capital, especially through urban redevelopment. Local government politics are increasingly determined externally. Urban cultures have become instruments of economic restructuring in the race among locations and planned "urbanity" is becoming an economic strategy (Esser and Hirsch 1989).

Glocalization and Global–Local Dynamics

The consuming and marketing of ethnicity are intriguing phenomena that give insight on the dynamics of local–global interaction and the features of economic and cultural globalization in our society. The growth and persistence of ethnic economies and cultures challenge the popular contention that globalization carries forth a process of Westernization through a mass monoculture created by transnational corporations headquartered in the U.S., such as McDonalds, Coca-Cola and Nike, that threatens to displace local, ethnic, and indigenous cultures. I argue for a more dialectical understanding of the relationship between local culture and global culture, where processes of globalization can also intensify the opportunities for local culture and community development.

As culture increasingly becomes a factor of production in urban economic development, many cities have sought to replicate the "Bilbao effect," achieved through "world-class" high-cultural construction projects such as the Guggenheim Museum designed by globally renowned architect Frank Gehry, which has made a great contribution to the recent economic revival in the declining provincial city of Bilbao, Spain. While elite landmark museums are one way of developing a cultural "sense of place" to assist in urban regeneration, there is growing interest in the role of bohemian and subcultural arts scenes at the level of the neighborhood or community. The impact of an abstract expressionist artistic colony on the revitalization of the declining industrial district of Soho in New York through the phenomenon of "loft living" was documented by Zukin (1982) and the subsequent displacement of artistic pioneers through gentrification and rising property values. Local cultural districts can be promoted for their artistic, hip, and subcultural qualities, such as New York City's East Village (Mele 2000) as well as "neo-bohemias" such as Chicago's Wicker Park (Lloyd 2006). In the postindustrial urban economy, the neighborhood is a growing force as a unit of cultural production.[10]

The concept of "glocalization" is pertinent. Glocalization is a conceptual portmanteau of globalization and localization that describes a world where global and local processes are not in binary opposition but intimately intertwined. Roland Robertson asserts the term originated in Japan (from *dochakuka*, meaning roughly "global localization"), to describe the transnational business practice of customizing international commodities to niche markets and local cultural tastes. The theory of glocalization describes intensification of local-level, "small box" processes in the midst of broader processes of globalization and social change. Roland Robertson (1992: 173–74) says that glocalization describes the simultaneity or co-presence of both universalizing and particularizing tendencies. From this standpoint, multicultural niche markets are particularized strategies to realize the universalizing global market. The local cultural particularism of ethnic enclaves and bohemian subcultures can be appropriated as by transnational corporate capital and the growth machinery of the world city to attract a broader diversity of urban visitors, tourists, and consumers.

While there are both economic and social dimensions to the process of localization, the process also has many ramifications in identity politics. Several convergent epochal trends, including the fall of the Soviet Union and its client states, the global proliferation of a mass media promoting secular values, and the spread of trade agreements such as the North American Free Trade Agreement (NAFTA), have stimulated the exploration of local and particularistic identities in the era of globalization and neoliberalism. This search for fundamentalism varies in its onus from ethnic nationalism in Eastern Europe and Central Asia, to Islamic and Christian fundamentalism, to the indigenous Zapatista rebellion in Chiapas, Mexico. While the anti-modern impulse that animates autochthonous movements seems to elevate atavistic or ancestral values, the nostalgic return to the traditional and the original can be understood as a response to globality. Local, ethnic, and fundamentalist movements in the global era are stimulated through social practices of interaction and reflexivity. Local culture comes to a new self-consciousness through seeing through the "looking glass" of global culture. Local culture is thus in dialectical interaction with global culture. There is a growing search for roots, ethnic identity, and autonomous homelands in the growing slippage between national identity and peoplehood. Opportunities for local–global exchange and transnational social movement building are opened up through mechanisms such as global human rights campaigns, worldwide ministries, cultural survival, and "first peoples" movements. The particularistically universal and the universalistically particular are two sides of the same coin. We can "think globally and act locally" as well as "think locally and act globally."

Projects of cultural survival and local development have emerged within the landscape of economic decline and neoliberal globalization. Assortments of initiatives have emerged amidst the landscape of deindustrialization, urban, and rural decline in America. They include marginalized farming communities such as the Pennsylvania Amish, sleepy seaside fishing villages and "cannery rows" such as Monterey, California (Norkunas 1993, Walton 2001), and deindustrialized mill towns such as Lowell, Massachusetts (Norkunas 2002) that have been preserving local heritage and using tourism as a redevelopmental strategy to renew their local economies. In some cases the adaptive re-use of declining industrial districts employs more inauthentic simulations of cultural heritage, such as the "festival marketplaces" in waterfront projects as Fanueil Hall marketplace in Boston, Harborplace in Baltimore, and Riverwalk in San Antonio that are built as top-down mega-redevelopment projects engineered by downtown growth machines and corporate developers. In other cases, localization projects are built from the grassroots and indigenous community through practices of historical preservation and community development. I am especially interested in ethnic localization projects that originate from the neighborhood and community level, and how they interact with economic and social forces from above.

In Great Britain, an early industrializing nation that is an environment of persisting decline and deindustrialization, we have seen the growth of an extensive heritage tourism sector. The particular strength of Britain in the global division of tourism relies upon its heritage, its popular historical reputation especially among Americans as the quaint "old country." Sites beyond London include Oxford, Cambridge, Stratford, York, and Edinburgh. Liverpool has capitalized on its Merseyside heritage in Beatles music and soccer, while Bradford has touted its status as "Worstedopolis" with a new presence of the Asian culture in restaurants, sari centers, and Asian markets, complete with curry tours and marketing pamphlets entitled "Flavours of Asia" (Urry 2002: 98–109). In the book *The Heritage Industry: Britain in a Climate of Decline* (1987), the author Hewison asserts that Britain has shifted from being global leader in the manufacturing of industrial goods, to global leader in the manufacturing of heritage. The superseding of industrial decline by heritage tourism is perhaps most visibly apparent at the Wigan Pier Heritage Centre of Great Britain, which is located on the Leeds–Liverpool canal in Lancashire, England. This former coal-mining capital has been restored into a tourist attraction through the refurbishment of canal warehouses into museum exhibition centers, a reconstructed nineteenth-century schoolroom with living actors in period costume, its canal boat rides and full-time Piermaster. There are also displays of old trades, including clog-making and textiles. The Heritage Centre presents a history of popular struggle and the heroic labor of the miners (Urry 2002: 102). The heritage tourism has stimulated the redevelopment of the city with a colorful market, elegant shops, sports facilities, attractive pubs and restaurants, and delightful canal-side walkways. Selling Wigan's heritage to tourists is part of the process of selling Wigan to potential investors.

Globalization and the acceleration of social change are among the new conditions producing changes in individual and group self-consciousness about identity and memory. With globalization, the experience of collective memory is both becoming more global as well as more local (Gillis 1994). With the increased mobility of labor and capital across national borders in the global economy, we also experienced greater interdependency between the fortunes of local economies and the global marketplace. Collective trauma increasingly has a global reach through events like the Holocaust, the Chernobyl disaster, the Tiananmen Square massacre, and the 9/11 disaster at the World Trade Center. At the same time, there is a growing density in local collective memories through the historical preservation of ethnic and vernacular cultures, the popular revolution in family genealogy, and other explorations in local particularity. The "roots" phenomenon has acquired a widespread popularity. We have achieved a popular democratizing of the past. The growth in the mass media, satellite telecommunications, and the Internet permit a compression of time and space in a "global village" where the opportunities for simultaneous transmission of cultural experiences to remote locations have led to an implosion of traditional center–periphery differences. The distances between the periphery and the center, the local and the global have shrunk. The global and the local interact with a greater intensity. Globalization is a phenomenon of economic and cultural change that connects the local and the global, the particular and the universal, in dialectical interaction.

Kevin Fox Gotham similarly sees the growth of localization processes in connection to the tourism industry in his book, *Authentic New Orleans* (2007). He similarly distinguishes between "bottom-up" community-level processes and "top-down" corporate and governmental dynamics, in which there are ongoing interplay and a struggle for definition and control, in which the very authenticity of local culture is at stake. By identifying the specific features of ethnic localization processes, I also work to identify some ways of fostering local social capital and sustainable economic and community development. Table 2.1 enumerates some of the characteristics of local processes that I have identified across a range of ethnic neighborhoods during the course of my research.

Local Culture and Ethnic History

Local culture is promoted by ethnic heritage preservation initiatives through oral history projects, local historical tours, "small press" publishing ventures and newsletters, historic preservation of important local buildings, and local cultural museum projects. Cultural heritage projects create particularistic stories, genealogical histories, and collective narratives to reclaim and preserve a strong sense of "place," "home," and biographical situatedness in the midst of the universalizing force that is the world city. The spread of the "little narratives" of ethnic

Table 2.1 Types of Ethnic Local Processes

Types	*Local Processes at Work*
Economic	Growth of ethnic enclave economies comprising local "mom-and-pop" businesses, limited partnerships, and other "little box" enterprises
Historical	Spread of "little narratives" including genealogy projects, oral history projects, and ethnic history museums
Preservational	Saving and preserving local historic buildings of architectural merit and ethnic importance
Cultural	Growth of local ethnic theaters, ethnic arts scenes, ethnic culinary districts, and ethnic festivals
Monumental	Erecting of statues and monuments to ethnic leaders and local heroes
Touristic	Marketing of ethnic neighborhoods and locations for recreational and educational tourism, through walking tours, street signage, information kiosks, websites, and promotional campaigns

popular history lead to a gradual and accumulative liberation from the repression and silence that was characteristic during earlier episodes of nation building, "ethnic cleansing," and forced cultural assimilation.

Heritage preservation has become an arena for ethnic communities to engage in contestation, preservation, and education. The impact in the urban arena is similar to that achieved by ethnic history and "ethnic studies" movements in the academic landscape.

While ethnic tourism has grown alongside the recent expansion in ethnic enclaves and economic partnerships between ethnic entre-preneurs with city government and other arenas of the public sector, the ethnic heritage movement has emerged as a product of the community action and preservation movement in ethnic neighbor-hoods. These urban movements are correlated with the "ethnic power" and "identity politics" movements taking place in American political and academic arenas since the 1960s in the wake of the civil rights movement and the Vietnam War. They connect with the "new social history" movement within academic intellectual history. Many different networks of ethnic community activists representing first- or second-generation backgrounds converged and cooperated to establish a variety of projects in heritage recovery and preservation, conducting oral histories, establishing museums, sponsoring festivals and other cultural events to honor the contributions of immigrant and minority ethnic people in American history. These activist networks helped to stop the destruction of poor ethnic places by slum clearance and urban renewal initiatives that held little appreciation for the neighborhoods or heritage of immigrants and minorities. These efforts have contributed to the stabilizing of inner-city neighborhoods and stimulate tourism. The growth of ethnic heritage preservation and ethnic tourism represents a kind of "coming of age" for ethnic groups in formulating a community history and a memory of their immigrant ancestors.

Chinese American history museums such as the Museum of the Chinese in the Americas in New York, the Chinese American Museum of Los Angeles, and the Los Angeles Chinatown Heritage and Visitors Center operated by the Chinese Historical Society of Southern California have emerged to claim a space in American public history for the previously unsung achievements of immigrant Chinese in America in the railroad industry, hand laundry work, restaurants, and garment sweatshops. Through oral history and popular documentary, they give voice to an ethnic group whose history was previously suppressed and undocumented. The Japanese American National Museum in Los Angeles' Little Tokyo similarly resurrects the collective trauma of dislocation and internment experienced by the "Nisei" generation of Japanese American immigrants. At El Pueblo Historical Monument in downtown Los Angeles, heritage preservation at the sites such as the Avila House, Sepulveda House, and Pico House highlight the legacy of Anglo conquest of Mexico and the dispossession and repatriation of Mexican Americans.

Many of these projects emerged out of organizing and consciousness-raising sessions conducted by ethnic activists during the 1960s and 1970s, to confront the racism and economic impoverishment that had left their neighborhoods displaced or threatened by urban renewal or abandoned through governmental neglect of public services in the inner city. These activist networks joined ethnic people who came of age in traditional inner-city ethnic neighborhoods with people who came into these neighborhoods from other ethnic places as well integrated suburban locations. Ethnic heritage projects concentrate the work of activists across time and space in one location. Second- and later-generation Chinese Americans coming of age in dispersed ethnic neighborhoods, the integrated suburbs, or remote locations will join first-generation activists in traditional Chinatowns.

There is great variation in the character and pace of this progress among the diversity of local ethnic enclaves and cultures. There is a question of who controls the progress of ethnic heritage preservation. The future of local cultures and communities is still under question insofar as they are still subject to future appropriation and displacement unless they can sustain local ownership. The fact that local heritage places are both subjects of representation as well as objects of tourism and popular consumption is a reminder of the dialectical nature of local–global interaction. The particularistic can be appropriated by the universal.

Ethnic Social Capital and Community Development

Sharon Zukin (1995) asserts the central importance of examining who controls the culture of a city, of deciding "whose culture" and "whose city." The creation of ethnic arts scenes and heritage districts for consumption and tourism are viable and potentially powerful strategies for fostering sustainable community development and cultural survival. Lily Hoffman (2003) asserts that tourism may act as an "equalizing force" in contemporary Harlem, a way of counteracting the social isolation and concentrated poverty of the racial ghetto experienced during the fordist phase of urban development. I similarly believe that tourism, the arts, and heritage projects can help to foster ethnic social capital and community development instead of economic and spatial isolation.

Robert Putnam, in his book *Bowling Alone* (2000), says the long-term decline in civic engagement in American life (as measured by declining participation in Boy Scouts, Parent–Teacher Associations, and the electoral system) has led to a decline in "social capital," or generalized relationships of trust and reciprocity. I would argue that Putnam overlooked immigrant social institutions and ethnic communities when he measured the decline of social capital in America.

Putnam distinguishes between *bonding capital* (exclusive) and *bridging capital* (inclusive) (2000: 22–23). Bonding social capital describes social networks among homogeneous groups of people, while bridging capital occurs among networks of more socially heterogeneous groups. Bonding capital can sometimes describe some negative social characteristics, such as the fraternal exclusivity of subcultural "gangs" and crime syndicates, the clannish insularity of ethnic patronage organizations, and the racial hatred of white supremacist organizations. In U.S. Chinatowns, the Consolidated Chinese Benevolent Association (CCBA, sometimes known as the "Six Companies") has historically represented the essence of the conservative and fraternal clan and kinship associations. The dense networks of ethnic enclave economies epitomize the reciprocity and solidarity of bonding capital, where ethnic labor trades exploitative working conditions for the social and cultural protections offered by co-ethnic bosses. When confronted with problems such as racism, prejudice, and sociospatial isolation in U.S. cities, the persistence of immigrant enclaves and greater stocks of ethnic bonding capital may have historically compensated for the lack of bridging capital.

Bridging capital, by contrast, is more often described advantageously, as a means to information and connections to external assets like jobs and public influence. The new entrepreneurs, political figures, and community leaders of today's Chinatowns build social bridging capital through their connections to the outside world and their access to external networks of investment capital, government funding, and philanthropy. They work through an organizational infrastructure that includes ethnic chambers of commerce, political organizations, community development corporations, heritage museums, churches, and other community-based organizations. The growth in these new ethnic actors is a product of economic globalization and neoliberalism, the Civil Rights movement, and other social movements of the 1960s and 1970s. While many of these organizations have a bonding aspect insofar as they have an ethnic-based identification, their memberships and boards of directors are increasingly diverse in terms of socioeconomic class, and often by ethnicity and national origin. They are bridging organizations also since they are connected with social and economic change.

The positive functions of robust and institutionally complete ethnic enclave economies are often compared with underclass black neighborhoods and "ghetto economies" that are challenged by poverty and disinvestment, social isolation, and lack of investment capital as well as social capital. The loss of a small business sector as well as vital bonding and bridging institutions has led to declines in trust, reciprocity, and civic engagement, hampering the process of economic and community development. The African American neighborhoods of Houston's Fourth Ward and Miami's Overtown, both subjected to condemnation and clearance during the fordist phase of postwar urban development, face huge obstacles in their efforts. The black community in New York City's Harlem, by contrast, survived the disinvestment process more institutionally and economically intact, and has been able to foster "ethnic-based" economic and community development in a fashion comparable to other dynamic immigrant enclaves, such as the Chinatowns of New York and Los Angeles, and the Cuban–Latin American enclave of Miami.

Ethnic culture and tourism initiatives can build social capital that bridges the relationship between ethnic insiders and nonethnic consumers, visitors, and audiences. Ethnic festivals, parades, and other public and performative events can be of significant impact in building this kind of bridging capital and collectivizing the recreational experience. Ethnic artistic, heritage and community organizations also contribute to the forming of ethnic bonding capital among co-ethnics through the organizational apparatus of nonprofit membership organizations that constitute the ethnic nonprofit sector. Ethnic good will and civic engagement can help to sustain the ethnic economy as well as altruism, volunteering, and philanthropy. The financial and social contributions of ethnic individuals and businesses are vital to the economic success of ethnic-based nonprofit cultural organizations and community groups. At the same time, ethnic community-based organizations and nonprofits help to sustain local businesses through their fundraising events, by renting the facilities of popular ethnic restaurants and meeting halls. The Versailles restaurant, for example, in Miami's Little Havana, is a sprawling landmark restaurant that has for decades been a gathering point for the community, anti-Castro protestors, and political fundraisers. The Chinese Museum of Los Angeles often uses the Golden Dragon restaurant for its seasonal banquet fundraisers.

Building ethnic good will and social capital is of major importance when considering the spatial dispersal of immigrants from their initial colonies in the inner city. Heritage, art and community development efforts in downtown, "core" Chinatowns must contend with the fact that the Chinese American population has spread into outlying clusters (such as the "satellite Chinatowns" of New York's outer boroughs) or extensive "ethnoburbs" (such as the suburban Chinese enclave of the San Gabriel Valley in Los Angeles). Another trend to contend with is the cultural assimilation of latter-generation Chinese Americans. Nonprofit arts and heritage organizations provide both a spatial and temporal focus for building ethnic social capital and community development. Ethnic arts also attract co-ethnics from home countries, giving these local arts scenes more of a diasporic and international character. Local fundraising campaigns can be transnational in scope. The Japanese American National Museum of Los Angeles, for instance, was able to tap significant corporate sponsorship in Japan, with assistance from Akio Morita, founder of the Sony Corporation, who had one of his executives garner support among the *keidenren* (the major Japanese business federation).

The development of local economies and cultures can help to sustain community development as long as local stakeholders are able to make effective bridges with outside public and private interests. Ethnic enclaves and communities gain positive access to consumers and tourists by playing to urban tourism and niche marketing strategies advanced by public officials, booster organizations, and private developers. At the same time, they suffer some negative consequences of ethnic marketing with respect to the degrading of authenticity and cultural ownership. Local ethnic residents and business owners are also exposed to the speculative pressures of appreciating property markets. I investigate the marketing of ethnic localities as a practice that creates costs as well as benefits.

3

ETHNICITY IN AMERICA FROM WORLD'S FAIR TO WORLD CITY

Cities are vehicles and barometers of economic and cultural change. Over the course of the last 150 years, U.S. cities have experienced periods of rise, decline, and rebirth through shifting economic cycles and changing paradigms of racial–ethnic relations. Looking at the past, we can put the present in clearer perspective. The growth of ethnic heritage places in our contemporary world cities recalls the phenomena of ethnic cultural attractions in the world's fairs in U.S. cities during the imperialist phase of capitalist development. In this chapter, I examine the changing ways that ethnicity has been represented in the American city through three successive phases of urban history from the nineteenth to the twenty-first centuries.

In Table 3.1, I distinguish three major periods in urban economic and cultural development in the U.S. from the 1870s to the present. From the antebellum period of the late nineteenth century until the 1910s, U.S. cities grew rapidly as the country made a drive to industrial maturity and nation building, and entered the world stage as an imperialist power. Cities staged international expositions by building grand temporary palaces and fairgrounds to promote urban and regional development and create collective images of prosperity, invention, national progress, and white supremacy. They were also celebrations of economic liberalism, free trade, and the world market, meant to generate public interest in foreign markets and cultures, and justify imperialistic interventionism abroad. They displayed foreign and indigenous peoples in educational and touristic environments. There were carnival "midways" that were like streets of all races and nations, and ethnological villages that were like human zoos where spectators could observe the exotic diversity of world cultures, sometimes as debased colonial subjects. The world's fairs gave impetus to the City Beautiful movement among urban planners and parks advocates, as well as movements for social reform, public health, and the education and moral uplift of the urban and immigrant poor in the U.S. The urban "slums" were viewed much like internal colonies similar to the external colonies that were in need of civilizing, reform, and moral uplift. The Neoclassical and Beaux Arts architecture of the time period celebrated European traditions, as aesthetic representations of American empire and white racial superiority. The Beaux Arts edifices of the 1893 Columbian Exposition in Chicago were known as the "White City." Immigration policy was generally liberal at this time, especially with regard to European immigration. Some groups suffered immigration control, such as the Chinese, who were subjected to exclusion in 1882.

The period from approximately the 1920s to the 1960s represented the maturation of the U.S. economy to the "fordist" mode of production and social regulation. "Fordism" describes the production paradigm named for Henry Ford, who pioneered mass production methods through use of the assembly line in the automobile industry, as well as a five-dollar, eight-hour working day. The theory of mass production derives from Frederic Taylor's concepts of scientific management derived from time and motion studies on workers in the production process. Key to Henry Ford's strategy was to use higher wages to stimulate worker motivation while intensifying efficiency in the work process. By creating a significant wage gap compared with alternative jobs, Ford's high-wage policy helped to limit worker turnover, while fostering worker morale and commitment as well as stabilizing family life and social integration. With higher wages, workers could also buy more of the products that they themselves created. The theory of fordism as a "mode of social regulation" that was developed by Marxist thinkers links the paradigm of mass production to that of mass consumption, thus representing a distinct regime in the mode of capitalist accumulation.[1]

The concept of fordism recognizes the importance of the consumption process in the social reproduction of labor. Ford was known to pay his workers high wages in order that they might be able to consume more, and the "feedback loop" between mass production and mass consumption describes a "fordist" regime of accumulation that brought capitalist profitability through the business cycle. Industrial conflict in the 1930s resulted in a growing number of collective bargaining agreements for organized labor. Fordism encompassed a "social contract" or "accord" between capital and labor. The spread of Keynesian policies of government spending to address unemployment and stimulate the economy during the 1930s also can be said to promote the social contract. Public spending during the New Deal spanned a range of areas including public works programs, public housing, and infrastructure development. In the postwar period, federal commitments were poured into a range of social programs, including the interstate highway system, public education, suburban housing development, and subsidized mortgage financing for homebuyers.

This was a period of protectionism and restrictions in U.S. immigration policy. The Quota Acts of 1921 and 1924 ended what were several decades of relative openness to immigration. Restrictions by national origin were codified in 1929. While discourses of white racial superiority and forced assimilation were more prevalent in the earlier period, assimilation assumed a softer and more voluntary nature as the paradigm of the "melting pot" became more commonplace. There was a revival of the international expositions in the late 1930s, but they did not feature the cultural diversity of the world's fairs of the imperialist era. Cities were perceived increasingly as places of decline and crime, and subjected to agendas of urban renewal. The spatial polarization between declining cities and expanding suburbs led to the growing segregation of underclass minorities in the inner city, contributing to the civil rights movement and the urban race riots of the 1950s and 1960s. The social disturbances of the 1960s further provoked white flight, leading to further urban disinvestment and a crisis of fordism by the 1970s, as many municipalities experienced fiscal bankruptcy.

The crisis of fordism shifted in the 1970s into the new mode of capitalist accumulation and social regulation known as postfordism. The postfordist mode of production is based on *flexible* specialization, small batch production rather than mass production methods. Postfordism also encompasses the growing impact of globalization and neoliberalism on the U.S. economy, including industrial outsourcing to offshore regions, deregulation of labor and capital flows, and support for neoliberal free trade agreements and institutions, such as NAFTA and the World Trade Organization (WTO). While offshore production has led to deindustrialization in many traditional industrial regions of the U.S., globalization has spurred the growth of certain world cities, which are advanced financial corporate headquarters complexes for the world economy and gateways of immigration and capital flow between the U.S. and its trading regions, such as New York, Miami, Houston, and Los Angeles. The growing economic clout of these world cities in the U.S. has abetted a resurgence in urban growth machines that were in relative decline during the previous episodes of suburbanization, urban decline, and fiscal crisis that marked the close of the fordist period. These growth machines have become more internationalized in their constituency and scope, and downtown redevelopmental schemes commonly tout the benefits of tourism and the world economy, through such devices of convention centers, performing halls, and world trade centers. Urban architecture increasingly features postmodern characteristics, communicating aesthetic qualities of parody, collage, cultural vernacular, historicism, as compared with the rationalized, bureaucratic, high technology, and international styles that characterized architectural modernism. New Urbanism has become popularized within both design and urban planning, to promote neotraditional community values including pedestrian scale, public spaces, and local cultural heritage and nature.

Ethnic enclaves and ethnic niche markets are increasingly prevalent in the postfordist U.S., especially in global and immigration gateway cities. This is a contrast to the fordist period of social regulation, which

Table 3.1 Historical Episodes of Urban Development in the U.S.

	1870s to 1910s	*1920s to 1960s*	*1970s to Present*
Mode of Production	Drive-to-maturity period of imperialist capitalism	Fordist period of industrial capitalism	Postcolonial (postfordist) period of global capitalism
Paradigms of City Building	World's fairs and City Beautiful movement	Urban renewal and suburbanization	Downtown redevelopment and global city
Styles of Architecture and Urban Design	Neoclassical and Beaux Arts	Modernism	Postmodernism and New Urbanism
Racial–Ethnic Relations Paradigm	White racial superiority and imperialism	Assimilation	Pluralism
Immigration Policy	Liberal immigration	Restrictionism	Liberal immigration with some restrictionism

promoted cultural assimilation, suburbanization, and the promise of the affluent middle-class "mass society." In the current period of neoliberal capitalism, ethnic cultures are again cultural attractions as they were during the days of the imperialist and expositional city. Where the ethnic representations of the world's fairs and the City Beautiful were degraded or exoticized within a paradigm of racial–ethnic hierarchy informed by white superiority and racial eugenics, ethnic attractions in the global city incorporate ethnicity into a paradigm of multiculturalism.

The City Beautiful Period: World's Fairs and the Representation of Empire

The 1870s to about the 1920s encompassed the expansionary take-off and drive-to-maturity stages in the industrialization of the United States. With the end of the Civil War and the abolition of slavery by the Emancipation Proclamation in 1864, the U.S. economy entered a period of national consolidation, including the settlement of the West and industrial development of the East. Borders were relatively open during this period of recurring labor demand, with generally rising immigration trends leading to a peak period between 1900 and 1910 when nearly one million immigrants per year arrived in the U.S. The period also marked a general shift in the national and regional origins of immigrant labor. Before the Civil War, the British Isles, Western Europe, and Scandinavia (the early industrializing "core nations" of the capitalist world system) were the main sources of labor. After the Civil War, immigrants to the Northeast and midwestern states increasingly came from Southern and Eastern European nations such as Austria, Hungary, Italy, Poland, and Russia, while East Asian immigrants such as Chinese, Japanese, and Koreans were of growing importance in the West. Immigration policy was not completely liberal during this period. Chinese immigration was initially encouraged through government acts such as the Burlingame Treaty established with China in 1868, but further immigration was subsequently halted with the Chinese Exclusion Act of 1882. Racism and nativist fears against Southern and Eastern European immigrants spurred the passage of restrictive U.S. immigration acts in 1921 and 1924.

This was a period when local industrialists, financiers, and real estate developers controlled the pace and development of cities in the U.S. These boosters and "place entrepreneurs" formed pro-growth coalitions to compete for federal financing of railroads and local economic development. Logan and Molotch (1987) call these interlocking networks of self-aggrandizing political and economic interests urban "growth machines." William Ogden, the railroad magnate who moved into real estate development and later became the mayor of Chicago, was a seminal place entrepreneur in the early Chicago growth machine.

World's fairs were tools of urban growth machines in the lively competitive spirit of capitalism among American cities in the age of the frontier. The expositions were inspired by earlier European events such as the 1851 Crystal Palace Exhibition in London, England, which commemorated the Victorian Age of Empire and Great Britain's importance as a workshop of the world. Paris also held a series of expositions, such as the 1889 Universal Exhibition that featured the erection of the Eiffel Tower. These events were grand celebrations of industrial progress, free trade, and imperialism. Through spectacular feats of engineering, they built magnificent palaces of exhibition in the midst of landscaped parks. They were commercial displays and emporia for the emerging world market in fine arts, manufactures, and consumer goods. The fairs also promoted the interests of empire and public support for overseas ventures through ethnographic displays of the peoples that inhabited the colonies. The display of these rustic and indigenous peoples in traditional states of dress and relative undress within an ethnic native village setting both degraded and exoticized them through the contrast between their "backwardness" and the "civilized" background of the beautiful grand buildings and well dressed spectators. The expositions had a didactic function in affirming the status of European and American white supremacy (Rydell 1984, Cocks 2001a). Expositions since the days of Xerxes, King of Persia, in the biblical book of Esther have been a way of showing off the glorious riches of conquest and empire (Luckhurst 1951).

Though there were some expositions after the Civil War, the first extensive American event was the 1876 Centennial Exposition in Philadelphia. Over the next 40 years, nearly one hundred million people would visit international expositions held in other cities such as New Orleans, Chicago, Atlanta, Nashville, Omaha, Buffalo, St. Louis, Portland, Seattle, San Francisco, and San Diego. The promoters of these events were primarily private capitalists, local entrepreneurs, and city governments that sought to boost urban and regional fortunes while advancing national interests as well. The federal government played a role insofar as the Congress approved appointed commissioners and established financial charters for the sale of private stock offerings, but disclaimed the state from financial liability. The Congress did appropriate federal funds for the construction of U.S. government exhibition buildings, as well as lending money. Ethnographic exhibitions curated by the Smithsonian Institution were main features at U.S. government exhibitions. Buildings were constructed to display the products of foreign nations, with the exhibition buildings of European nations aligned to emphasize their hierarchical separation from the buildings of the less advanced Latin American and Asian nations. Hierarchical ideas about social Darwinism in race and culture articulated by public officials and intellectuals at dedications and international congresses held at the expositions helped to promote mass support for immigrant restriction.

The world's fairs provided manufacturing and commercial enterprises spectacular exhibition spaces to promote and market the mass consumption of their products. The exposition grounds were landscapes of genteel leisure, representing the world of urban prosperity and harmony. They highlighted new architectural forms, especially associated with the Beaux Arts (after the French École des Beaux Arts) or Classical Revival style, which comprised an amalgamation of Greek, Roman, and Renaissance forms. Advocates of the City Beautiful urban planning movement promoted the expositions and the Beaux Arts architectural movement with the intention of generating popular support and funding for ambitious plans to restructure U.S. cities around monumental civic buildings and high cultural principles. The City Beautiful movement failed to implement these ideals systematically in any American city. The expositions served mainly to promote capital accumulation and commercial extravagance and to manufacture popular consent through new mediums of entertainment, representation, and tourism. The staging of exhibitions and voyeuristic attractions displaying the cultural diversity of the world for popular consumption gave legitimacy to larger ideologies of racial hierarchy, national progress, and imperialist hegemony (Rydell 1993, Cocks 2001a). The moral and ideological functions of national celebration were important in the minds of those that inspired and created the 1876 Centennial Exhibition of Philadelphia. Rapid industrialization was accompanied by significant episodes of labor conflict, which were intensified by an economic depression in 1873. The exposition offered an opportunity for commerce, edification, and diversionary entertainment to help temper the shock of social and economic change.

The Chicago World's Columbian Exposition of 1893 celebrated the quadricentennial of Christopher Columbus' landing in the West Indies. This was the penultimate U.S. world exposition of the City Beautiful era. Prominent railroad titans, developers, bankers, and public officials from New York cooperated with their counterparts in Chicago to lobby for the federal charter and funding for the event. Renowned architect and urban planner Daniel Burnham oversaw the design and construction of the buildings and grounds. The magnificent palaces of the "White City" occupied prime positions at the lakefront, while a Midway Plaisance receded away to a giant Ferris wheel. The midway was the honky-tonk sector of the fair, a carnivalesque strip of popular amusements, restaurants, and ethnic villages. The historian Hubert Howe Bancroft described the scene as follows:

> Entering the avenue a little to the west of the Woman's Building [the visitor] would pass between the walls of medieval villages, between mosques and pagodas, past the dwellings of colonial days, past the cabins of South Seas islanders, of Javanese, Egyptians, Bedouins, Indians, among them huts of bark and straw that tell of yet ruder environment. They would be met on their way by German and Hungarian bands, by the discord of . . . camel drivers and donkey-boys, dancing girls from Cairo and Algiers, from Samoa and Brazil, with men and women of all nationalities, some lounging in oriental indifference, some shrieking in unison or striving to outshriek each other, in the hope of transferring his superfluous change from the pocket of the unwary pilgrim . . . Finally they betake themselves to the Ferris Wheel, on which they were conveyed with smooth, gliding motion to a height of 260 feet, affording a transient and kaleidoscopic view of the park and all it contains.
>
> (Rydell 1984: 60)

The evolutionary spectrum of human types along the midway leading up to the White City evoked the eugenicist idea of a great chain of being. The philosopher Herbert Spencer, a proponent of eugenics and social Darwinism, was keynote speaker at the Congress on Evolution, part of the conference on the "Intellectual and Moral Exposition of the Progress of Mankind" held at the exposition. Another important paper was delivered at the exposition at the Congress of the American Historical Association by a promising new historian called Frederick

Figure 3.1 Chinese Theater at the Chicago World's Columbian Exposition of 1893. Paul V. Galvin Library of the Illinois Institute of Technology.

Jackson Turner, "The Significance of the Frontier in American History," a defining essay in the annals of U.S. intellectual history.

As international expositions continued to be organized throughout the U.S., they expressed the special character of regional economic sectors, industrial products and racial–ethnic minority subcultures. The southern expositions (New Orleans 1885, Atlanta 1895, Nashville 1897, etc.), for instance, featured cotton and brewery production exhibits as well as "Negro" ethnological displays, "Old Plantation" villages, and minstrel

Figure 3.2 Javan settlement at the Chicago World's Columbian Exposition of 1893. The Ferris wheel can be seen in the background. Paul V. Galvin Library of the Illinois Institute of Technology.

sideshows. The Trans-Mississippi Exposition at Omaha in 1898 featured Native Americans. The Louisiana Purchase Exposition of St. Louis in 1904 rivaled the impact of the 1893 Chicago exposition. The fair was held in conjunction with the first Olympic Games ever held in the Western hemisphere. Displays of new inventions such as airships and automobiles attracted many spectators. A series of international congresses brought speakers from around the world, such as Max Weber and Henri Poincaré. While celebrating the 100-year legacy of the Louisiana Purchase, the St. Louis fair reflected the theme of American imperialism abroad. As a result of the 1898 Spanish American War, the U.S. had acquired the Philippines and Puerto Rico as protectorates. By displaying the indigenous peoples as backward, the exhibits had the effect of justifying imperialism by showing the beneficial effects of Western rule. The Philippines Reservation included a colonial administrative building, educational building, and a commercial museum. The anthropological exhibits organized by the U.S. government portrayed various ethnic groups including the "high and more intelligent" Visayans and an assortment of "lost tribes" including the Islamic Moros, the "savage" Bagobos, the "monkey-like" Negritos, and the "picturesque" Igorots in open-air villages. The scantily clad Igorots, with their elaborate dances, were one of the main attractions of the entire fair. The great promise for American imperialism to civilize the "savages" was demonstrated through an exhibit on imperial schooling, and the more educated Visayans were displayed in theatrical productions wearing Western dress.[2] Hemispheric themes and Latin American trade were features of the 1901 Pan-American Exposition in Buffalo (Rydell 1984), as well as San Francisco's Panama–Pacific International Exposition of 1915 and San Diego's Panama–California Exposition of 1915–16.

Expositions were always temporary, with the magnificent buildings eventually demolished, though the landscaped grounds persisted as parks. They gave great impetus to the City Beautiful movement, which originated in the mid-nineteenth-century parks movement and village improvement societies, growing increasingly coherent after the Chicago Columbian Exposition of 1893. The City Beautiful movement was associated with the concerns of the Progressive movement for political and social reform in the cities, but with more emphasis on the aesthetic dimensions of bringing beauty and republican grandeur to cities. They criticized the individualism and commercial utility of the gridiron pattern in American cities, emphasizing monumental civic centers amidst radial avenues and concentric boulevards to create greater pride in citizenship and community (Cocks 2001a: 130–31). Like the Progressive social reformers, the parks' advocates and urban planners of the City Beautiful movement were devoted to urban improvement as a practice of "moral uplift." They sought to reconstruct the social bonds that were destroyed by the progress of industry and urbanization. They championed a kind of "civic renewal" (Cocks 2001a: 132) that linked economic reform with spiritual and aesthetic beautification. Beauty would take a defining role in the construction of moral order and social improvement. They linked the well-being of the public to an ideal of national citizenship. City business associations gave active support to the City Beautiful movement, but the movement made only partial progress as a national urban planning and parks movement. Daniel Burnham played a leading role in the movement and designed unified city plans for Chicago, Washington, San Francisco, and Cleveland. New York made great strides with the vision of Frederic Olmstead in creating Central Park, but Washington, D.C. represents perhaps the fullest expression of the City Beautiful movement, where a Commission on Fine Arts headed by both Burnham and Olmstead created an array of monuments and boulevards that extended the neoclassical framework already laid by Thomas Jefferson and Pierre L'Enfant.

Though expositions were transient, they were huge celebrations that transformed city landscapes for the sake of commemoration and commerce. They featured speeches, parades with historical floats, and dedications of monuments, and dominated a city's newspapers, streets, and squares for successive days and weeks. Educators used the events to discuss issues of local and national significance. Through the forging of links between history and national industrial achievement in an atmosphere of touristic celebration and festivity, the expositions legitimated social inequalities and elite cultural authority. They promoted tourism and leisure for city dwellers while simultaneously acting as a vehicle of Americanization and helping to blunt class and ethnic conflict. The growing urban tourism industry served both civic and commercial goals (Cocks 2001a: 178–80). The emergence of urban tourism to fulfill leisure time was important to social reproduction of a proletariat that was experiencing the onset of industrial capitalist work and time discipline, and the volatility of the capitalist business cycle. There were financial panics in 1873 and 1893, and the 1880s were an era of recurring labor conflict, including the nationwide Pullman railroad strike of 1894 and the "Haymarket riot" of 1886 in Chicago. The public mixing permitted at expositions, also, exposed officials to public attack, and President William McKinley was famously assassinated while on location at the Pan-American Exposition of 1901 in Buffalo, by Leon Czolgosz, a reputed anarchist. The event triggered state repression of anarchists and socialists throughout the country and the fair recovered to be eventually judged a success (Rydell 1984: 152).

The world's fairs influenced the growth of city parades, carnivals, and the boosting of urban tourism (Cocks 2001a). Parades had originally emerged as phenomena of oppositional public culture in Europe and among European immigrants to America. Whether staged for protest or revelry, street parades had a certain unpredictability that could degenerate into social disorder. By the time of the American Revolution, parades had become more institutionalized and routinized, with military troops and brass bands, trades and labor associations, schoolboys and public officials taking the streets for the Fourth of July and other patriotic holidays (Davis 1986). A more carnivalesque celebration of historical, allegorical, and ethnic themes for entertainment and the boosting of commercial interests gradually superseded the spirit of revolutionary and proletarian solidarity during the City Beautiful period. Just as in exposition midways, parade float processions were staged to communicate a narrative of racial–ethnic succession and evolution, with exhibits of "primitive" and "savage" cultures making way to the more "modern" and "civilized." The floats, displays, and carnival amusements separated spectators from the objects of display while making the objects more visible, condensed symbols of racial difference. These urban public entertainments represented the racial–ethnic "other" as different, exotic, or degraded, while dramatizing their integration into a rational economy in the spirit of commercialized leisure and national celebration (Cocks 2001b: 96–101). The spontaneity of oppositional public culture had been succeeded by a public culture of racial–ethnic containment within a framework of civic unity and social progress.

The condition of racial–ethnic "otherness" was staged in urban festivals with an increasing concern for authenticity. At the Hudson–Fulton Celebration of 1909, for example, the festival organizers retained a contractor with the understanding that 125 authentic Iroquois Indians (not halfbreed) would be delivered with costumes and accoutrements, with proper attention to coaching of the performers for the exciting rendition and stylistic choreography of performances rather than appearing as dying souvenirs of a vanishing culture. At the San Francisco Portolá Festival of 1909, organizers took great concern in appointing Nicholas A. Covarrubias as an "authentic" presider of

Californio descent to play the part of the first governor of the state, Don Gaspar de Portolá (Cocks 2001b: 98–99).

Los Angeles was later in its metropolitan development, remaining a dusty frontier pueblo dominated by booming San Francisco to the north until the arrival of the Southern Pacific Railroad in 1887. Los Angeles never staged an international exposition, though it promoted a festival that evoked New Orleans Mardi Gras and the racial–ethnic pageantry of the world's fair period. The Los Angeles Merchants and Manu-facturers Association (M&M) organized an annual La Fiesta de Los Angeles beginning in 1894, a year after the hugely successful 1893 Chicago exposition. The fiestas, which originated at the Plaza, the old center of Los Angeles, had been a popular annual phenomenon of the city's Latin American community for religious rites and ranching celebrations since the *pueblo* period of Spanish colonization and Mexican rule in California. The M&M successfully appropriated the religious connotations of the fiesta to more commercial purposes, with floats to advertise sponsoring businesses and products. For the grand finale of the week's events, it organized a parade as a moving multicultural tableau of regional diversity that included Native American, Mexican American, African American and Chinese American participation. A float of angels began the procession, moving through Spanish cavaliers into pueblo Indians. The parade romanticized the Spanish American heritage and American conquest while ignoring the Native American genocide. It displayed the transition into U.S. rule as one marked by social progress and national integration (Deverell 2004).

The growth in the urban travel tourism spurred the development of an urban guidebook and sketchbook industry. Emulating the city guidebooks published for the urban expositions, national companies like Rand, McNally and Appleton began publishing travel guidebooks of cities. With the public interest in foreign and exotic cultures stimulated by the midways and amusement zones of the world's fairs, an oppor-tunity arose for local companies and authors to create guidebooks and walking tours of local racial and ethnic minority communities. They stimulated the phenomenon of "respectable" middle-class tourists "slumming" in minority neighborhoods to pursue voyeuristic, exotic, and "authentic" experiences in the heart of the inner city. Urban guidebooks and slumming tours of minority communities during the turn of the twentieth century stimulated middle-class interest in ethnic restaurants, souvenirs, and curio shopping. The work of Hutchins Hapgood in New York's Lower East Side is typical in this respect (Cocks 2001a). The work of photographer Arnold Genthe in portraying San Francisco Chinatown is also illustrative. In capitalizing on the voyeuristic craze for slumming, historian John Kuo Wei Tchen points out that Genthe effectively "orientalized" his photographs to make them appear more authentically Chinese by retouching, erasing, or cropping out images of Western pedestrians.[3]

The Case of the Statue of Liberty

The Statue of Liberty is a relic of the City Beautiful period of American urban history. It is a monumental evocation of the Neoclassical and Beaux Arts architectural movement that communicates messages of republican grandeur, liberty, and enlightenment. As an icon of American political liberty and nationhood, its grand representation of womanhood is a stark contrast to the historical hegemony of the male image in other famous monuments, such as Mt. Rushmore and the presidential monuments in Washington, D.C. It was through the efforts of Jewish American leaders and visionaries and the support of the American general public that the statue became a symbol of America as a refuge for immigrants and slaves from persecution, oppression, and intolerance. While still essentially a white representation of the American motherland, the iconic meanings of the image have become more pluralized over time. We can see that American collective memory is not an immutable creation of political and cultural elites through the example of the changing social meanings of the Statue of Liberty. The heritage represented by our greatest cultural monuments can be subject to transformation.

The statue was a gift from the French government intended to mark the American Centennial. Construction was delayed, however, and only the arm and torch were available for the Philadelphia Centennial Exhibition of 1876. The statue was completed, shipped, and dedicated ten years later in New York in 1886. The French elite were hesitant to fund the statue, and monies were eventually generated through public lottery sales. As a gesture of collaboration, the U.S was expected to fund the construction of the base and pedestal. The French politician and author Édouard de Laboulaye and others opposed to the regime of Napoleon III conceived it as a way of immortalizing ideals of liberty and republicanism in the U.S. at a time when these ideals were threatened in France. French sculptor Frédéric Auguste Bartholdi was commissioned to design the statue, and he drew his inspiration from Marianne, the powerful female symbol of the French Revolution. Marianne originated in the vernacular culture of peasants in the south of France before she became an official symbol of French national culture (Bodnar 1992: 18).[4]

The representation of enlightened womanhood represented by the Statue of Liberty was also famously foreshadowed in a painting (circa 1872) by John Gast called *American Progress* that represents an allegory of Manifest Destiny. In the scene, an angelic woman (sometimes identified as Columbia, a nineteenth-century personification of the United States) carries the light of "civilization" westward with American settlers, stringing telegraph wire as she travels. Native Americans and wild animals flee—or lead the way—into the darkness of the "uncivilized" West. A female figure representing the U.S. called Columbia had similarly been in use since the time of the American Revolution. Popular in political cartoons, Columbia was the female equivalent of Uncle Sam.

The Statue of Liberty is a contrast to other U.S. monuments that are mainly representations of great statesmen, such as Mt. Rushmore and the Washington, Lincoln, and Jefferson Memorials in Washington, D.C. Its origins as a gift from a European ally rather than a creation of the U.S. government made the public ambivalent about the statue. Many Americans were suspicious and some clergymen saw pagan and idolatrous values connected with the icon. Efforts were slow in obtaining government funding for the base and pedestal for the statue until the intervention of the publisher Joseph Pulitzer, who spurred fundraising through the editorial pages of his newspaper, *The World*. Pulitzer was a Jewish Hungarian immigrant with allegiances to the Progressive urban reform movement. Using the ploy of promising to publish the name of every contributor no matter how small the donation, Pulitzer eventually raised $100,000, mostly in small donations from 120,000 people from all walks of life, including children and senior citizens. The statue also pays homage to the abolition of slavery, as represented by her feet, which trample chains of bondage at the base: African Americans were major contributors.[5]

The Jewish historian and poet Emma Lazarus wrote the poem, "The New Colossus," which renamed the statue "Mother of Exiles," as an auction piece during fundraising efforts for the statue in 1883. Her poem celebrating the Statue of Liberty as a beacon light and new homeland for foreign immigrants and refugees of persecution did not immediately capture national attention in the atmosphere of labor unrest and immigrant restriction of the late nineteenth century. In his brief speech at the statue's dedication, President Grover Cleveland described the statue as "our own peaceful deity keeping watch before the open gates of America"; as, therefore, a watchful guardian rather than an international symbol of liberty and refuge (Perea 1997). Sympathetic Jewish American interests financed the placing of a bronze plaque containing the poem on an interior wall of the statue in 1903. More popular interest grew when the icon was associated with advertising promoting Liberty Bond drives sponsored by the government during World War I, as well as in posters promoting immigrant loyalty to the war effort. But the poem remained outside of the American popular imagination during the climate of immigrant restrictionism of the 1910s and 1920s. In the 1930s, Jewish American refugees from Nazism gave renewed impetus to reviving the Lazarus poem which has become a durable icon for the oppressed and persecuted in the national collective psyche. The journalist and writer Louis Adamic was leader in these efforts to persuade public school teachers to acknowledge the statue as an icon of the immigrant contribution to American history.[6]

Immigrant "Slums" and Progressive Reform

While marginalized immigrant and ethnic interests sought representation and inclusion during the City Beautiful period of U.S. urban growth, they were also the object of reform by the Progressive movement for urban reform. Even though the industrial revolution kept labor demand high during the City Beautiful period, there were recurring calls for immigrant restriction as well as the perception that immigrants and ethnic groups were closely linked to the problems of "slums" and "ghettos" in U.S. cities. Immigrants congregated during this historical period in American seaports and manufacturing centers near waterfront, warehouse, and factory districts of emerging central business districts. Rapid industrialization and immigration in many cities led to the conversion of some existing residential neighborhoods into higher density tenement housing districts with infilling of rear yards and vacant land. The incidence of residential congestion was coupled with problems of abandonment by absentee landlords, and public neglect by City services such as street paving and lighting, plumbing, and policing. These factors bred social problems and public health hazards. The American use of the term "ghetto" originated with reference to the neighborhoods of Eastern European and Russian Jews in the northeastern cities in the late nineteenth century (Ward 1989). During the City Beautiful period ethnic "slums" and "ghettos" were perceived as urban spaces plagued by residential overcrowding, unsanitary conditions, vice, and other social pathologies. A focus on the "moral uplift" of the poor prevailed among urban missionaries, charity workers, and settlement house workers, such as Jane Addams who opened Hull House in Chicago in 1889. Jacob Riis brought the spirit of reform to journalistic and photographic realism with his reportage from the tenements of New York in *How the Other Half Lives*, published in 1890. The urban poor were seen to be the product of the psychological and moral deficiencies of individuals rather than the victims of an adverse environment. Reformers were preoccupied with behavioral uplift and hygiene, though there were also efforts toward housing reform such as the Model Tenements movement, as well as urban parks advocacy.

Revival of the World's Fairs

There was a revival of the world's fairs in the 1930s, beginning with the Chicago Century of Progress Exposition of 1933. Science and technological progress were the prevailing themes of world's fairs in this period, with architecture expressing modernistic industrial design and the machine age. Main attractions included the latest modern appliances displayed in "model kitchens," the introduction of Formica, and demonstrations of long-distance phone calls at the Bell Telephone display. In 1939 came two fairs, which achieved a quintessence of the modern revival of world's fairs, the San Francisco Golden Gate International Exhibition of 1939, and the New York World's Fair of 1939. The San Francisco fair celebrated the earlier completion of the Golden Gate and San Francisco/Oakland Bay Bridges, the two largest suspension bridges in the world. The fair was a celebration of modernism and technological innovation. It marked the achievements of city building in the broader context of hemispheric relations in Latin America and the Pacific Rim. There were exhibits on the railroad industry, mining, and recreational industries in the American West (Rydell 1993). The interwar period was a more isolationist period of U.S. history, and the world's fairs of this period were less replete with exhibitions on ethnic diversity. There was a stronger cultural discourse of assimilation and the design features of the fairs conveyed the aesthetics of technology and modernism.

The New York World's Fair of 1939 and its overarching theme, "The World of Tomorrow," was perhaps the epitome of the Depression-era world's fairs. Two monuments were constructed, the Trylon and the Perisphere, which apparently were inspired by the Eiffel Tower and Celestial Globe built for the 1889 Paris Exposition. The Trylon was an equilateral triangular right prism that evoked the Eiffel Tower in a more modernistic and abstract way. This was a contrast from the more ornate and neoclassical design of the Beaux Arts architecture of the City Beautiful. Rather than representing the golden age of cities as a revival of the classical past, the modernism of the architecture in New York represented the golden age of cities as the future. The modernism of the exhibition buildings reflected the design aesthetics of streamlining, machinery, and uniformity. They communicated the promise of science and technology, the bureaucratic rationality of the corporation and nation state, and the abundance of the society of mass consumption. A main attraction was the "Futurama" exhibit inside the General Motors building, created by the stage designer Norman Bel Geddes. The exhibit gave a utopian view of cities in the future with automated super-highways and landscaped suburbs. Visitors sat in comfortable armchairs on a ride through a succession of displays that gave the illusion of flying over a city from an airplane, with a narrator giving an inspiring lecture on the wonders of the future including mass airplane travel, mass automobility, and the promises of science and technology.[7] The Futurama exhibit represented the affluent society in the era of fordism.

With the crisis in overproduction represented by the Great Depression, the revival of world's fairs gave people a sense of diversion from the economic uncertainty that confronted them, while inspiring hope for better times in the future. The federal government also promoted tourism and leisure through the work of the U.S. Parks Service, the Federal Writers' Project of the Works Progress Administration, and the creation of the U.S. Travel Bureau in 1937. Rather than being seen as non-essential activities compared with economic sectors such as agriculture and manufacturing, tourism and leisure were increasingly seen as sectors that could help promote economic stability by helping cities and regions weather business cycles and make up for losses in stagnant or declining industries (Berkowitz 2001).

Slum Clearance and Urban Renewal in the Fordist Period

With the Depression and widespread unemployment of the 1930s came a shift in the national paradigm of city building. There was a growing discourse of urban decline and a transition from city beautification and urban reform movements to slum clearance and urban renewal. The discourse became particularly pronounced after World War II, with the outmovement of people and industry to the suburbs, the urban unrest of the 1960s, and the perception of a growing problem of entrenched urban poverty and ghettoization. U.S. cities generated collective representations of social disorder and dereliction, or what Robert Beauregard (2003) calls "voices of decline." There was a growing concern with the problems of slums and blight and the rise of a rational–scientific approach to urban planning (as opposed to moral uplift in the earlier period), with the increasing participation of the federal government in the rebuilding of cities through urban renewal.

The fordist tradition in urban renewal began to prevail with the Wagner Housing Act of 1937, which established a tradition of public housing construction by the federal government. The Wagner Act has also been criticized however for establishing a legacy of constructing public housing "slab towers" in many American cities, which hurt the fabric of urban life by destroying the defensible and intimate spaces necessary to sustain healthy urban communities. In the 1930s, a variety of U.S. cities demolished inner-city residential and commercial areas. Manhattan's Lower East Side is a case in point; deteriorated piers and tenement buildings along the East River were razed to make way for expressway arterials and public housing (Buttenweiser 1987). In downtown Los Angeles, Chinatown was cleared in order to make way for the Union Railroad Station during the 1930s. Other neighborhoods were demolished for the building of the Arroyo Seco Parkway.

The Housing Act of 1937 gave way to the Housing Act of 1949, during which slum clearance became the main operation of a rational–scientific planning project of eradicating "blight" from the city (Villa 2000). Blight was identified through a variety of administrative and economic indicators such as structural deterioration of the infrastructure and poor sanitation, and falling under a threshold of minimally acceptable housing and living standards. But blight was defined not just as an aspect of things, but also as a judgment of them (Greer 1965: 22). The stigmatization of social actors accompanied urban renewal in the prosecuting of an agenda toward urban social problems, such as crime, juvenile delinquency, and venereal disease. The Taft–Ellender–Wagner Bill of 1949 offered some continued federal funding for public housing, but marked an increasing shift towards outright slum clearance for urban renewal. Urban expressways continued to be built in the postwar era, including the giant Cross-Bronx Expressway project of New York City's master planner Robert Moses, which severed a huge Jewish neighborhood, especially the "tragic mile through East Tremont" (Caro 1975: 885), paving the way to the future deterioration of the South Bronx. New York City was especially active during this period, with $267 million spent on urban renewal between 1949 and 1957, on the construction of parkways, bridges, tunnels, expressways, and public housing, while all other cities in the U.S. spent $133 million. In Miami, the African American community in Miami's Overtown was cut apart by the construction of Interstate 95, a raised-above-ground "concrete monster" that eviscerated the heart of the community and eventually led to a population loss from 40,000 to 10,000 (Mohl 1993b). The impact of urban renewal and expressway construction on African American communities in the postwar era was pervasive, causing some to describe urban renewal as a project of "Negro removal."

In Los Angeles, slum clearance and urban renewal involved more of a process of "Chicano removal" (Parson 2005). There were two distinct episodes in the early twentieth-century history of urban renewal in Los Angeles. A liberal administration led by Mayor Fletcher Bowron endorsed a plan led by Frank Wilkinson of the Housing Authority of the City of Los Angeles to apply for federal 1937 Wagner Act funds for slum clearance of the Mexican American neighborhood of Chavez Ravine, to be replaced by the Elysian Heights public housing project. The European architect Robert Neutra was commissioned to draw up a visionary plan for the giant housing project. The plan was blocked by critics who opposed the "socialistic" tendencies of the housing project, and subsequent red-baiting of the Frank Wilkinson and Fletcher Bowron administration eventually led to the election of a pro-growth coalition promoting Norris Poulson for mayor, who was elected in 1953. In a nod to middle-class versus working-class constituencies, Poulson subsequently gave the Chavez Ravine site to Walter O'Malley, owner of the Brooklyn Dodgers baseball team, to attract him to move the team to Los Angeles. Mexican American neighborhoods downtown were also removed to make way for urban expressway construction.

A mural was painted by Judith Baca and her followers in the Tujunga Wash area of the Los Angeles River channel called the "Division of the Barrios" as part of a larger set of murals called the "Great Wall of Los Angeles." This particular mural panel depicts the displacement and destruction of the Latino neighborhood at Chavez Ravine for the building of Dodger Stadium. This slum clearance project, along with downtown freeway arterials, effectively critiques policies of urban renewal for destroying the social fabric of the downtown Latino community by dividing the barrio. The mural is representative of the views of activists in a variety of racial–ethnic minority communities since the 1960s and

1970s, that urban renewal was a horrific episode in government policy that eviscerated whole neighborhoods, cut off many minorities from easy pedestrian access to the city center, and abetted urban decline in these same neighborhoods. The recent growth of interest in preserving ethnic heritage places often carries with it a spirit of fierce resistance and opposition to the legacy of slum clearance and urban renewal.

Ethnic Heritage in World's Fairs Compared with the World City

The recent growth of ethnic heritage preservation in the contemporary era of the world city invites comparisons with ethnic representation in the era of the world's fairs. To be clear, ethnic participants in the imperialist era of U.S. city building were quite subordinate to the white visitors that thronged the urban expositions. They were brought to the fairs as displays from the colonies and emerging trading regions of Latin America, Asia, and Africa. The ethnological displays of the world's fairs exhibited the ethnic other in primitive, degraded, and exotic contexts, with the exception of groups like the Japanese, who were a world imperialist power in their own right.

We can compare this with the contemporary world city, which has emerged in the postfordist (or postcolonial) period in which ethnic participants have acquired civil rights to become more equal part-ners in the economic and political structure of the American city. The economic liberalism, free trade rhetoric, and internationalism of the turn-of-the-twentieth-century period of capitalist imperialism com-pares with the neoliberalism, free trade, and globalization discourse of the contemporary period. Postcolonial ethnic actors however are more liberated and empowered to determine the destiny of their communities in an era of greater international mobility of labor and capital, and to create economic enclaves and ethnic cultural heritage places. Rather than being victims of state subordination and the expansion of capitalism, they are increasingly part and parcel of the governmental establishment and the capitalist system. In the case studies that follow, I examine in detail the economic and social dynamics taking place as ethnic actors take the stage and ethnic enclaves are increasingly interpenetrated with the urban growth machine.

4

ETHNIC PLACES, POSTMODERNISM, AND URBAN CHANGE IN HOUSTON

Houston and its gleaming skyscrapers rise over a landscape of wooded prairie and riparian bayou, where the U.S. South meets the Southwest. The city was named for General Sam Houston, who in 1836 led the Texas Army to victory over Mexican forces in nearby San Jacinto. The frontier spirit of Manifest Destiny and legacy of southern segregation have faded to reveal a more multicultural metropolis coming to grips with its turbulent past and moving towards a more international future. Leaders in the Chinese, Mexican, and African American communities are creating places of ethnic cultural heritage and tourism. Plural images of multiethnic diversity are superimposed upon an existing local culture of Anglo patriotism and free enterprise. An eclectic cast of characters (including heroic pioneers, cowboys, wildcatters, oilmen, and spacemen) has historically imbued a forward-looking rugged individualism in the metropolitan cultural iconography. In the wake of a postmodern archi-tectural building episode, which crowned the severe regional recession of the mid-1980s, new ethnic place entrepreneurs and community leaders have emerged with new power and potential to contribute to the economic revitalization of Houston and its cultural self-definition as a headquarters of the world petrochemical industry.

I taught for three years in the early 1990s in the Sociology Department at the University of Houston. I did research on economic as well as cultural features of the inner-city ethnic enclaves of Houston, including Chinatown, the Mexican American East End, and the African American Third and Fourth Wards. I did field interviews with minority business leaders and directors of community-based organizations, city planning officials, and architects. I consulted architectural guidebooks and criticism on local buildings and landmarks and attended meetings of the American Institute of Architects. I also directed a survey of households at the Allen Parkway Village public housing project in the Fourth Ward, working with students and the resident council president, Lenwood Johnson. I attended many community meetings at Allen Parkway Village and at the home of William Simon, my sociologist colleague at the University of Houston, working to build local support for the preservation of low-income housing units rather than the plan for demolition and redevelopment favored by public officials and the Housing Authority of the City of Houston.

The movement for preservation at Allen Parkway Village was a social cause that had occupied many local activists and residents of Houston since the late 1970s, when the housing authority began deferring maintenance and depopulating the housing project. To African American leaders, the disinvestment and neglect occurring at Allen Parkway Village were further expression of a longer history of governmental destruction of the Fourth Ward under the aegis of slum clearance and urban renewal policies. While I was in Houston in the early 1990s, there was new interest in reinvestment and repopulation of downtown neighborhoods as the region was coming out of a regional recession in the 1980s, and the problems of urban sprawl drove new interest in downtown residential locations. The governmental and corporate establishment was keen to stimulate redevelopment and gentrification downtown as well as convention and tourism activity. City officials and urban boosters increasingly touted the international diversity and rich racial–ethnic heritage that Houston had to offer for visitors and investors. Chinese and Mexican American place entrepreneurs saw the promise for investment and new cultural visibility.

Postmodernism and Urban Change in Houston

In the 1980s, the corporate interests of Houston erected a series of postmodern architectural showpieces including several skyscrapers and a landmark opera house. These postmodern buildings evoked qualities of cultural heritage, parody, and grandiosity through designs that incorporated architectural styles such as Dutch gables and Mayan temples. These landmarks paid homage to Houston's economic prosperity and its rise as a refining and shipping center and a key corporate headquarters complex in the international petrochemical industry. But the promises of globalization in Houston had also brought the specter of greater uncertainty fostered by financial deregulation, oil price shocks, and international economic interdependence. The Houston that I encountered in the early 1990s was a "postmodern" metropolis that was prosperous, but also challenged by a recent banking crisis and regional recession, urban sprawl, and central city decline.

My viewpoint at the time drew much from an academic vogue in postmodernist readings of the city, especially from the standpoints of cultural studies, urban planning, and architectural criticism (Jameson 1984, Davis 1985, Dear 1986, Soja 1990, Smith 1992, Sorkin 1992, Parson 1993). I drew especially from David Harvey (1989), who saw a historical shift from urban planning policies of slum clearance and urban modernization towards preservation of urban neighborhoods and the use of postmodern architectural designs that incorporated more culture and history rather than the bureaucratic rationality of modernism.

I distinguish postmodernism, then, as both an aesthetic–architectural movement and as a historical phase in urban development under advanced capitalism. Postmodernism may also refer to a point of view employed by individuals interested in "reading" and interpreting the links between cultural and political economic change in the city.

Following architectural convention, I make a distinction between early and high modernism. On the Houston skyline, an architectural historian can clearly trace the changing imprints of twentieth-century movements in architecture: decorative early modernism of the Zigzag Moderne, Art Deco, and Streamline styles, the high-tech, austere, and functionalist International style of high modernism, and the surreal and eclectic neohistoricism of postmodernism. These design phases aesthetically "crown" the historical ebb and flow of building episodes that also correspond to stages in the changing political economy and spatial character of Houston's urban development (see Table 4.1).

By examining the disposition of ethnic spaces as a changing urban category, I aim to better examine the links between political economy and cultural change. The political economy of postmodern Houston is increasingly decentralized and polyglot. By linking the changing utility of ethnic places to broader trends in urban capitalist development and architectural design movements in Houston, I seek to clarify modernism and postmodernism as conceptual categories.

A Note on Urban Iconography and Culture in Houston

General Sam Houston proclaimed the independence of the short-lived Texas Republic with his victory over Mexican General Santa Anna's army at the battle of San Jacinto in 1836.[1] Later that same year, the Allen brothers, two real estate speculators from New York City, procured the Texan general's surname for their new city in exchange for several parcels of land. In an expression of the frontier patriotism that typifies

Table 4.1 Historical Periods of Urban Development in Houston

	Early Modernism	*High Modernism*	*Postmodernism*
Architectural Styles	Zigzag, Streamline, and Art Deco	Glassy International and high-tech futurist	Eclecticism, historicism, and parody
Urban Political Economy	Local Anglo power elite (Suite 8F crowd)	Transnational corporate elite	New ethnic actors and place entrepreneurs
Urban Geography	Centralization	Decentralization	Decentralization with some recentralization
Policies toward Ethnic Places	Invisible minorities and Jim Crow segregation	Slum clearance of ethnic places for freeways and urban renewal	Urban revitalization with some re-use of ethnic places

Houston, a young soldier shimmied up the flagpole to unfurl the tangled Old Glory during the city's dedication, and was ceremoniously awarded with a parcel of land for his initiative. The Allen brothers were boosters of shameless entrepreneurialism. In their promotions to Eastern investors, Houston was falsely advertised as being immediately proximate to beautiful mountains (like Denver), while the city is actually situated on a flat, hot and humid coastal plain. Rapid growth following the discovery of oil in East Texas in the early twentieth century brought windfall revenues for Houston's entrepreneurs and corporations, financing an opulent display of architectural showpieces.

As a primarily new, automobile-centered city, Houston sprawls over a huge network of highways that crisscross some 600 square miles of prairie and woodland. The city may be characterized (along with Los Angeles) as a futurist paradigm of the sprawling postmodern metropolis, a decentered profusion of "suburbs in search of a city." Since World War II the core central business district has been surrounded by a patchwork multinucleation of peripheral business centers or "edge cities" (Garreau 1991) that have sprouted along major freeway arteries and interchanges.

Guided by a laissez-faire, "free enterprise" (Feagin 1988) political culture that vociferously resists regulation and planning, Houston's urban character at street level is similar to the desert boomtown gambling center of Las Vegas. The quintessential American commercial strip of parking lots, shopping malls, and motor hotels is common to Houston.[2] The anonymity of the strip contrasts with the thriving civic quality of other urban public spaces like Parisian boulevards, Italian piazzas, or New York City's Central Park. Houston had only two public squares in its original city plan (County Courthouse and Market Square), on either side of a central thoroughfare (Main Street). In Houston, huge billboards advertise places as commodities in a city experienced by automobile rather than by foot. Along the commercial thoroughfares and freeways, low-rise buildings form spatial relationships across huge spaces. There are few central public spaces in Houston because the "front spaces" are typically highways and parking lots. Since there is no zoning, vacant lots proliferate (Houston is the largest

American city without land-use zoning regulations). Lack of regard to uniformity of land use has led to odd juxtapositions of institutional, commercial, residential, and industrial buildings. The architectural critic Ada Louise Huxtable has observed:

> Houston is a study in paradoxes. There are pines and palm trees, skyscrapers and sprawl; Tudor townhouses stop abruptly as cows and prairie take over. It deals in incredible extremes of wealth and culture . . . Houston is all process and no plan . . . One might say of Houston that one never gets there. It feels as if one is always on the way, always arriving, always looking for the place where everything comes together.
>
> (1976: 144)

Houston's place identity crisis is mirrored in the profusion of adjectives used to describe the metropolis: magnolia city, freeway city, mobile city, high-tech city, space city, speculator city, strip city, oiltown, cowboy city, and "shining buckle of the Sunbelt." The motif of paradox and iconic oxymoron is explored by director James Bridges' *Urban Cowboy* (1980), which features John Travolta and Debra Winger in the rowdy bar scene of Gilley's, a famed honky-tonk saloon popular with petro-chemical and ship-channel workers in the east Houston community of Pasadena. The saloon crowd line dances to country and western music and rides mechanical bucking bull machines. German director Wim Wenders hauntingly represents Houston in a starkly existential ambience of family separation in his film *Paris, Texas*, which is based on the play by Sam Shephard. A colliding entourage of overdramatic personas populates the novels of Larry McMurtry, who depicts Houston as a provincial oil capital reaching for nationally minded sophistication, though still lacking a coherent local culture.[3] The characters in McMurtry's Houston trilogy (*All My Friends Are Going to be Strangers*, *Moving On*, and *Terms of Endearment*) lack a strong sense of both self- and group identity (Dixon 1979).[4]

The variegated landmarks and urban iconography of Houston can be read on a deeper level like a cultural palimpsest. I interpret the cumulative texture of its "place culture" as proceeding through historical episodes.

Ethnic Insignificance in the Modernist City

Race and ethnic neighborhoods in the early part of the twentieth century were segregated and "invisible" to the Anglo middle classes and elite of Houston, since they generally inhabited unwanted land adjacent to downtown and on the industrial east side of the city. An approximate band of African American neighborhoods (the Third, Fourth and Fifth Wards) surrounded the central business district. The Mexican American barrios of El Segundo (Second Ward) and Magnolia filled a vast wedge east of downtown adjacent to the ship channel (Bullard 1987, De Leon 1989). A small Chinatown sprouted between the southeast fringe of downtown and El Segundo.

This ring of minority settlements around Houston's traditional downtown was essentially comparable to the "zone-in-transition" found

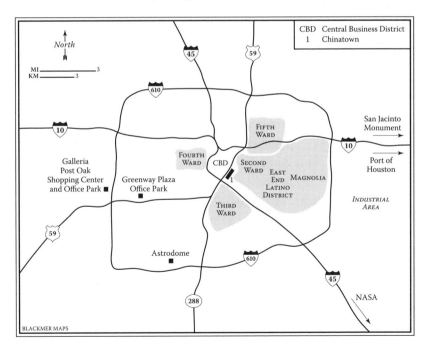

Figure 4.1 Ethnic neighborhoods and major landmarks in Houston.

in other U.S. cities, such as Chicago in the 1920s. At that time, Houston was not only spatially, but also politically, centralized, run by a downtown power elite of "wildcatter industrialists" and "society tycoons" with interconnected interests in oil and gas, real estate, construction, and banking (Feagin 1988). These power brokers were locally dubbed the "8F group," a reference to the downtown Lamar Hotel suite at which they would informally meet (Fisher 1989: 148). This group essentially controlled economic and urban development in Houston for the next 30 years.

In the midst of Houston's first oil boom, the Suite 8F crowd erected a series of tall buildings in the downtown district, including the Houston Cotton Exchange and Board of Trade Building (1924), the Petroleum Building (1927), the Niels Esperson Building (1927), and the Gulf Building (1929). The 36-story Gulf Building, built by the developer and banker Jesse H. Jones, remained Houston's tallest building until 1963. Jones, who was appointed by President Franklin D. Roosevelt to head the Reconstruction Finance Corporation in 1932, procured many Works Progress Administration civic projects for Houston in the 1930s, including Houston City Hall, Sam Houston Coliseum and Music Hall, and Jefferson Davis Hospital, all built in early modernist styles. Art Deco, Zigzag, and Streamline architectural designs were common in this era of early modernism.

The 1930s was a period of widespread inner-city slum clearance and waterfront redevelopment in many American cities. Manhattan's Lower East Side is a case in point; deteriorated piers and residential tenement buildings were demolished to make way for expressway arterials and public housing (Buttenweiser 1987). Slum clearance became even more systematic with substantial federal financing in the postwar era through the urban renewal programs of the Housing Act of 1949 and construction of the interstate highway system. The fabric of giant urban neighborhoods was demolished. The more dramatic cases include the Cross-Bronx Expressway designed by New York City's master planner Robert Moses after World War II, which destroyed a huge Jewish neighborhood in the South Bronx. In Boston's West End, Herbert Gans (1962) depicted the social life of an immigrant Italian American "urban village" just before its wholesale demolition.

In "free enterprise" Houston, there was no master planned urban renewal in the fashion seen in some northeastern cities, but federal funding was procured to demolish condemned neighborhoods (particularly African American ones) to build highways and public housing. Fourth Ward, or "Freedmen's Town" (the original settlement site of the first emancipated slaves after the Civil War), faced the wrecker's ball in 1944 when 37 acres of housing were demolished to make way for San Felipe Courts, wartime housing for families of white defense industry workers. Moreover the Fourth Ward was dealt a death blow when it was bisected by the Gulf Freeway (I-45) in 1953; Fifth Ward was similarly divided by the construction of Interstate 10.

In Houston, the building of the highway system served the interests of middle-class Anglo suburbanization at the cost of near-city minority neighborhoods, which did not have the political clout to contest these land-use decisions. In northern cities, the destruction of white ethnic neighborhoods contrasts to some extent with the blunt racism and segregation of Jim Crow in southern cities. Minority enclaves were not just "in the way," but "invisible" to the southern Anglo industrialists of Houston. Integration would await the Civil Rights movement of the 1960s.

The construction of the postwar highway system spurred the decentralization of Houston's urban development. Federal aeronautic contracts prompted development of the southeast corridor to the National Aeronautic and Space Administration (NASA) Manned Spacecraft Center, built in 1962–64. The Astrodome, the nation's first fully enclosed, climate-controlled geodesic stadium, was built in 1965.[5] These two projects, both sterling examples of high modernism, capped Houston's new image as a high-technology and space-age city. Both landmarks are located far from the central city, as were many ensuing development projects, such as the Greenway Plaza office park (1969–73) and the Galleria/Post Oak shopping and office complex (1970–86).

The decline of spatial centrality was paralleled by a decline of political economic centrality. National and international oil and gas corporations increasingly sited their production facilities and headquarters offices in Houston. The power of the old Suite 8F crowd diminished with the entrance of these corporate monopoly and global interests. There was a partial resurrection of the local power elite by the Houston Chamber of Commerce in the 1970s, but this organization never attained the authority of the Suite 8F group.

Ethnicity Preserved in the Postmodern City

From approximately 1982 to 1987, Houston experienced a sharp economic recession that was mainly regional in scope, since most of the remainder of the country was experiencing an economic boom. The immediate cause of this economic bust was the dramatic fall in oil prices between 1982 and 1983. This was the first serious setback to Houstonians after seven decades of seemingly limitless growth; it led to a reassessment of some fundamental assumptions and conventions relating to the character of urban life and development. The possibilities of better planning and public services (anathema during earlier years) entered popular discourse. Various dimensions of urban planning and policy were considered: zoning, mass transportation, housing, and community development. Unfettered, unregulated growth and "modernization" were no longer patently accepted as a universal, unquestioned good. There was also a new interest in reviving the downtown area.

Downtown cultural sites are primarily located on the western edge of downtown, near Houston City Hall. Even as Houston decentralized, this "civic center" area grew during the 1960s and 1970s with the building of the Jesse H. Jones Hall for the Performing Arts (1966), Alley Theatre (1969), Houston Public Library (1975), and a "postmodern opera house," the Gus S. Wortham Theater Center (1987). Major modernist office towers continued to be built downtown as well, including Houston's two largest buildings, Texas Commerce Tower (1981) and Allied Bank Plaza (1983). This contributes to the reviving of downtown primacy, through the intersecting interests of Houston's high cultural establishment and corporate elite interests of national and international scope.

This points to opposing dynamics in urban development as Houston recovers from the economic bust of the mid-1980s. The city shows some signs of spatial recentralization even as it continues to decentralize with the growth of suburban office locations. There is continuing residential outmovement to exurban master-planned communities appealing to the corporate workforce, including the Woodlands, Sugarland, First Colony, Cinco Ranch, and Kingwood. The tension between decentralization and recentralization is reflected in opposition between downtown and the Galleria/Post Oak edge city that is locally dubbed "uptown."

Philip Johnson and John Burgee's Art Deco "steeple," the Transco Tower (1983), was built adjacent to the Galleria shopping complex. The architects' inspiration was Chartres Cathedral, which rises from the flatness of the northern plains of France. The Transco Tower is chameleon-like in its tonal variability, the product of an alternating opaque and translucent glass exterior. A rotating beacon crowns the tower at night, self-consciously proclaiming its status as the tallest American skyscraper outside of a traditional downtown. It stands somewhat as a symbol of the decentered metropolis, as does the Orange County complex to central city Los Angeles in the "60-Mile Circle" of that metropolitan region (Soja 1990).

As Sharon Zukin (1988: 434) suggests, however, postmodernism probably best describes central-city and waterfront redevelopment schemes created by mega-developers and superstar architects, linked with local historic preservationist and artistic interests. Two examples of spectacular postmodernist office development can be seen in downtown Houston. The RepublicBank Center (1983), also designed by Johnson and Burgee, conjures a romantic historicism with its red-granite stepped Dutch gables and Gothic spires. Even more "exhibitionist" is the surreal parody of Heritage Plaza (1987), a glassy International Style blue tower capped incongruously by a Mayan pyramid (architect Mohammed Nasr was inspired by a visit to the Yucatan Peninsula). Both office towers are near the growing "civic center" on downtown's west side. The George R. Brown Convention Center, which somewhat resembles a postmodernist ocean liner (homage to Houston's role as a port), was built on the downtown's east side in 1987.

Two new urban plazas, Tranquility Park (1979) and Sesquicentennial Park (1989), have been built downtown along with a refurbishment of the old Market Square with art works embedded in plaza stone, giving downtown revitalization a public spatial focus. These are the sites of major outdoor festivals and cultural events, including the hugely popular "Art Car Parade" and the International Festival, which both take place in May (the seasonal height of outdoor events, since Houston summers are brutally hot and humid). Historic preservationists have also attempted to link new development of the civic center with redevelopment further east of downtown, along Main Street, which is the site of some remaining nineteenth-century architecture and early modernist landmarks of the 1920s and 1930s.

These efforts to link historic preservation and municipal arts to the redevelopment of downtown have provided an opportunity for minority interests seeking to revitalize their own neighborhoods. Proposals for waterfront revitalization along the Buffalo Bayou have been extended further east to link with Mexican American community interests. The construction of the Brown Convention Center on the downtown's

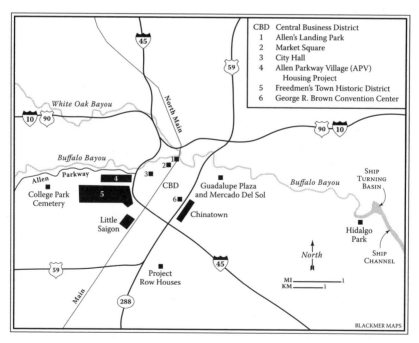

Figure 4.2 Ethnic sites and downtown landmarks of Houston in detail.

southeastern periphery near Chinatown has given the Asian community interests an opportunity. Along the bayou on the west side, however, Houston's oldest African American neighborhood faces the contrasting prospect of redevelopmental demolition even as its residents seek to preserve their district historically.

East End Redevelopment: Bayou Revitalization as Latinized Spectacle

The East End Area Chamber of Commerce,[6] with support from a local Mexican American councilperson (Ben Reyes), is seeking to revitalize Buffalo Bayou from Allens Landing[7] to the Turning Basin for purposes of tourism. A promenade/bike trail is planned, as is a continuous "urban historical park" along the length of the bayou, which would be punctuated at intervals by sites of natural (e.g., trees at Magnolia Park), historical (McKee Street Bridge and Navigation area cemetery pillars), and ethnic significance (Mexican culture at Guadalupe Plaza and Hildalgo Park).

Efforts are somewhat anchored around the partially constructed Mercado del Sol, a would-be Latino "festival marketplace" that occupies a former mattress factory along the bayou's edge. Adjacent to Mercado del Sol is the Mexican-themed Guadalupe Plaza, landscaped with palm trees and bright colors for civic occasions. Across the street is Our Lady of Guadalupe Church, historically an important community center for the Second Ward Mexicans of Houston. The East End Area Chamber of Commerce is promoting the construction of Mercado del Sol and planning for another ethnic market in the Harrisburg/Wayside area near Magnolia (with a planned studio/workshop of Latino folk artists).

These efforts at bayou revitalization and commercial development on Houston's near east side essentially mimic the successful strategy pursued by the city of San Antonio. Here, an elaborate Riverwalk was created in the city center, with associated Latino markets (El Mercado and La Villita). Southwestern and Latino heritage permeates the whole of central-city San Antonio's revitalization (with associated hotels, shopping malls, and museum exhibitions) in a "spectacle" of urban tourism and retail consumption. San Antonio's Riverwalk is comparable

Figure 4.3 Mercado del Sol Latino-themed market, with water steps to bayou in foreground and downtown towers in background. Photo by Jan Lin.

with a number of other "festival marketplaces" (Baltimore's Harbor Place, Boston's Faneuil Hall, San Francisco's Fisherman's Wharf, London's Covent Garden) where urban theatrical spectacles have been created.

The skeptical eye that some postmodern observers cast to these efforts at revitalization is rooted partly in the perception that the nostalgic urban narratives created by these touristic consumption landscapes in the central city essentially camouflage an underlying history of struggle (inner-city rioting in 1960s Baltimore, revolutionary struggle in Boston, Mexican defeat at San Jacinto east of Houston, Mexican American working-class struggle in the East End). The benefits of these spectacular developments, furthermore, go chiefly to large-scale developers (e.g., James Rouse in Boston and Baltimore) and city treasuries (in the form of boosted tax revenues), and not to the retail trade and service sector work forces that are employed by festival marketplaces. Thus, any tourist/commercial employment generated by bayou revitalization on Houston's East End will never replace the higher wages offered by manufacturing or construction employment associated with the Port of Houston. The charm and tourist potential of a bayou "festival space" in the shadow of what is essentially still a very industrial port/manufacturing district is still uncertain. There are other attractions in Houston like the huge Galleria shopping complex in west Houston (locally known as uptown), the Museum District, the Astrodome and Mission Control of NASA.

Efforts to refabricate a Latinized East End bayou for urban tourism also project a distorted picture of current Latino settlement and community in Houston. Newer Central American migrants have been concentrated on the west side since the 1970s, and upwardly mobile Mexican Americans are increasingly assimilated into the suburbs (Hagan and Rodriguez 1992).

Chinatown Redevelopment and Conventioneers in the "World City"

The Houston Chinatown Council, with some backing from overseas Chinese investors, is seeking to redevelop Houston's old Chinatown, which is adjacent to the newly built George R. Brown Convention Center. A mixed-use development covering some six square blocks is envisioned, with a variety of restaurants (offering Chinese, Vietnamese, Korean, Thai, Mexican, Italian, and Texas-style barbecue cuisine), a farmer's market, a community center, a theater with Chinese opera and other cultural performances, a concentrated area of Asian wholesale importers, and even some housing. A giant stone Chinese gate complete with guardian lions has been donated by representatives from Houston's Chinese sister city of Shenzhen.

This central-city Chinatown is no longer the city's only Asian enclave, as a new "suburban Chinatown" has emerged since the 1980s on Houston's west side. There are also areas of Korean business development on the west side, and a Vietnamese "Little Saigon" close to downtown on the south side. The businesses of the "downtown Chinatown" have benefitted from the growth of other Asian immigrant enclaves because they operate in wholesale trade to Asian food and restaurant product retailers. These wholesalers import their products through the Port of Houston for sale to Asian restaurants and businesses in Houston as well as throughout the South and Midwest.[8]

The Bush Administration used Houston as the site for the 1990 Economic Summit, the meetings of the advanced industrialized Group of Seven nations. Houston's image as an "international city" was touted. The proposed Chinatown redevelopment is predicated on the notion that Houston conventioneers would be attracted to the "world city" atmosphere created by an adjacent Chinatown development. Houston Chinatown Council, led by seafood wholesaler and developer Dan Nip, garnered considerable investment capital, but project ground-breaking never took place as public infrastructural improvements including an expanded sewage line to service large restaurants never materialized. The redevelopment has stalled for years despite Dan Nip's persisting efforts, which included a campaign to lure overseas investors through the U.S. Immigration and Naturalization Service EB-5 visa program, which

Figure 4.4 Rear view of Chinatown businesses with George R. Brown Convention Center and downtown towers in background. Photo by Jan Lin.

grants the visa and progress towards permanent residency for investing US$500,000 and creating two jobs for ten years. The program normally requires an investment of US$1 million, but the economically distressed neighborhood qualified as a special investment zone for the lower threshold. The area received a boost with the opening of Minute Man Park in 2002 for the Houston Astros baseball team, along with some new town homes and lofts. But many lots are still vacant and commercial properties warehoused in anticipation of greater development.

While the East End Chamber of Commerce's proposal for bayou revitalization presents Latino culture in the context of local history, the Chinatown redevelopment scheme presents a mosaic of ethnic diversity in the emerging globalized metropolis. Rather than historicizing ethnicity to celebrate the past, it presents ethnicity as a culinary experience while presenting an image of the evolving urban future. While the redevelopment of Houston's east side Chinatown has been stalled, there has been dramatic growth in Asian American business interests in the southwestern suburbs surrounding Bellaire who now promote the suburban Chinatown as an urban destination. While both Chinatowns can claim to be gateways to the global marketplace, the east downtown original Chinatown has greater historical significance.

The Destruction and Renewal of the Black Wards

On the west side of downtown, a different dynamic is being played out between the African American community and developers, who are much more interested in the potential value of the land for the westward expansion of the downtown business district. Indigenous community interests here have been seeking to preserve sites of African American historical significance, partially achieved through the federal designation of a Freedmen's Town historic district in 1984.

Fourth Ward or "Freedmen's Town" was the site of the settlement of the first emancipated slaves in Houston following the Civil War. Many of the woodframe houses are architecturally significant as examples of "slave era" building styles common throughout the nineteenth-century American South. Some of the one-floor row houses were popularly known as "shotgun houses" (or "shacks") because you could shoot a bullet

down the linear arrangement of rooms from the front door straight out
the back. Introduced to the U.S. by freed Haitians, the shotgun houses
became symbols of freedom for African Americans who built them in
clusters in Freedmen's Town. Until the 1920s, Freedmen's Town was the
"mother ward," housing some one-third of Houston's African American
population, but the center of Houston's black population shifted to Third
Ward, as Fourth Ward was disinvested and depopulated by the removal
of black-owned homes and businesses to permit the construction of San
Felipe Courts housing project (later "Allen Parkway Village" or APV).[9]
Built during World War II, the public housing project was designated
for white military families and a brick wall was built as a kind of de facto
physical barrier segregating the white housing project from the black
Fourth Ward (APV was integrated later in the 1960s). Fourth Ward's
neighborhood vitality was further destroyed by the construction of the
Gulf Freeway in 1953. The center of African American economic and
cultural life shifted to Fifth Ward then Third Ward. Meanwhile,
redlining by banks, the loss of economic, religious, and professional
leaders, and the neglect of absentee landlords led to severe deterioration
of the Fourth Ward by the 1960s.

Emerging developer interest in Fourth Ward essentially stems from
two earlier developmental events. One was the construction of Allen
Parkway (1926) along the scenic bayou in the north section of Fourth
Ward to provide a convenient highway arterial from the newly built
affluent garden suburb of River Oaks to the central business district.
The other was the siting of the American General (the largest insurance
company in the South) office complex between River Oaks and APV
in 1965. Developmental interest did not arise again until the late 1970s,
when the Housing Authority of the City of Houston (HACH) became
aware that new developmental activity in the civic center area was
raising the potential value of Fourth Ward land. A $10 million federal
grant designated in 1979 to modernize APV was shifted elsewhere
while some funds were spent on consultant studies that recommended
demolition. HACH began to disinvest and depopulate the site,[10]
household by household, even though thousands of Houstonians were
still on the public housing waiting list. They promoted a scattered-site

approach in their metropolitan housing policy. The facilities fell into a depressing state of disrepair for the remaining families. A resident housing survey that I directed in the fall of 1992 found widespread evidence of major and minor problems, including plumbing leaks, broken tiles, peeling paint, improper security, rodent and roach problems. Every household reported an interest in staying at APV because of convenience to churches, schools, and downtown. Many reported feeling a strong sense of community in view of the proximity to Fourth Ward.

In 1990, American General Corporation and Cullen Center, Inc. (which owned property on opposite sides of APV) announced a giant plan, "Founders Park," to clear and redevelop some 600 acres of Fourth Ward (including APV) land in favor of an extensive mixed-use development that would include mid-rise office towers, upmarket condominiums and shopping centers. Vociferous community resistance (representing a coalition of liberal preservationist interests, single-family property owners, and the low-income African American community), however, was eventually successful in swinging public opinion against the proposal, which was dependent on a special municipal bond issue for infrastructural improvements.[11]

American General and Cullen interest in the area waned, but acrimonious debate and a series of opposing lawsuits over the disposition of APV continued between housing bureaucrats at HACH (which sought legal authority to demolish the housing project) and "friends of APV" (who sought to renovate and refill the site with public housing residents). As part of their preservationist rhetoric, these activists point to the "sacred" importance of the "mother ward" to the African American community of Houston. Preserved homesteads and cemeteries which mark the resting places of the ancestral founders of the community are held in high regard, historic places which are "off limits" to the bulldozer. The two-decades-long campaign to save APV was led by resident council president Lenwood Johnson and his supporters in the black Fourth Ward as well as white supporters such as Joan Denkler of Houston Housing Concern (representing suburban church and community groups), sociologist Bill Simon of the University of

Houston, and Sissy Farenthold, a prominent community activist and former state legislator. The documentary filmmaker Christine Felton videotaped much of the campaign in a film entitled *Location, Location*.

An important factor in these negotiations is the fact that though the local housing authority (HACH) owned the buildings, the federal HUD owned the land, and thus retained considerable jurisdictional oversight over the project. Preservationist interests had an ally in senior U.S. Senator Henry Gonzalez (a New Deal-style Democrat from San Antonio), who held a congressional field hearing at Allen Parkway Village in December 1993. The architectural historian Stephen Fox of Rice University brought attention to the low-density design of the APV housing units, which were arranged in *Zeilenbau* configuration, a formation of low-rise rectangles in parallel rows rather than high-rises. Adapting utopian German social housing designs of the 1920s and 1930s, APV designers had a noble and humane vision of public housing.

Figure 4.5 Allen Parkway Village housing project before redevelopment, with downtown towers in background, including postmodern Mayan-themed Heritage Plaza in center and stepped Dutch gabled RepublicBank Center to the left. Photo by Jan Lin.

The park-like campus of APV was intended to provide the apartments with maximum sunlight and fresh air. APV was put on the National Register of Historic Places of the U.S. Department of the Interior in 1988.

Sustaining community development is a difficult undertaking, as there is a plethora of ethnic advocates, but a paucity of ethnic entrepreneurs in Houston's Fourth Ward. Most of the property is under absentee ownership, a common phenomenon in inner-city African American neighborhoods. One community development corporation exists, however, the Freedmen's Town Association. In a 1992 interview with me, executive director Gladys House discussed her interest in preserving the traditional architecture of the slave era "shotgun shacks" as an affordable housing stock that celebrates black history. To raise public interest, she had discussions with downtown interests to develop a tourist trolley car which would shuttle between downtown and Fourth Ward historical sites. Some of these historical sites include hand-laid

Figure 4.6 Fourth Ward church and woodframe "shotgun" row houses. Photo by Jan Lin.

brick streets constructed by Reverend Jeremiah and his congregation, the historic home of Reverend Yates, historic churches, and Houston's first cemetery, Founder's Cemetery, which contains graves of soldiers from the Civil War, and John and Augustus Allen, the founders of Houston.

In 1996, Henry Cisneros, the secretary of the U.S. Department of Housing and Urban Development, brokered a compromise and signed an agreement that would give the City of Houston the authority to demolish 677 of the 963 units at Allen Parkway Village to permit redevelopment into a complex of mid-rise apartment buildings and upscale townhomes. The remaining public housing was rehabilitated and along with 220 newly-constructed units, was renamed the Historic Oaks of Allen Parkway in 1999. There were 156 low-income elderly people resettled in the public housing.

The focus of heritage work in Houston's African American community shifted to the Third Ward. A project to rehabilitate the "shotgun shacks" emerged from a group of artists dubbed the "Magnificent Seven" led by Rick Lowe. They acquired eight properties on Holman Street beginning in 1992 with public, private, corporate, and foundation grants, and gave birth to "Project Row Houses," a community-based project to rehabilitate dilapidated properties and convert them to studio and exhibition spaces that would showcase black arts and history, while also providing a similar number of houses for affordable housing, educational classrooms, and child care, with the focus on single mothers, dubbed the Young Mother's Residential Program (YMRP). The YMRP women are entitled to one-year renewable contracts for free housing and participation in parenting and life-skills workshops. There are recurring reunions of YMRP partici-pants and a resident "mentor mom" who is a graduate of the program. Educational programs include a computer lab and interdisciplinary art-based afterschool and summer programs in local parks, encompassing sculpture gardens and an annual music and arts festival. Artists from local to international are encouraged to interact and dialogue with the surrounding community while developing their studio and gallery space (Lopate 2000).

The project began a new phase of expansion working in a larger 35-block area through preservation of existing units, construction of new duplex buildings, and restoring the Eldorado Ballroom, a gift property to the project. Formerly a mecca for black jazz and blues musicians in the 1940s and 1950s, the Eldorado was renovated and reopened as a performance and exhibition space in 2003. The Eldorado project includes an oral history program and a series of community gatherings to "Share Third Ward Stories" to help create an archive of old photographs and documents marking the musical and residential history of the neighborhood. A blues vocalist, Carolyn Blanchard, recalled, "The Eldorado Ballroom made us feel like we were kings and queens. We always held our heads a little higher after leaving the Eldorado" (Lesh 2003). There is collaboration with a Rice University architecture and design program that applies the work of faculty and students to the projects. Project Row Houses has become a major player in the economic and cultural revitalization of the Third Ward. It is hugely successful at stimulating volunteerism and giving among the middle-class and black elite of Houston. Its annual fundraiser held at the Eldorado attracts 250 guests and fashionistas in a "Steppin' Out in Style" event that is given splashy reporting in the *Houston Chronicle*.

Though long associated with poverty, shotgun houses have become more respectable and even chic, as contemporary architects have learned from the affordability, honesty, and simplicity of the gabled vernacular home design style, which originated in the hot tropical climates of West Africa and the Caribbean. The front-to-back alignment of rooms without a hallway allows for cross-ventilation and piers beneath the floor allow circulation of air underneath. Shade is provided by front porches that also stimulate neighborliness. Houston architects such as Brett Zamore worked with the Fifth Ward Community Redevelopment Corporation to do shotgun house restorations to the Fifth Ward. Bert Long, Jr., an international acclaimed sculptor who recently bought a renovated shotgun home back in his old neighborhood, asserted, "One of the biggest tragedies in African American communities is that we have tried to escape from our history. These houses are an important part of who we are and should be preserved. They are a symbol of the power of our people to survive" (Dietsch 2000).

Meanwhile, back in Fourth Ward, the greater proximity to downtown has spurred the ongoing demolition versus preservation of the original shotgun house inventory, with some properties getting relocated to Third Ward or concentrated in a "historic district" on several blocks of Fourth Ward along Andrews Street. Upscale new row houses built by speculating private developers and housing authority-built apartment complexes have replaced the affordable row house inventory in Fourth Ward. In the historic district on Andrews Street, preservationists are staging a last stand, including an effort to restore a street inlaid brick pattern that local archaeologists and historians say has historic roots in Africa. Cross patterns were often laid in streets by African Americans in the post-abolition Reconstruction-era South in honor of the followers of the BaKongo religion of West Central Africa, who etched chalk patterns in their streets as a way of invoking spirits to protect local villages. Catherine Roberts, a board member of the Rutherford B. H. Yates Museum in Freedmen's Town, says some elderly residents have memories of their grandparents going out to the center of the intersections to pray. Christopher Fennell, an anthropologist and expert on African American culture says:

> That would be consistent with the beliefs derived from the BaKongo religion. The significant part for them was the intersection. That is different from Christians. The cross line itself was an invocation point. You want to invoke the ancestors to come from the spirit world to the world of the living and the cross point was what enabled that.

(Harkinson 2004)

Conclusion

The racial–ethnic minority communities of Houston have had uneven experiences in their efforts to preserve their historically significant places and revitalize their communities. The movement to preserve the Allen Parkway Village housing project and the historic Fourth Ward black community on the west side of downtown was overcome because of the prime real estate value of the land adjacent to the central business district and interests of the governmental and corporate establishment. This could be interpreted to some extent as an expression of the triumph of land values, of "economics vs. culture" in locational decision making,[12] since there is a generally increasing land value gradient towards Houston's west side, since the east side is mainly industrial. Allen Parkway Village occupied prime real estate valuable to the establishment. Looking deeper, however, I have shown how decline of the Fourth Ward was less a result of natural market forces but more an intentional outcome of removal, disinvestment, and depopulation by the governmental establishment during the modernist period of slum clearance and urban renewal in Houston. I find that in the postmodern period, the urban growth machine is more internationalized and less centralized around an exclusive political and economic set of lead actors. Ethnic leaders and place entrepreneurs have gained new political and economic influence in affecting developmental decision making.

Racial and ethnic heritage has thus been represented through the lens of history (by African Americans) or the emerging global marketplace (by Latinos and Asian Americans) in ways to advance neighborhood revitalization through selective preservation and growth. Black efforts in the Fourth Ward have been restricted by a scarcity of indigenous businessmen, landowners, and other place entrepreneurs in their neighborhoods. Like other minority communities, however, they have a new negotiating space among city officials and planners in Houston's postmodern, postboom era of urban development. Mexican American and Chinese political and business leadership has moved forward in its efforts to preserve heritage and create viable ethnic urban destinations. The black community has experienced a split decision in its efforts. While the majority of units at Allen Parkway Village were destroyed and Fourth Ward has shrunk in the face of speculative redevelopment, the Third Ward has launched a new "row house" paradigm of heritage preservation and community development.

In a broader urban geography in which many minority households have assimilated or formed secondary enclaves in the suburbs, central city ethnic places in American cities are often "vestigial" districts, symbolic arenas of history, recollection, and sentiment, as much as they persist as enclaves of vital residential or economic life. In this sense, ethnic places in the postmodern city may be "manufactured" as much as they are "preserved." This reiterates the image of the "growth machine" propounded by new urban sociologists. From this vantage, ethnic entrepreneurs in postmodern Houston project ethnic places as "commodities" in the same way that the city's superpatriotic Anglo founders have historically done.[13]

Where I have interpreted these trends as evidence of a period of "postmodern" urban development and planning, a symbolic interactionist perspective may be just as useful. A progression of literature in this vein has examined the importance of culture in urban development. Walter Firey's seminal work (1945) is instructive, as he suggested that "sentiments and symbolism" were just as salient as economic variables in determining the ecology of land uses in Central Boston, as evidenced by locations such as Beacon Hill, the Boston Common, colonial cemeteries, and the Italian North End. Wohl and Strauss (1958) and Suttles (1984) have also drawn our attention to the locational significance of emotive and narrative sources (such as literary texts and folklore) as well as material artifacts (such as statues and street names). These "interactionist urbanists" have shown how texts and landmarks, in the evoking of certain symbolic representations, are the fundamental means by which humans and societies comprehend the lifeworld of cities. Hummon (1988) has examined the concept of state and regional tourism as a social ritual that augments meaning and identity by providing a break from everyday life. Maines and Bridger (1992) have examined the defensive use of historical narratives, or "story telling," of Amish life and heritage by community activists in Lancaster, Pennsylvania as a means of challenging and slowing rampant urban sprawl. Lofland (1991) has similarly highlighted the role of imagery in public debates concerning development in Davis, California.

Symbolic interactionism and postmodernism both recognize the importance of culture in the growth and development of cities. They both read the cultural meanings of urban signs, symbols, and literary texts, as well as landmarks and artifacts (such as statues, parks, historic homes, and cemeteries). There is also somewhat of a common endorsement of preservationist or "anti-modernist" sentiments among both schools of thought. Symbolic interactionism and postmodernism have more in common than previously thought.[14]

5

HERITAGE, ART, AND COMMUNITY DEVELOPMENT IN MIAMI'S OVERTOWN AND LITTLE HAVANA

Miami is a provocative case of urban development and race relations. Urban boosters have historically projected an image of a "magic city" and an "American Riviera" by the sea, a resort paradise of tourism and architectural spectacle. The fanciful Spanish Mediterranean mansions and hotels of the 1920s, such as the landmark Coral Gables Biltmore Hotel, have given way to a twenty-first-century Gold Coast of spectacular high-rise condominium and hotel towers along the shoreline of Biscayne Bay. Beachside promotional images of a "city at play" have whitewashed a starker real history of Jim Crow segregation and postwar racial removal that bred disinvestment and the creation of extensive black "ghetto" neighborhoods such as Overtown and Liberty City, which erupted with incendiary violence in the 1960s and 1980s. The black community was hit hard in the postwar fordist period of Miami's development, when the construction of Interstate 95 and associated urban expressways devastated the commercial and residential heart of Overtown, the city's original black neighborhood. The urban express-ways further contributed to the decline of the inner city with the out-movement of people to newer subdivisions in the suburban periphery. This period of "black removal" under fordism has been followed by a period of "black renewal" under postfordism as preservationists and place entrepreneurs work to revitalize the ghetto and reclaim the historic community through the development of an Overtown "Folklife Village" that joins heritage and cultural tourism with strategies of local economic development. Progress has been gradual for three decades, with many lots still vacant, but Overtown is now poised for change as the rise of Miami as a global trade entrepôt and the "gateway to Latin America" has stimulated the revival of downtown and corporate investment in urban ethnic niche markets and neighborhoods.

More advanced efforts of ethnic-based community development are taking place in the nearby inner-city neighborhood of Little Havana, especially along "Calle Ocho," or SW 8th Street, the traditional commercial artery for the Cuban American immigrant community in Miami. The renovation of the historic Tower Theater and the opening of the Latin Quarter Cultural Center have abetted an economic and cultural revival that includes a buoyant arts and commercial scene that features over a dozen Cuban-owned art galleries, clubs, and community theaters. A monthly event called Viernes Culturales (Cultural Fridays) showcases the artistic and musical effervescence in Calle Ocho. While African American efforts in Overtown are premised more on resurrecting a historic community destroyed by fordist urban renewal, Cuban Americans (who did not experience this kind of racial removal) join nostalgic Cuban recollection in Little Havana with the vision of a pan-Latino hemispheric future.

The Lyric Theater in Overtown and the Tower Theater in Little Havana are both focal sites for the ethnic community to preserve cultural heritage and sustain an ethnic cultural arts scene. The spatial expression of ethnic heritage and culture is further localized through the preserving of landmark homes of ethnic ancestors, and the creating of ethnic monuments, parks, and artistic sidewalks. There is also a temporal experience as these ethnic arts and cultural scenes are celebrated through monthly showcase events, seasonal artistic and lecture calendars, and annual festival events such as the Calle Ocho festival (now Carnival Miami). Especially in Little Havana, there is a set of intersecting cultural and economic "localization" processes that work through the relationships between the art galleries, restaurants, and other small businesses that cater to the growing throng of local audiences and consumers as well as external visitors and tourists. The agglomerative clustering of creative activities is particularly advanced in Calle Ocho, where the efflorescence of ethnic creative capital further builds social networks of ethnic social capital in service of community development. A back-to-the-city movement of middle-class blacks and Latinos living in suburban and exurban locations has also been stimulated, with homebuyers drawn by the inventory of historic homes, the buzz of the arts scene, and somewhat of the rhetoric of return to ethnic roots and giving back to the community.

Urban tourism and booster organizations, developers, and public officials have also promoted these ethnic heritage and arts districts. Ethnic tourism has grown in concert with the rise of Miami as a nexus for global trade, investment, and finance in the Latin American and Caribbean region. Globalization has assisted the growing renewal and transformation of downtown Miami through a high-rise office and condominium tower building boom that began in the 1980s and reached a superheated apogee at the turn of the twenty-first century. The promise of a growing residential and touristic population down-town has also been encouraged with the construction of the Bayside Marketplace in 1987, which has brought brand-name chainstores, restaurants, and entertainment to the marina. Encouraged by these developments, the City of Miami cooperated with private investors to build the Carnival Performing Arts Center on Biscayne Boulevard, designed by internationally renowned architect Cesar Pelli in an effort to further enhance the city's image as a "world-class" tourist destination and investment environment for global capital. The hot high-rise condominium market is associated with an overseas circuit of capital investment from the Latin American region, as well as European investors.

The Greater Miami Convention and Visitors Bureau, which has had great success luring visitors to the "sun-and-surf" tourism of Miami's beach and bayside neighborhoods, has also begun promoting local heritage tourism through its "Sense of Place" marketing campaign. Neighborhoods such as Overtown and Little Havana, previously seen as the "hole in the doughnut" of downtown renewal, are now ripe for tourism and redevelopment. The growth of tourist and convention traffic and the construction of landmark museums downtown relate to the ascension of "culture" as an engine of economic development in Miami. The cultural economy of Miami can be seen in three senses: a) the high cultural realm of museums and concert halls, b) the culture of the quotidian realm and its ethnic cultures, cuisines, and festivals, and c) the creative cultural industries such as music recording, television, fashion and design (Yudice 2005). Ethnic cultural heritage is a feature of Miami's urban ethnic places through the proliferation of ethnic histories, arts, and festival cultures and cuisines. The Cuban enclave has been grown through the arrival of a pan-ethnic spectrum of Latin American immigrants representing the hemispheric global culture. While ethnic tourism and niche marketing constitute an opportunity for economic and community development, the local culture can be easily appropriated and its residents and small businesses displaced through the gentrification process that is sparked by external larger corporate investment and redevelopment interests.

In the course of doing research for this chapter, I made two field research trips to Miami, in June 1996 and June 2007. I conducted interviews with representatives of community stakeholder groups, including heritage preservation organizations, community-based organizations, businesses, and governmental, as well as nongovernmental, organizations that were identified in the journalism or by reputation and word of mouth as being a stakeholder. I was interested to know the specific dynamics of collaboration or conflict between stakeholders and investment interests, as well as the overall balance of power between nonprofit community interests, quasi-public interests, and governmental interests. I sought to understand best practices as well as the kinds of challenges that were being confronted. I was interested to know what kinds of opportunities and risks were offered to stakeholders through the growth of tourists and visitors, gentrification, and redevelopment change. I wanted to understand the process of economic localization and community development amidst the broader dynamics of urban and regional globalization.

I examine the case of South Beach, where the experience of an earlier neighborhood preservation movement formulates some object lessons for emerging preservation movements in the ethnic communities. The movement to preserve the Art Deco hotels in South Beach is celebrated by local preservationists, but the subsequent redevelopment and gentrification of the district suggests that heritage can be appropriated by capitalism as much as heritage can help to sustain local communities. Overtown represents a racial–ethnic "ghetto," Little Havana is an ethnic "enclave economy," and South Beach is a bohemian subcultural community.

The Gold Coast and the Slum

Miami has always been a city of images, dreams, and spectacles. Julia Tuttles sent the railroad magnate Henry Flagler a fresh orange blossom after a hard freeze hit North Florida, to tempt him to extend his railway to Miami. It was coined the "magic city" by promoters of Flagler's Florida East Coast railway line, which propelled the incorporation of the city in 1896. Through the real estate boom of the 1920s, Miami was represented as a place of tropical romance, health and fitness, and the leisurely life. A popular love song was recorded by Caesar LaMonica in 1925, "Miami: Playground of the USA." The Anglo tycoons and developers built lavish hotels, mansions, and luxurious residential subdivisions such as Coral Gables, utilizing Near Eastern and Mediterranean Revival architecture, as popularized by the City Beautiful urban planning movement (Bush 1999). Miami, the Biscayne Bay metropolis, was like an American Riviera (Portes and Stepick 1993). The booming resort city was also highly segregated. Bahamian immigrants and African Americans were an important labor force in the building of the railroad, but their residential neighborhoods were segregated away from valuable beachside property, on the west side of the railroad tracks in an area known as "Colored Town." There is a stark contrast between the Gold Coast along Biscayne Bay and the "slum" of Overtown.

A new period of city building came after the Depression and World War II with the arrival of Jewish Americans from the Northeast. The

Jewish population of Miami increased from 5,500 in 1940 to 55,000 in 1950 as Jewish investors from New York led a building boom in luxury hotels and high-rise residences on Miami Beach. They popularized both "Art Deco" and "Miami Modern" (MiMo) styles of architecture that were less ostentatious than the earlier Mediterranean revival styles. This was akin to a transition from "early" to "late" modernism. There is a parallel between the architectural modernism of MiMo and the principles of standardization and bureaucratization underlying the fordist mode of regulation. The Jewish enclave on Miami Beach was not the classic "ethnic enclave" of working-class immigrants and small business owners historically found on the Lower East Side of Manhattan, but more a secondary enclave of upwardly mobile entrepreneurs and retirees drawn to "golden cities" such as Miami and Los Angeles in the postwar period (Moore 1994). Jews were assimilating into whiteness in the migration to locations like South Beach. The representation of Miami in the national media increasingly shifted to Miami Beach during the 1950s. There was a boom in Miami in the 1950s and 1960s and the Republication convention was held on Miami Beach in 1968.[1]

The postwar period also brought the construction of the interstate highway system, which brought Interstate 95, originating in Maine, down the east coast of Florida, to its terminus in the heart of Miami. I comprehend the U.S. interstate highway system as a Keynesian public spending project that, along with government-subsidized mortgage lending and higher education, was a hallmark of American fordism and the postwar mass society. Miami's downtown power elite made use of federal highway monies (under the aegis of the Miami First Committee, first organized in 1955) to condemn and destroy the "blighted" neighborhood of Overtown, displacing tens of thousands of residents and businesses, to make way for the elevated expressway and associated cloverleaf interchanges. The expressways and cloverleaves were destructive "concrete monsters" that destroyed the commercial and residential heart of Overtown. I-95 became effectively a "Chinese wall" physically segregating blacks from whites in desirable neighborhoods towards the bayside and downtown. A "second ghetto" was built by developers for black residential settlement fanning towards the northwest in such areas as Brownsville, Liberty City, and Opa-locka (Mohl 1993a). Fordist-era highway building led to sociospatial polarization that further compounded the impoverishment and social isolation of the Overtown ghetto. Poverty, overcrowding, and substandard housing contributed to social unrest and Liberty City eventually exploded in riots in 1968 and again in the 1980s.

The early 1980s were real watershed years in Miami history. The "Mariel boatlift," beginning in early April 1980, started to bring tens of thousands of new refugees from Cuba on a "freedom flotilla" of boats and rafts. Three weeks after the Mariel exodus began, the acquittal of police officers in the follow-up trial to the "McDuffie beating" of the earlier year led to the most violent riot in Miami's history. During their resettlement in Miami, the Mariel refugees were held for a while in the Orange Bowl, and then transferred to a makeshift "tent city" under the I-95 after the start of the football season. There is a defining scene in director Brian de Palma's film, *Scarface* (1983), about the life of Cuban American refugee Antonio "Tony" Montana (placed by Al Pacino) and his rise in the cocaine trafficking underworld in Miami, when he is housed in a tent city called "Freedomland," which is a detention center for Mariel refugees. Tony Montana takes part in a riot at the detention camp and during the melee he kills a man for his green card under the looming trestles of the I-95.[2] The screenplay by Oliver Stone featured extremely graphic violence and was shot in Los Angeles as Cuban Americans protested against location shooting in Miami and publicly denounced the film's subsequent release because of its negative cultural representations.

Miami acquired a notorious reputation in the media in the 1980s as a vice and crime capital. *Time* magazine ran a 1981 cover story entitled "Paradise Lost" reporting that rapid economic growth had generated costs including poverty and crime. Miami was first in total crime as well as violent crime, according to FBI statistics, among the 79 major U.S. large metropolitan areas in 1992 and 1993 (Nijman 2000). Although crime continues to be a social reality in their city, Miamians are unsupportive of unfavorable media representations of their city.

Figure 5.1 I-95 construction through Overtown looking south. Historical Museum of South Florida.

Director Anthony Yerkovich's 1984 film, *Miami Vice* (subsequently syndicated on television from 1984 to 1989) did much to contribute to Miami's image as a place proliferating with crime, drug trafficking, and other urban vices. *Miami Vice* also generated enduring scenes of Miami's glitzy high-rise skyline, pastel-colored Art Deco hotels, and handsome

Figure 5.2 I-95 ramp construction. Historical Museum of South Florida.

men sporting fashionable white linen suits. It was a glamorous look that juxtaposed a city that pulsed with "life in the fast lane" and a shady international underworld.

Immigration and the Rise of the World City

Miami made the transition from a segregated southern fordist city to a postfordist world city with the arrival of Cuban exiles following the revolution of 1959. From 1959 to 1961, 135,000 exiles, especially of the elite and middle classes, left Havana while regular flights to Miami were still available. The flow continued in more clandestine fashion through the failed Bay of Pigs invasion of 1961 and Cuban Missile Crisis of 1962 until the number reached 210,000. Fidel Castro reinitiated official emigration in 1965 to allow family reunification among exiles, and the U.S. negotiated for daily flights of refugees, or "freedom flights," which brought 340,000 new Cubans over the next eight years.

While U.S. authorities tried to resettle the refugees throughout the country, they reconcentrated in Miami and by 1979 about 80 percent of Cubans in the U.S. lived in Miami (Portes and Stepick 1993). The Cuban influx was the main factor as Miami went through the period of its most rapid population growth in the third quarter of the twentieth century, tripling from about 500,000 in 1959 to 1.5 million in 1975 (Nijman 2000).

The Cuban ethnic "enclave economy" emerged as a sub-economy of ethnic entrepreneurs and firms providing a route to social mobility for immigrants. The enclave economy is a contrast from the existing segmented labor market, comprising a primary sector with good job ladders providing upward mobility versus a secondary sector with poor mobility ladders such as the service sector. The Cuban enclave grew and diversified from an initial enclave of cigar companies to become an institutionally complete sub-economy that includes garment manufacturing, construction, retail and wholesale trade, finance, insurance and real estate, and the service sector, including governmental, non-governmental, and community-based organizations (Portes and Bach 1985). As other Latin American groups fled civil wars and political instability in countries such as Nicaragua and Guatemala in the 1980s and 1990s, these immigrants became integrated with the Cuban enclave or established separate enclaves. Along with the Haitian enclave, these enclave economies constitute the ethnic niche markets of international Miami. A circuit of middle- as well as upper-class capital investment in Miami was also established among other Caribbean, Central American, and South American visitors, immigrants, and resident aliens, lured by Miami's growing status as a place for shopping, establishing business activities, and making profitable investments in real estate.

There were also geopolitical, military, and symbolic "logics" surrounding the growth of the Cuban enclave. After the Cuban revolution, Miami became the center for counter-revolutionary activities involving anti-communist Cuban exiles, the displaced Cuban mafia, and the U.S. Central Intelligence Agency (CIA). The University of Miami during the 1960s operated the second largest CIA station in the world, after the headquarters in Virginia. The State Department funneled millions of dollars to help subsidize many Cuban-owned businesses that served as fronts for CIA operations, revenues that recirculated throughout the Cuban ethnic economy. Miami also became a center for drug smuggling during this period (Grosfoguel 1995).

During the early 1970s, Miami increasingly became an important city in the regional division of labor within the Caribbean, with the spread of export-oriented manufacturing, financed often by U.S. corporations, in Puerto Rico, the Dominican Republic, Haiti, and Jamaica (Grosfoguel 1995). Transnational corporations and banks opened up regional offices in Miami. As the hub of Pan American Airlines (Pan Am), Miami International Airport increased its growth and prominence in the Caribbean and Latin American region (Nijman 2000). A free trade zone was established near the airport for import–export companies to store, manufacture, and re-export goods free of tariffs. The port also became a principal embarkation point for cruise ships departing for the Caribbean.

Miami lacks local manufacturing activity, when compared with other global cities, like Los Angeles and New York, which have enterprises manufacturing garments, toys, furniture, and other products. Its producer services, moreover, are more oriented to the international versus the local economy (Nijman 2000). Miami ranks relatively low on the scale of world cities in terms of corporate headquarters, command and control functions. Its globalization index is higher on the level of relations and connections to other cities in the hierarchy, in terms of flows of trade, people, information, and capital (Nijman 2000). It has become popular for American blue-chip companies headquartered in New York to site their Latin American regional offices in Coral Gables.

So much of Miami's growth has taken place in the postwar period of U.S. history that the Anglo power elite never developed exclusive control of the local economy and political machinery. Thus the Miami growth machine has increasingly become permeated with Cuban and other Latin American interests, including corporations, developers, bankers, and politicians. Mayor Manny Diaz is Cuban American, and there are Cuban Americans on the City and County Commission and other elected and appointed public offices. Small businesses in Miami are owned largely by Cubans and other Latino immigrants, while corporate "branch" offices are American owned (Portes and Stepick 1993: 8). Miami has the highest foreign-born population of any city in the U.S., 61 percent, according to the 2002 American Community Survey. Miami's highly bilingual and binational labor force with an affinity to both North and South American cultures is a highly valued asset by international businesses.

The bilingual and bicultural Miami created by Cubans also became popular for other Latin Americans from throughout the hemisphere to travel and shop. Wealthy Latin Americans invest their money in local banks and condominiums along the bayshore or homes in new subdivisions in western Dade County. They shop in trendy boutiques in South Beach as well as suburban malls in Dadeland and Aventura. Part of the allure stems from the emergence of a "Latin Hollywood" of celebrities that have bought residences in Miami, such as Gloria Estefan and Julio Iglesias. In a 1993 *Time* magazine cover, entitled "Miami: The Capital of Latin America," Ray Rodriguez, the Cuban-born president of Univision, the No. 1 Spanish language television network in the U.S., said: "Miami has become the meeting place of the Americas for the Spanish-speaking world." Other Latin American stars residing in Miami are the Venezuelan singing idol Jose Luis Rodriguez, known as El Puma, the Dominican merengue star Juan Luis Guerra, and Don Francisco, the jovial and pudgy host of Latin TV's popular show, *Sabado Gigante* (Booth 1993).

The High-Rise Condominium Building Boom

Since the 1990s, Miami has been undergoing an unprecedented real estate boom, especially in high-rise luxury condominiums. A December 2006 *Wired* magazine (Di Justo 2006: 52–53) article predicted the number of skyscrapers in Miami will rise from five in 1999 to 71 in 2012, with 36 of them in the downtown area. Cities experiencing comparable high-rise building booms include Dubai, Las Vegas, and London. Tall, glassy and sleek, the condominium towers are built to inspire buyers to fantasize and dream. Some are named for precious

stones like Onyx, Emerald, Platinum, and Jade. Others evoke colors of
the sea, like Acqualina and Blue, or states of rapture like Nirvana and
Apogee. A pioneering firm and a major player in the Miami high-rise
architecture market is Arquitectonica, which designed the Atlantis
Condominiums. The Atlantis was featured on the opening credits of
the television series *Miami Vice* in the 1980s.[3] An internationally
renowned firm now, Arquitectonica has been involved in numerous
projects associated with Miami's latest vertical building surge, such as
Icon Brickell, Brickell CitiCenter, Infinity, Latitude, Axis, and Bentley.
In April 2005, *USA Today* reported some 69,000 condo units were in
the permit pipeline, under construction, or completed, surpassing Las
Vegas, the perennial U.S. leader in the high-rise condo market. Special
demand-side factors in Miami's hot condominium market are buyers
from outside the local economy. There is the impact of well-heeled baby
boomers nearing retirement, part of the historic flow of "snowbirds"
from the Northeast and Midwest. American developers such as Donald
Trump target this market. International demand is even greater, with
a range of Latin American investors lured by business connections and
the status that comes with buying Miami real estate. There is growing
participation from European investors armed with the euro, which
carries a strong exchange rate relative to the U.S. dollar. The Jade
Residences, a luxury 50-story high-rise, featuring $7 million penthouse
condos on its top floors, targets Latin buyers. Ana Cristina Defortuna,
vice president for sales, estimates that 90 percent of buyers are foreign
nationals, with people from every Latin American country, including
royalty, singers, and actors. Mexicans are among the top Latin buyers
now. Mexican pop music star Luis Miguel bought a penthouse. So did
Colombian racing car driver Juan Pablo Montoya (Adams 2005).

   The media touted the Miami real estate market in 2005, with an
article in the newspaper *USA Today* (Adams 2005), and a segment on
the ABC News television show *Frontline* entitled, "Boomtown Miami."
A year-and-a-half later, ABC News revisited the story, with the title
"Miami Condo Boom Goes Bust," chronicling how developers were
shifting from new projects to completing construction under way
and sales of existing condominiums. Speculators, who had bought

preconstruction units with the intent of flipping with the booming market, were reducing their expectations of quick profits and often looking to retain their condos to rent for a while. One analyst, Jack Winston of Goodkin Consulting, estimated that speculators make up to 70 percent of the demand in the Miami real estate market and that some time in the fall of 2005 new sales had come to a halt. The sagging sales reflected the superabundance of supply as well as rising insurance rates from the battering that Florida received in eight hurricanes in 2004 and 2005, and rising property taxes because of increasing property values (Kofman 2007).

There were voices of exhilaration amidst the sure signs that a slowdown was impending. At an Orlando homebuilder conference in July 2007, Florida Governor Charlie Crist quipped, "Have you been to Miami lately? It's like we have a new state bird: the building crane." The Miami construction boom helped drive Florida's robust growth from 2001 to 2005, with construction, finance, insurance, and real estate sector jobs. Financial observers were growing increasingly pessimistic, however, with Lewis Goodkin, president of Goodkin Consulting, predicting a regional recession to hit soon. South Florida and regional lenders, such as Alabama-based Regions Bank, foresaw the glut and stopped financing Miami condos in 2005, leaving the job to other banks such as Chicago-based Corus Bankshares. The decline in the market had put some projects in jeopardy. Jade Residences was one of the more troubled condominium towers, where the buyers initially snapped up 338 units following its June 2004 opening. By July 2007, 112 had put up their units for sale. Buyers of 17 units totaling $17 million had gone into foreclosure, leading to a special assessment on the remaining buyers to cover the maintenance money lost. Puig Development Group, a real estate management company with many Miami properties, based in Hialeah, Florida, went bankrupt in May 2007. Still there were some signs that overseas capital would help alleviate some of the decline. Projects such as Asia on Brickell Key, by Hong Kong-based developer Swire Properties, Inc., with 123 luxury units was completely sold out through preconstruction sales. Swire is heavily invested in Brickell Key, the 44-acre island made of dredged sand connected to Miami by a 1000-

foot four-lane bridge that has ten high-rises under construction, adding an element of Pacific Rim participation to the Latin American and European capital investment activity in Miami (Ivry 2007). Public officials such as Mayor Manny Diaz continued to boost downtown high-rise condominium construction, contending it would reduce sprawl and bring more people and money into Miami. "We will continue to build because I see more and more interest from foreign investors coming into Miami," Diaz said in a 2007 interview with Bloomberg.com reporter Bob Ivry, "I don't think we're done." Dana Nottingham, executive director of the Miami Downtown Development Authority, asserts that "We want to be a premiere urban center, not just nationally but globally, and downtown residential development is part of the formula for a great city" (Ivry 2007).

The decline in the condominium property market, however, is real. Miami's sagging real estate market has drawn the growing interest of so-called "vulture fund" or "vulture capital" investors, who are "circling the skies" or "waiting in the trees" of the forest of downtown construction cranes. The troubles at projects like Jade Residences portend the real possibility that a developer may go bankrupt soon, passing on their indebtedness to banks, which will offer these construction loans at a significant discount of typically 50 percent to vulture fund investors. Vulture capitalists will then resell or rent these units at a 15–30 percent discount to what buyers first paid in 2004 or 2005, and pocket the difference. Vulture fund investors are also willing to convert from condominiums to rental apartments to anticipate a future recovery in real estate values.[4]

New Urbanist Master Planning in High-Rise Miami

While Miami experienced the climax of a real estate boom around the turn of the twentieth century, local forces were also at work to undertake urban master planning. The development of a comprehensive metropolitan master planning process was sparked in 2001 upon the election of Mayor Manny Diaz, with Elizabeth Plater-Zyberk of Duany Plater-Zyberk (DPZ) and Company, Architects and Town Planners, hired as the lead consultant.[5] DPZ is a leader in the National Congress of the

New Urbanism. New Urbanism is a planning and design movement working to address the ills of urban sprawl by reducing automobile
congestion, returning social life to city streets, creating more public
green and pedestrian-friendly spaces, and celebrating local history and
the environment. New Urbanism also favors use of neotraditional
design elements and to increase the supply of affordable housing while
achieving a balanced mix of spaces for employment and housing.
While New Urbanism is perhaps best known for new town construction
of elite neotraditional "privatopias" such as the Florida Panhandle
town of Seaside and Orlando's Disney-sponsored Celebration, the
movement has also worked to restore depressed urban neighborhoods into functional and sustainable communities (Congress for the
New Urbanism 1999). In the 1990s, the U.S. Department of Housing
and Urban Development began integrating some principles of New
Urbanism into its multibillion-dollar plan to rebuild public housing
projects throughout the nation. In Miami, DPZ has also worked with
the Black Archives in the master planning process in Overtown, before
the entry of the Collins Center into the neighborhood. DPZ is
headquartered in east Little Havana.

The Miami 21 plan that emerged was not a comprehensive master
plan, essentially a rezoning plan that accepted the existing landscape of
capitalist urban development while coordinating six elements, including
economic development, transportation, parks and public realm, arts
and culture, and heritage preservation. It was implemented beginning
in 2005. It promotes a "form-oriented" zoning code that stimulates
community dialogue through planning charrettes among neighborhood
stakeholders. It tries to marry some of the principles of New Urbanism,
such as lower-density pedestrian-friendly neighborhoods and heritage
preservation, with the high-density skyscraper cityscape of booming
twenty-first-century Miami. New Urbanism promotes "glocalization"
insofar as it tries to create dynamic, compact, walkable, vibrant local
neighborhoods within the broader rubric of the global metropolis.
It does not oppose density, but promotes *transitions in density*, and
mixed-use spaces, with tall buildings stepping down to lower-density
residential buildings and commercial streets that feature pedestrian-

conducive environments where automobiles and parking are concealed. Public spaces and access to open spaces like the waterfront are also encouraged.

The wedding of high and low density through transitions in scale and "stepping down" is a promising planning strategy, but high and low density can also clash, as in the case of the restored Cuban American Freedom Tower and Miami's new "Gold Coast" of luxury bayside condominium towers along Biscayne Boulevard. These upscale condo towers offer spectacular views of the emerald green waters of Biscayne Bay and are walking distance to public amenities and entertainment at the waterfront including the American Airlines Arena, Carnival Center for the Performing Arts, and the Bayside Marketplace. The neoclassical architecture of the 17-story Freedom Tower is a contrast to the high-tech modernism of the 65-story Marina Blue luxury condominium tower, at 800 Biscayne Boulevard. One of Miami's most active high-rise building developers, Hyperion Development, is the developer of the Marina Blue project, and the architect is Arquitectonica. Rising behind Marina Blue up Biscayne Boulevard are 900 Biscayne Boulevard (by Terra Group), Ten Museum Park, and the Marquis Miami. The Marquis Miami is the crown jewel of the collection, with a plan for 67 stories and luxury condominiums that will range from $900,000 one-bedroom units to a $14 million penthouse, as well as a 56-suite boutique hotel.

The Cuban American Freedom Tower is located at 600 Biscayne Boulevard. It was constructed in 1925 in the Spanish Renaissance style, and like the Biltmore Hotel in Coral Gables, is a copy of the Giralda Tower in Sevilla, Spain. For its first 25 years, it was home of the *Miami News* newspaper, then was abandoned and fell into government ownership. From 1962 to 1974, it was used as a station for the processing and documenting of Cuban refugees and immigrants and providing for their medical and dental needs. Preservationists were able to gain recognition from the U.S. National Register of Historic Places in 1979, but the building fell into dilapidation and it passed through several private owners, until 1997, when a member of the Cuban American community, Jorge Mas Canosa, purchased it for $4.1 million and spent $16 million

Figure 5.3 Cuban American Freedom Tower in foreground with Marina Blue condominium tower and others rising in background. Photo by Jan Lin

on renovations. The tower has acquired a reputation within the Cuban American community as their "Ellis Island" or "Statue of Liberty," a symbol of promise and freedom. The building is being restored as a monument to Cuban America, housing a museum, library, meeting hall, and the offices of the Cuban American National Foundation.

The Freedom Tower has been the site for many collective demonstrations and protests, marches, prayer vigils, and hunger strikes. On the eve of Pope John Paul II's visit to Cuba in 1998, the Cuban American National Foundation presented an exhibit of civil rights abuses in Cuba at the tower. Later that year, it was a collection spot for relief supplies for Nicaraguan victims of Hurricane Mitch. Upon her death in 2002, the "queen of salsa," singer Celia Cruz lay in state on the ground floor of the tower as hundreds of thousands of Cuban Americans filed past to mourn and pay their last respects. The tower is an important icon of Cuban American political consciousness and for the continuing experience of Cuban ethnicity and collective identity in America.

In 2005, a major player in the Miami property market, the Terra Group, bought the building from the family of Jorge Mas Canosa, who had passed away. The president of Terra Group, Pedro Martin, despite being a Cuban American, announced the intent of demolishing 75 feet of the original tower to develop 683 condominium units. Preservationists were able to block the demolition and a deal was brokered with the City of Miami whereby the building was donated to Miami Dade College while Terra Group was granted approval to build a 62-story high-rise condominium tower (currently dubbed Paramount Park) behind the 17-story tower. Miami Dade College will be responsible for managing the Freedom Tower museum, creating exhibits, and running educational programs on the Cuban American immigration experience, arts, and culture. The Freedom Tower has been saved, a relic of history in a new forest of 50- and 60-story skyscrapers lining Biscayne Bay and the mouth of the Miami River. The Freedom Tower preserves the style of neoclassical architectural and the scale of the neotraditional city amidst the modernism of the high-rise city. The distinction between the low-scale neotraditional city and the

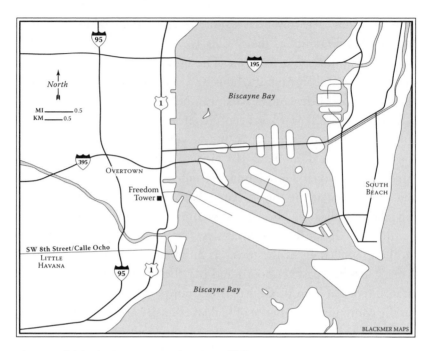

Figure 5.4 Major heritage preservation sites of Miami.

high-rise modernistic city has its parallel in the contrast between the New Urbanism of Duany Plater-Zyberk and the modernistic sky-scrapers designed by firms such as Arquitectonica.[6] The Cuban American Freedom Tower was saved from demolition by preservation interests amidst the pressures of a high-rise luxury condominium market fueled by global investment capital.

Preservation and the Dynamics of Gentrification in South Beach

The story of South Miami Beach provides lessons in how the govern-mental and corporate establishment has capitalized on the success of a local preservationist movement to restore deteriorating classic Art Deco hotels. Preservation stimulated neighborhood revitalization, which then led to dynamics of redevelopment and gentrification, eventually threatening the existing community of retirees and small business owners with displacement by corporate place entrepreneurs and upscale residents. The South Beach story started in the 1970s south of Lincoln Road, when it was still a depressed property market of senior citizens living in hotels and low-income cooperative housing. While more affluent Jewish Americans had moved to nicer hotels and condominiums further up the beach, poorer families were left in South Beach. The urban historian M. Barron Stofik (2005) called South Beach "God's waiting room" for elderly working-class and middle-class Jews, who subsisted on pensions and social security checks in small apartments, cooking on hotplates. She depicts the daily rituals of their social life that included sitting on folding chairs on front porches, shifting from one side of the street to the other, or into interior lobbies, as the sun made its trajectory through the sky and intensified from morning to afternoon.

The local preservation movement was born in the 1970s with the work of activists like Barbara Baer Capitman, Leonard Horowitz, and Nancy Liebman in Miami Beach, who organized the Miami Design Preservation League (MDPL) to block historic Art Deco buildings from destruction and eventually procured support for a historic district of some 300–400 buildings. They were not able to save the area south of 6th Street, which was declared "blighted" by the City of Miami Beach in 1975 and designated for redevelopment as the "South Shore" (now South Pointe). The preservationists had initially planned to save historic buildings and hotels to maintain the inventory of affordable housing for the elderly, but they eventually had to adjust their vision to attract public officials and developers to the idea that historic districts could enhance rather than impede the economic revitalization process. The Art Deco district occupies several dozen prime blocks in the middle of South Beach, splitting the redevelopment area to both the north (the convention center and new hotels were built north of Lincoln Road, near City Hall and the museum/theater district) and south (the South Shore area sports high-rise condominiums like the 44-story Portofino Tower). The Art Deco district became a popular place for artists, gays, and lesbians to visit and live in the 1980s.

Many historic hotels fell to the wrecking ball during the conflicts and negotiations between activists and developers, such as the

New Yorker and the Senator, seen by preservationists as two of the finest examples of Art Deco architecture. The Capitman family had purchased the Senator along with several other buildings in an effort to restore them with public funds, but a weak housing market in the 1980s made banks and public officials wary of investing in South Beach. They lost ownership of the building to private developers, the Royale Group, which decided to demolish the Senator. The Save Our Senator campaign was able to delay the demolition of the hotel for a year, leading to a final incident in May 1988 when Barbara Capitman chained herself to the railings of the Senator while dressed in a black caftan that resembled a judge's robe. She suffered a heart attack during the episode and the demolition proceeded as she was led away by police. She suffered congestive heart failure and died several months later. The episode brought attention to the fact that developers could still circumvent protections such as designation on the National Register of Historic Places as well as City and County of Miami preservation ordinances passed in the early 1980s (Stofik 2005).[7]

Many South Beach hotels were saved from demolition by the efforts of the MDPL, however, and the Miami Beach Development Corporation also began to implement a color scheme of pastel tones like peach, cream, mauve, and aqua, created by architect and MDPL co-founder Leonard Horowitz. The pastel-colored Art Deco hotels were popularized by the film and TV series *Miami Vice* in the 1980s, which assisted in the transformation of the popular perception of South Beach. The 1990s brought a new booming economy and real estate market to Miami, and South Beach emerged as "SoBe," a trendy and fashionable community that attracted the fashion models, photographers, and legendary designers such as Gianni Versace (brutally murdered in front of his Casa Casuarina mansion in 1997) and a more upscale residential population.

The Art Deco hotels were like the proverbial "goose that laid the golden egg," said Gene Barfield, of the Metro Dade County Historic Preservation Board, in a June 1996 interview. South Beach became one of the paradigmatic illustrations in urban America of a historic preservation district that became an engine of urban revitalization.

The Art Deco district had the unintended consequence of assisting the redevelopment and gentrification process that eventually would threaten the pre-existing low-income community and mom-and-pop businesses.

South Miami Beach went through a sequence of urban historical phases that included abandonment, preservation, residential colonizing by artistic and gay subcultures, and subsequent gentrification as an enclave for high-end international tourism, global fashion and design activities, and affluent high-rise residential condominiums. South Beach provides lessons on the opportunities and risks for preservationists and stakeholders in Overtown and Little Havana. On the matter of ethnic identity, South Beach represents more a case of transformation and fluidity. The historic Jewish American community was assimilated into the more general white population. During the more recent process of urban revitalization, the district has acquired a more gay and Latin-inflected atmosphere, represented through caricature in films such as *Birdcage* (1996).

Heritage Preservation in Overtown

Heritage and community development efforts in Overtown have been based around the preservation of the Lyric Theater and other key buildings, linked together in a pedestrian "Folklife Village" that mixes residential housing with businesses. The Overtown preservation movement has owed much to the seminal efforts of Dr. Dorothy Jenkins Fields. A school librarian and reading teacher in the Miami public schools, Dr. Fields became motivated in 1974 to establish a black photographic archive for the celebration of the 1976 U.S. Bicentennial. This grew into a larger interest in historic preservation of significant heritage sites in Overtown as she grew acquainted with historians and preservationists at the Historical Museum of Southern Florida, the National Trust for Historic Preservation, and the Dade Heritage Trust. During the summer of 1977 she grew inspired while visiting the Foxfire Oral History Program in Rabun Gap, Georgia, which was doing pathblazing work to preserve and disseminate Appalachian heritage, culture, foodways, and music through several linked programs in oral history, public education, musical recording, book publishing, and architectural

preservation of historic log cabins. Dorothy Fields translated the
tradition of folk culture revival into a movement of black cultural
renewal in Miami's Overtown.

Upon returning to Miami, Dr. Fields began to set up a board of
directors and founded the Black Archives, History, and Research
Foundation, Inc. She set to work preserving historic buildings and
creating a historic district. Personal and collective memories of Over-
town in its heyday among her extended family as well as her board of
directors motivated their efforts. Intensive research work supported the
election of six buildings that were eventually recognized by the National
Register of Historic Places, namely the Lyric Theater, the Dorsey
House, the Cola Nip Bottling Company, the Greater Bethel A.M.E.
Church, Mt. Zion Baptist Church, and the St. John Institutional
Baptist Church. The Lyric Theater drew the particular attention of
Dr. Fields because of its beauty and the story of black businessman
Geder Walker, who was inspired to build the theater from trips to opera

Figure 5.5 Lyric Theater after renovation. Photo by Jan Lin.

houses in Paris, France. Built in 1913, it showcased stage and film performances of gospel, jazz, vaudeville, and literary arts of the Harlem Renaissance.

In a June 2007 interview, Dr. Fields spoke very much in the idioms of family genealogy, historic preservation, and racial–ethnic rediscovery. While Alex Haley went back to Africa on a global voyage of ancestral self-discovery, Dorothy Fields went to Georgia, and then back to Overtown to discover her racial–ethnic roots. She describes the decision to begin preserving buildings in Overtown:

> I thought that if a black man built this, he built it for us. I felt obligated to restore the building. I think of those buildings as footprints that connect generations of the past, whom we shall never see, with the generations of the future, whom we shall never see.

The Lyric Theater renovation was achieved through a mix of funding from the State of Florida, the City of Miami, and a $4.3 million add-on to a $250 million bond issue for the Miami Performing Arts Center complex built just beyond the eastern edge of Overtown (Borrup 2003). The Black Archives moved on to acquire and reconstruct the Dorsey House, which was built in 1915 by a real estate agent and Overtown's first black millionaire, D. A. Dorsey, for his wife.

The Lyric Theater was originally the centerpiece of a two-square block area once known as "the strip" or "Little Broadway," then eventually "The Great Black Way" that in its heyday contained two theaters, three dance halls, and six restaurants. There were five hotels with nightclubs, including the Dorsey, the Marsha Ann, the Lord Calvert (renamed the Sir John), and the Carver hotels. It became fashionable for black leaders, sports figures, and celebrities to stop in Colored Town. Black entertainers performing in Miami Beach couldn't stay there because of racial segregation laws, so they stayed in Colored Town's hotels. The entertainment promoter Clyde Killens booked the black musicians in the Colored Town clubs, and sometimes they held jam sessions at the nightclubs until dawn (Fields 1998).

Figure 5.6 Dorsey House. Photo by Jan Lin.

The Lyric Theater is central to the Black Archives and to the revitalizing of Overtown. Dr. Fields' idea to link several sites together in a folklife village emerged from influences like the Foxfire Appalachian folklife project in Georgia and the Smithsonian Institution Folklife Festival, held on the grounds of the National Mall in Washington, D.C. since 1967. Dr. Fields wants to create spaces for "cottage industries" such as artist and handicraft entrepreneurs operating in combined work/retail spaces. The village would cater to outside visitors and tourists through walking tours and public education on the cultural heritage of Overtown as well as showcasing the present-day "creative capital" of African American artists. There have also been plans floated for a "Jazz Walk of Fame," an associated sculpture garden, and rehearsal and studio spaces for literary, folk, visual, and performing arts. Comparable black historical areas can be found in other cities such as the Sweet Auburn Avenue district of Atlanta, the Savannah Historic District, and the Black Historic Trail of Boston, Massachusetts. The Overtown Folklife Village can be seen as a project of black economic and cultural localization.

Figure 5.7 Mt. Zion Historic Baptist Church. Photo by Jan Lin.

In 1980, a first master plan for the Folklife Village was developed by architectural firm Ronald Frazier and Associates through a charrette held in town hall style with significant community stakeholders. The idea for a mixed-used cultural/entertainment district with a retail corridor and affordable/workforce housing was developed. A second master plan was created by the New Urbanist architectural firm Duany Plater-Zyberk which convened a 1998 charrette in a neighborhood church, bringing together participants from a variety of community, public, and private interests. The plan incorporated artists' housing as well as commercial/retail space, mixed-income residential housing, and historic structures. It presented a tourism plan aimed at attracting outside visitors, especially through the hosting of family reunions, targeting black families who were formerly residents (Borrup 2003). The phenomenon of black family reunions is common in Miami and other southern cities such as Atlanta, where black families are dispersed into suburbs and neighboring cities and will converge in downtown hotels for holidays and celebrations. Family reunions can help to foster relations of trust and reciprocity, and ethnic social capital, which are valuable tools for community development.

In 2001, the dynamic of redevelopment in Overtown took a dramatic change with the announcement of $7.5 million in funding by the Knight Foundation to be devoted to a neighborhood revitalization initiative. Three million was granted to the Collins Center for Public Policy to fund the Overtown Civic Partnership and Design Center to involve residents in a range of sustainable development exercises and for a community land trust that would acquire and hold land for the benefit of residents. Two million was granted to the Local Initiatives Support Corporation (LISC) to develop linkages with an umbrella of local community-based organizations, including the Black Archives/ Lyric Theater, the Bethel A.M.E. (BAME) Community Development Corporation, and the St. John's Community Development Corporation. Monies were also targeted for Habitat for Humanity to build ten houses in Overtown, for a community center called Miami Inner City Angels, and for the Trust for Public Land to construct pedestrian-friendly greenways.

The Collins Center hired Philip Bacon in 2002 as executive director of the Civic Partnership and Design Center (CPDC). Four charrettes were held with over 200 stakeholders invited to develop a new, yet more comprehensive master plan, and the CPDC was housed for a while in the Dorsey House. Ray Guidros, a New Urbanism-type planner with Urban Development Associates, was recruited to lead the planning process. The Collins Center also took a group of collaborative partners on trips to a conference in Los Angeles, a visit to LISC in Chicago, and then to the Pittsburgh offices of Ray Guidros. A much larger area surrounding the Folklife Village site was identified that encompassed the holdings of the collaborative partners, as well as several vacant lots owned by the City of Miami and the CRA.

The larger area encompassed five-and-a-half vacant parcels that were mostly parking lots previously servicing the now defunct Miami Arena. The development rights over some of the parcels were mired in a lawsuit between the CRA and private developer Ted Weitzel, who had previously cooperated with the CRA to build Poinciana Village, a

low-rise, 64-unit condominium complex on the southern fringe of
Overtown. Although the disposition of land was tied up in litigation,
the Collins Center moved ahead with plans to develop the sites and
issued a Request for Letter of Intent (RLI) from prospective developers.
A successful RLI process, it was thought, would impress upon City and
County officials and planners the seriousness of the Collins Center-led
plan. Philip Bacon brought a keen acumen for engineering private-sector
participation in master planning into the developmental dynamic in
Overtown that he had acquired in his previous position as executive
director of the CRA of Fort Lauderdale. He had worked earlier with
Crosswinds Communities, Inc., a private developer based in Michigan,
which had narrowly missed being awarded a contract with the
Ft. Lauderdale CRA, and invited them to submit a bid in Overtown.
Crosswinds proposed a 1300–1500-unit mixed-income residential
project, called "Downtown Overtown," which would be adjacent to the
proposed Folklife Village.

The Collins Center was also gradually acquiring some 20 properties
in the surrounding area. Philip Bacon stated in a June 2007 interview:

> It's new for Collins Center to be a property owner. We are civic
> entrepreneurs; we are not a community development corporation.
> We've used our land holdings to influence what was happening
> here, to attract a major developer. We are using the rest of our
> land holdings to influence the larger redevelopmental area of
> Overtown.

The Crosswinds "Downtown Overtown" project attracted the interest
of other developers including Miami's Codina Group and former
basketball star Magic Johnson's Canyon–Johnson Urban Fund. Private
investors had long seen Overtown as the "hole in the doughnut" of
Miami's downtown redevelopment boom, which could be seen in
areas like Brickell Avenue, Biscayne Boulevard, the Miami River, and
Edgewater, booming in construction cranes. Public officials such as City
Commissioner Johnny Winton and Mayor Manny Diaz gave their
endorsement to the project (Viglucci and Yardley 2003).

Opposition emerged from some several sectors of the community including African American City Commissioner Art Teele. Commissioner Teele said in a *Miami Herald* article that he was concerned the Crosswinds proposal was a "gentrification project" that would hurt Overtown's historically black character. As chairman of the Miami CRA since 1997, he told City Commissioner Winton that he wanted to exclude the two CRA parcels, and Crosswinds subsequently reduced the scope of their project from five-and-a-half to three-and-a-half lots (Corral 2004). While the legal dispute between Crosswinds, the City, and Ted Weitzel was eventually settled, two new lawsuits emerged. One was from Glenn Straub, owner of the Miami Arena, contending the City should have put the land out to bid. Power U, a community group comprising professional organizers, filed the second lawsuit, contending the project was "racist and classist" because the condominiums were unaffordable to the majority of Overtown residents. They also worried that redevelopment and residential gentrification would raise property values that would eventually displace the black residents (Viglucci 2006).

The $200–220 million Crosswinds proposal now plans for some 1050 mixed-income condominium units in high-rise towers that step down gradually to the low-rise heights of the Folklife Village. The four residential buildings will be mixed with 75,000 square feet of retail and office space. The name has been changed from "Downtown Overtown" to "Sawyer's Walk" to suggest a more pedestrian and folkloric setting that evokes the atmosphere of Mark Twain's 1876 novel, *The Adventures of Tom Sawyer*. The story of Tom Sawyer fooling his friends into helping him whitewash the fence becomes a parable of gentrification as a latent "whitewashing" process according to some opponents to the Crosswinds project. Twenty percent of the condos are slated to be affordable housing, with 160 projected as "workforce" housing targeted at middle-income buyers such as police officers, teachers, and clerical workers, and 50 units set aside to be sold by the City to qualifying low-income households, with a preference for Overtown residents. The market-rate condos were projected to sell for up to $300,000 (Viglucci 2006).

In November 2006, City commissioners voted to grant a building permit to Crosswinds for Sawyer's Walk, with a promise that affordable set-aside condos for Overtown residents would be increased from 50 to 112 and middle-income workforce condos would be increased from 160 to 210. The City also granted a $12 million subsidy for infrastructure and parking. In return, the City will earn millions in tax-increment funds generated by the massive development. While the City owns the land, Crosswinds owns the development rights. A lingering legal barrier, however, was a "reverter clause" stipulating that the ownership of the three vacant lots could revert from the City to the County if construction wasn't under way by August 2007 (Del Campo 2006). At the time of my field research visit to Miami in June 2007, it appeared that construction would not begin that summer, but that an agreement was close between the City and the County to extend the deadline on the reverter clause. Meanwhile, the two lawsuits were in the process of final settlement, opening the way for construction.

Figure 5.8 Site of the Crosswinds Sawyer's Walk project with downtown towers in the background. Photo by Jan Lin.

While community residents and stakeholders are quicker to welcome more affordable housing projects like the Villas of St. Agnes, they were initially skeptical of the Crosswinds project. Still, the major community-based organizations, like the Black Archives/Lyric Theater, the St. John's CDC (Community Development Corporation), the BAME CDC, and the Overtown chapter of the Miami-Dade Empowerment Trust, had become invested as stakeholders in the Collins Center-led Overtown Civic Partnership, although they also operate independent civic partnership organizations. They have pressed for minority contractor agreements for the local CDCs, as well as job creation and skills training for the local labor force, and an increase in affordable set-aside condominium units for local residents. They secured the drafting of a community benefits agreement with Crosswinds in October 2006 in the process of endorsing the project at public hearings. The agreement lists only general language with the specifics to be worked out later, on issues such as parking for the Lyric Theater and Longshoremen's Union.

Dorothy Fields of the Black Archives is very concerned about the issue of community participation and ownership in the redevelopmental process. She said in a June 2007 interview:

> We must be a part of the process. Part of the reason we can insist and demand to be part of the process is because we hold the records of the families and the collective memories, of the community organizations and the indigenous people. It's our land. It was assigned to us by Julia Tuttle, the Mother of Miami, who in her deed stated that Negroes and factories would be on this side of the railroad tracks. And we're not going to let it go. We can't just sit back and let development come and wipe us out. This is our land; it was assigned to us. It was thought to be worthless, and now it is worth so much that everybody wants it. We're not going to give it away. This is our land.

Kris Smith of the Local Initiatives Support Corporation is also supportive of the Collins Center and the Crosswinds proposal, but he voices concerns about matters of zoning and scale. He observes that the

Collins Center/Guidros and Associates master plan has diverged from the original master plan created by the Black Archives/Duany Plater-Zyberk:

> The DPZ master plan of 1997–98 is the original vision of the Black Archives, with Caribbean style architecture and small businesses, shops, cultural amenities, beauty shops, travel agencies and theater-related industry. Ice cream shops helped to animate the space. Phil Bacon's plan, a larger and broader view of the area, articulated the need for a catalytic development like Crosswinds. Those are two diametrically opposed plans. Black Archives had market-rate housing also, but at a smaller scale. Black Archives also wanted to create a greater cultural aesthetic, attracting artists back to the area, not just repopulating the area residentially. There were smaller footprints and buildings of three to four stories. The desire was to build live–work spaces for artists and handicraft makers; people could do their work and live there in an affordable way.

Timothy Barber of the Black Archives brings up the same point with reference to the divergence from the original DPZ master plan, which featured New Urbanist principles and neotraditional design elements such as low-rise residential and commercial buildings, human scale and pedestrian walkability, as well as central civic and public spaces sensitive to local history. The Crosswinds plan initially relied upon high-rise condominium towers, but a subsequent revision by architect Clyde Judson and Associates better integrates some guiding principles of New Urbanism insofar as the high-rise towers step down gradually to the lower-scale buildings of the Folklife Village. The construction of the 9th Street Pedestrian Mall between 2nd and 3rd Streets by the Miami CRA reinforces this focus on pedestrian walkability. It features brick inlay in a multicolored African kente design.

Kris Smith believes that redevelopmental master planning must take a holistic and moral approach that is sensitive to the current conditions. He also draws attention to the need to remove the stigma of dilapidated buildings, homelessness, and perceptions of crime and social disorder in Overtown, in order to attract art galleries, theatrical audiences, and tourists and to residentially repopulate the area. He suggests the idea of an open house program to celebrate the remarkable assets in the neighborhood, and signature events in order to introduce people to the area. He cites the success of black entertainment and business districts such as U Street/14th Street in Washington, D.C., Bronzeville in Chicago, as well as 18th and Vine area in Kansas City. He also cites the need for amenities like public and green space in order to create healthy and sustainable neighborhoods, as well as green building issues such as energy efficiency. He said that LISC was exploring the idea with the Department of Transportation of taking water runoff from I-395 to create gardens and landscaping and green the neighborhoods.

When I asked Kris Smith about whether efforts were leading blacks to start a "back-to-the-city" movement to neighborhoods like Overtown, he responded:

> There is a greater back-to-the-city movement among Caribbean blacks rather than African Americans. The Bahamian tradition is strong in Overtown; it is historic. Their cultural forefathers came here and settled. Bahamian culture was once a thriving culture and celebrated here. African Americans do not participate as much in returning to Overtown. Other neighborhoods, like Richmond Heights, Liberty City, Miami Gardens, and Carol City have attracted African Americans. Social networking through civic groups and churches will also need to play into luring people to return. St. Agnes Church brings black people back on Sundays. The Villas of St. Agnes housing community, furthermore, attracted both African Americans and Caribbean blacks because of location and affordable housing well below market cost. I moved here from Jacksonville myself and I live in Overtown by the Miami Arena.

Irby McKnight, chairperson of the Overtown committee of the Miami-Dade Empowerment Trust, is similarly interested in attracting middle-class and suburban black residents back to the inner city by building more affordable housing in Overtown. In September 2006, the community celebrated the opening of the Villas of St. Agnes, an 80-unit complex of single-family three- and four-bedroom, pastel-colored Bahamian-style houses, featuring wraparound porches and grassy lots. The St. Agnes Rainbow Community Development Corporation, associated with St. Agnes Episcopal Church, partnered with the Miami-Dade Empowerment Trust to build the ten-acre project on the site of a long-demolished public housing project at NW 3rd Avenue between 18th and 19th Streets ten blocks north of the Lyric Theater. The County contributed $10 million to the project. The Empowerment Trust oversaw the construction of the project.

Overtown residents have welcomed the affordable housing project as a hopeful sign after years of mismanagement, misspending, and neglect by the Miami-Dade Housing Agency. The home prices ranged from $95,000 to $125,000 and 32 of the buyers received a subsidy toward their mortgage or purchase costs, financed by the Knight Foundation and governmental sources. As reported in a *Miami Herald* article, Sharmin Crumbley, 43 years old, was able to buy a $95,000 home with the help of subsidies, with mortgage payments of less than $100 a month. She had lived on the streets from 1985 to 1996 as a self-described alcoholic and drug addict. After treatment in the late 1990s, she now earns $19,000 a year working at the Homeless Assistance Center. Said Ms. Crumbley: "This means the world to me. This has given me the opportunity to experience the American Dream. God gave me a blessing with this house" (Arthur 2006).

While Mr. McKnight criticizes the Collins Center for budgetary overspending and moving too slowly, he is generally supportive of the Crosswinds project because he believes it will help to bring households of a range of income levels into the area, contributing towards community stabilization. He said in a June 2007 interview: "We need to have middle-class professionals so children will have mentors and have hope and be inspired to go to school instead of being in the streets." He observed that the St. Agnes Villas were already bringing in more working- and middle-class people back to Overtown and even some professionals such as lawyers.

Irby McKnight was also concerned that policy makers give more attention to the existence of an informal sector economy. He suggested the U.S. census undercounts the actual Overtown population by up to 10,000 or 15,000 people. He also said that public officials often overlook the existence of hidden financial flows and significant spending power in the inner-city sub-economy. He cited what he called the phenomenon of predatory processing of government transfer checks by some retail businesses in Overtown, such as butchers and mini-markets, which charge exorbitant service fees. His organization, Overtown Benefits, Inc., advises residents on finding less exploitative avenues for processing their government entitlements.

Arts and Culture in Little Havana

The commercial and cultural heart of Cuban Miami is in "Little Havana," especially along SW 8th Street (Calle Ocho). Little Havana is the traditional reception center of Cuban exiles to Miami, beginning with a group in the 1930s, who mingled with the largely Jewish residents who developed SW 8th Street as a commercial alternative to Anglo-dominated West Flagler Street. The neighborhood near the Miami River was known as Riverside, with Shenandoah further west. The Cuban exile flow widened since the 1960s into an immigration stream that began to include a range of other Latin American refugee and immigrant groups, such as Nicaraguans, Guatemalans, Colombians, and other groups.

The refugee flow after the Cuban Revolution in 1959 had by the time of Mariel in 1980 begun moving into the Miami suburbs, especially to the south and west of Calle Ocho, leaving East Little Havana an urban transitional zone replete with boarded-up store fronts, vacant lots, commercial and residential decline. The kind of gentrification beginning in some other American cities in the early 1980s was for a while delayed in Miami's Little Havana because the continuing influx of refugees kept building occupancies at near capacity. Some historic bungalows were converted to architecturally unremarkable multistory buildings (George 1991). Preservationists would begin fighting to save some of Little Havana's historic structures from

Figure 5.9 Tower Theater. Photo by Jan Lin.

abandonment, however, in the 1980s. The Tower Theater, located at SW 8th Street and 15th Avenue in the heart of Calle Ocho, was their initial focus.

This historic theater was built in 1926 and transformed into an Art Deco gem with a prominent 40-foot steel tower for the Wometco Theater chain by architect Robert Law Weed in 1931. In early 1960, it was the first theater in Miami to show movies with Spanish subtitles. Many immigrants have fond memories of going to the theater for their first exposure to American popular culture. The theater eventually added movies completely in Spanish. As the Little Havana neighborhood began to decline with the outmovement of residents to suburban locations, the theater started to decline. It was closed by 1984, and preservationists in the community worked with the City of Miami to protect the building and raise funds for a $3 million restoration as a center for art, film, and culture for Cubans and other Latin American immigrants to Calle Ocho. The efforts of Jack Luft, director of the City of Miami Planning Department, and planner Jose Casanova were crucial during this period. The site earned National Register of Historic Places status in 1993 and the renovation was completed in 1997. In March 2002, the City entered an agreement with Miami Dade Community College (now Miami Dade College) authorizing it to manage and operate cultural and educational programming at the theater. From June 1 to 3, 2007, for instance, there was a photographic exhibition, *Havana Today in Images*, of high-definition huge-scale images of buildings and streetscapes in Havana, Cuba. On the evening of June 2, there was a screening of a documentary film critical of the Castro regime. There are periodical artistic exhibitions, poetry and book readings, film screenings, and theatrical productions on Cuban and Latin American culture and politics throughout the year. Some events are held in the Latin Quarter Cultural Center, across the street, which opened up new offices at 1501 SW 8th Street.

Calle Ocho has been redubbed the "Latin Quarter" to recognize the growing presence of Latin American immigrants from beyond Cuba, such as the Nicaraguans, who have established a "Little Managua" in

Figure 5.10 Latin Quarter Cultural Center. Photo by Jan Lin.

the northeast sector of the neighborhood,[8] as well as Hondorans, Colombians, and other groups. The Latin Quarter Specialty Center was built, a project of the East Little Havana CDC. This is a mixed-use project featuring 45 middle-income condominiums in a low-rise building with street level commercial storefronts. At the time of my last visit in June 2007, construction was finished but a legal dispute with the developer delayed occupancy, with a Great Florida Bank branch the only retail tenant. City signage and tourist promotional literature increasingly identifies the area as the Latin Quarter.

Sites, Rites, and Tourism in the Latin Quarter

A number of other important sidewalk, statuary, and monument sites have also emerged through the years that help demarcate a landscape of Cuban American public history and exile politics in Miami. A succession of memorials and statues are located just off Calle Ocho on SW 13th Avenue between 8th and 12th Streets, now dubbed "Cuban Memorial Boulevard." One of the most poignant memorials is the

Figure 5.11 Eternal Torch of Bay of Pigs memorial. Photo by Jan Lin.

Eternal Torch of Brigade 2506, a memorial to the soldiers killed in the 1961 Bay of Pigs Invasion of Cuba. There is also a bronze statue of Nestor "Tony" Izquierdo, a Cuban revolutionary hero, a bronze bust of General Antonio Maceo, an Afro-Cuban general who died while fighting for Cuban independence, a statue of the Virgin Mary, and a bronze map of Cuba. There is a large Ceiba tree with its roots sometimes filled with candles, of religious importance to those practicing Santeria. Also located on the boulevard is a memorial to Cuban journalists well known for their criticism of the Castro regime.

There is also the Plaza de la Cubanidad (Plaza of Cuban Patriots), at West Flagler and 17th Avenue. The artistic fountain in this plaza includes a sculpture of the island of Cuba, a boat and life preserver, honoring the *balseros* (rafters) who came on boats and rafts to the United States, and the patriot José Martí, a leader of Cuban independence from Spain, also a renowned poet and writer. There is a bust of José Martí in a park dedicated to his name along the Miami River in

Figure 5.12 Plaza de la Cubanidad. Photo by Jan Lin.

Figure 5.13 Close-up of artistic fountain honoring the *balseros* (the rafters) at Plaza de la Cubanidad. Photo by Jan Lin.

East Little Havana. There is also a Bay of Pigs Museum, at 1821 SW 9th Street, which displays pictures, uniforms, and flags of the soldiers of Assault Brigade 2506 that invaded Cuba on April 17, 1961 in an effort to oust the Castro regime. The 1500-strong exile army was recruited and trained by the CIA.

While the majority of memorials are dedicated to the patriots, liberators, and political leaders of Cuban American public history, there are other sites and rites that preserve and celebrate the contributions of Cuban Americans and other Latin American immigrants to American cultural life. Maximo Gomez Domino Park was established at SW 8th Street and 14th Avenue, named after the Dominican-born general who was chief of the Cuban Liberation Army in the wars of independence against Spain. Cuban American seniors and retirees frequent the little pocket park to play dominos and chess. A bus stop is located just in front of the domino park, where tour companies disembark for visits

Figure 5.14 Calle Ocho tourist bus stop. Photo by Jan Lin.

Figure 5.15 Seniors at Maximo Gomez Domino Park. Photo by Jan Lin.

to Little Havana. Next to the domino park is Little Havana To Go, a souvenir and gift shop popular with tourists.

The Calle Ocho Walk of Fame is located on SW 8th Street between 12th and 17th Avenues. This collection of star-shaped plaques embedded in the sidewalk recognizes the contributions of important Cuban American and other Latin American artistic and cultural figures. The idea came about following the dedication of Celia Cruz, the Cuban American "queen of salsa," with a star at the Hollywood Walk of Fame, in Los Angeles, California, in 1987. A Miami publicist named Javier Soto formed a company called Latin Stars, Inc. in 1988 to develop a Latin Walk of Fame. They gained City approval for the project, and in 1989 the first star was dedicated to singer Gloria Estefan and the Miami Sound Machine. After installing some 23 stars, Latin Stars, Inc. ran into financial difficulties and trouble with City officials. In 1995, a new company called Stars of Calle Ocho was created to manage the Walk of Fame, which continued to have conflicts with the City over financial issues and the criteria for screening and selecting stars on the

Figure 5.16 Star of Celia Cruz on the Calle Ocho Walk of Fame. Photo by Jan Lin.

walkway. Over the years, there has been significant controversy in the Cuban American and Latino community of Miami, as the Walk of Fame broadened its selection process to honor Latin American entertainers in general, such as Enrique Iglesias (the Spanish-born singer is based in Miami), Selena (the Mexican American *tejano* singer), and Sammy Sosa (the Dominican-born baseball player). Featuring the panethnic Latino diaspora seems to reflect the real situation of growing diversity in the Latin American community of Miami, but the presence of a star for Sylvester Stallone (the movie actor is of Italian/Jewish origin, and he attended the University of Miami) has tended to fuel allegations that stars are being "sold" to artists who can provide the $10,000 needed to finance one. It seems that the criterion that is evolving is that the stars have some kind of connection to Miami, whether or not they are Latin.[9]

The Calle Ocho festival and Carnival Miami

Preceding the artistic renaissance and redevelopment of Little Havana was the Calle Ocho festival, now called Carnival Miami (also Carnaval Miami). Billed as the "world's largest block party," the festival started out in 1978 as the Calle Ocho Open House 8, a street event started by the businessman Leslie Pantin, Jr. and his associate, Willy Bermello, with the support of the Kiwanis Club of Little Havana. In a June 2006 interview, Mr. Pantin reported that sources of inspiration were Mardi Gras in New Orleans, as well as ethnic festivals held in Philadelphia in the 1970s. Now more than one million people typically descend upon Miami for a ten-day extravaganza of events that includes an 8K run, a domino tournament, a golf classic, and the Calle Ocho street festival on the concluding weekend, with food vendors, a parade, outdoor music, and street dancing in what is billed as the "world's longest conga line."

The Latin Quarter stakeholders I spoke with in June 2007 felt that the Calle Ocho street festival had begun to transcend the local scene and appeal to a larger Latin American mass market that is more international in scope. The street festival has grown from a block party to a large corporate-sponsored commercial affair that shuts down the

majority of the small businesses on Calle Ocho for a weekend in order
to prepare the onslaught of tourists, curiosity seekers, and people
coming for free entertainment and great food from vendors on the street.
Robert Parente, of the City of Miami Office of Cultural Affairs, said
Calle Ocho was like "the proverbial snowball going downhill; it just got
bigger and bigger." While local stakeholders such as Tony Wagner of
the Latin Quarter Cultural Center support the Calle Ocho festival, he
also must close his center to prepare for the massive crowds. He believes
that smaller-scale monthly events such as Viernes Culturales (Cultural
Fridays) better contribute to sustaining local economic development and
the creative talents of local artists and musicians. Tanya Bravo, the
director of Viernes Culturales, said:

> Calle Ocho is like the Nuyorican Day parade in New York, which
> has a very urban feel, with a mixed-race crowd that comes out.
> When I used to attend Calle Ocho as a teenager, it was somewhat
> of a scary experience. The crowds are not contained, and you'll
> get people from all over the place. It's begun to transcend the locals.
> There are huge international acts that play here, including
> reggaeton and other urban music.

Viernes Culturales (Cultural Fridays) and the New Art Scene

Viernes Culturales is a cultural event held on the last Friday of each
month that features a live stage showcasing musicians from all over the
city as well as artists exhibiting in the "Latin Quarter Plaza" on SW
8th Street and 15th Avenue next to the Maxilo Gomez Domino Park.
It is also a chance to introduce visitors to the art galleries, restaurants,
and other small businesses operating on Calle Ocho. Tanya Bravo,
director of Viernes Culturales, spoke of reprogramming in a July 2007
interview, to reflect the cultural and generational diversity of the Latino
community:

> There are two challenges, the older audience and the younger
> audience. The older audience has been coming to Viernes
> Culturales for years, and they come to dance salsa all night. Some

Figure 5.17 Viernes Culturales banner on Calle Ocho. Photo by Jan Lin.

people come all the way from Palm Beach to dance. Then there is also the second and third generation that are in tune with what is new musically, a Hispanic fusion. These are people who have grown up in the U.S., of Cuban, Colombian or Puerto Rican background, mixing cumbia, salsa, merengue, and hip hop music that is a fusion representing Miami and what is in the U.S. The music of this new generation mixes with the root element that is Afro-Cuban and salsa. Viernes Culturales mixes the nostalgia of the older generation with the energy of the younger generation.

She observed that people were initially very skeptical about going into Calle Ocho at night to enjoy Cultural Fridays, because of the perception of crime and urban decline in Little Havana. She felt they had been successful in getting tourists to take time away from the sun-and-surf tourism of the beach to enjoy the Latin Quarter as a cultural hub to see live art, music, and culture and enjoy Latin American food. She observed that white and Cuban American young professionals and artists were coming back to the inner city, attracted by high-rise condominium projects such as Havana Lofts and the historic homes in Little Havana, sometimes even homes in the more affluent community of Coral Gables.

Tony Wagner of the Latin Quarter Cultural Center distinguished between the overseas Cubans, who he felt are lured more by the high-rise condominium market, versus second-generation Cuban Americans, who are moving into the historic homes. Mr. Wagner spoke optimistically about the prospects for economic development in the Latin Quarter, currently concentrated on Calle Ocho between 14th Avenue and 16th Avenue, to spread south to 12th Street and north to 22nd Street where there are new art galleries opening up. He and Tanya Bravo both cited the emergence of three nightclubs featuring music and dancing in the district, including Alfaro's, Hoy Como Ayer, and Kimbara Cumbara. Alfaro's offers traditional salsa and Afro-Cuban music. Hoy Como Ayer, at 22nd Street, is a new club that was formerly the site of Cafe Nostalgia, popular among Cuban old-timers, now a magnet for younger Latin hipsters more attuned to modern DJ-spun dancing music.

I spoke with Luis Molina, who is the owner of Molina Fine Art Gallery and Studio at 1634 SW 8th Street. He was very upbeat about the success of his art business. He is a Cuban immigrant who made money running flower shops in New York City before he was lured by the experience of Viernes Culturales to move to Miami and fulfill his long-sought dream of becoming a successful artist. He thought it would be a good opportunity to open a Little Havana location to develop his artistic interest in modernized folkloric Afro-Cuban themes, which includes bright colors and images such as roosters and African goddesses. He moved to Miami in 2001 and has been operating

Figure 5.18 Molina Fine Art Gallery and Studio. Photo by Jan Lin.

Figure 5.19 Luis Molina in his gallery. Photo by Jan Lin.

the studio/gallery since 2002 with paintings now selling for thousands of dollars. His was among the pioneering galleries on Calle Ocho. There are now 11 art galleries, mainly with resident artists that also operate studios in the heart of SW 8th Street. The owner of Cremata gallery is the president of the Latin Quarter Art Association. There are also new galleries opening up further south on Calle Ocho, such as Zu Galeria, at 22nd Avenue. Zu Galeria promotes emerging and mid-career artists still establishing their reputations. Manny Lopez, the owner of the gallery, reported that he felt there was a good opportunity to open a gallery in the lower-rent 22nd Avenue section of Calle Ocho while anticipating the spread of the art district further down the boulevard from the Tower Theater site.

Corinne Moebius, who was Tanya Bravo's predecessor as the director of Viernes Culturales, is not very sanguine about the impact of redevelopmental trends in the Latin Quarter:

> My perception is that as the city develops, there is increasing pressure downtown, for people that want a downtown location. People get tired of commuting. It's a double-edged sword. There is an aim for a pedestrian scale and family-friendly atmosphere. But Miami doesn't have a lot of room to grow horizontally, that is why we have high-rise condos emerging, and some of that pressure can move into Little Havana.
>
> There is a fear of what gentrification could bring, how it will change the unique flavor of the community that makes it so special right now. I personally think some of our biggest assets are small businesses. I think it is important the City and the County look at culture in its full range, including small businesses, a taken-for-granted daily kind of culture. Calle Ocho connects immigrant people with their roots, which they left because they wanted or had to. One of the biggest fears is that Calle Ocho will lose that, and that the local economy will become dominated by chain stores and not [be] for local residents anymore. How do you bring more commercial vitality? Will that push out small businesses and residents? Will the seniors that play at Domino Park be under threat?

As redevelopment and gentrification proceeds, public agencies such as the Little Havana Neighborhood Enhancement Team (NET) of the City of Miami support the effort by addressing crime, sanitation, and beautification projects to support the popular appeal for a new residential population. The Miami Police Department also operates a special problem-solving team, or PST, in the neighborhood to prosecute undercover drug operations. There are also issues of homeless people, alcoholics, and loiterers trespassing in the entranceways of commercial businesses. Little Havana has a population of over 50,000 and has the highest residential density of any neighborhood in Miami, which contributes to the size of the homelessness problem. The ethnic community in general is somewhat tolerant of the homeless and they can be found on a Sunday morning sleeping in building entranceways or in public parks underneath the sheltering trees.

Pablo Canton, who has worked with the Little Havana NET for 15 years, says that the intersection of Flagler Street and 7th Avenue was initially an area of public vice activity, with 20 to 30 people in the street selling drugs and engaging in prostitution quite openly in the late night hours. He identified the police and the NET as responsible for bringing down crime and assisting the improvement in the local real estate market. He cited several new condominium projects in Little Havana, including the Neo-Loft building, a 15-story high-rise with prices up to $300,000, and the Havana Loft, with units up to $400,000. He observed that middle-class Cubans were beginning to move from suburban subdivisions like Kendall to downtown locations like Little Havana.

Concluding Comparison of the Case Studies

Table 5.1 provides a broad comparative analytical overview of Miami's Overtown and Little Havana. While there are general similarities in the historic preservation, tourism, and local economic development efforts in Overtown and Little Havana, there are significant differences related to: a) the urban historical experience of each community, b) access to investment capital, and c) the mix of nonprofit, quasi-public, and public stakeholders involved. Each neighborhood can thus be understood as separate modes of "localization" or local incorporation into the postfordist metropolis of Miami. The fordist era urban renewal that led to the destruction of the original commercial and residential

Table 5.1 Miami Case Studies Compared

	Overtown	Little Havana
Historical Experience	Fordist urban renewal created a socially isolated ghetto marked by disinvestment, population loss, poverty, and vacant lots	Principal reception center for Cuban immigration and site of ethnic enclave economy that is a feature of postfordist economy
Planning Initiatives	DPZ/New Urbanist master plan, Overtown Civic Partnership and Design Center master plan	Miami Planning Department-led plan for Latin Quarter Cultural District
Stakeholders		
Nonprofit	Black Archives	Latin Quarter Cultural Center
	BAME CDC	Kiwanis Club Little Havana
	St. John's CDC	East Little Havana CDC
	St. Agnes CDC	
	Local Initiatives Support Corp	
Quasi-public–private	Knight Foundation/Collins Center	
	Miami CRA	
Public–government	Miami Planning Department	Miami Planning Department
	Miami-Dade Empowerment Trust	Miami Dade College
Cultural Focus	Preservational focus	Arts and culture focus
	Planned Folklife Village	Viernes Culturales (Cultural Fridays)
		Calle Ocho festival/Miami Carnival
Cultural memory	Family reunion	Memories of Americanization
	Musical nostalgia	Patriotism
	History of urban removal	Exile/refuge in the U.S.

heart of Overtown has hampered cultural and economic recovery efforts, while Cuban Americans never faced such challenges as they began to populate Little Havana as Miami was beginning its transition to the postfordist global city. While Overtown is trammeled by lack of investment capital, there are continuing flows of Cuban (and other Latin American) labor and immigrant capital to Little Havana to sustain the local economy.

Cuban American community leaders and stakeholders are more clearly in control of their tourism and community development efforts in Little Havana. They have worked in close cooperation with the Miami Planning Department, which has since the 1980s shepherded the urban revitalization process in the district, from the preservation of the Tower Theater to the development of the Latin Quarter Specialty Center. African American stakeholders in Overtown, by contrast, are confronted with quasi-public stakeholders such as the Miami CRA, and the Knight Foundation-funded Collins Center and Crosswinds, Inc., the developer of the Sawyer's Walk condominium/mixed-use project. I list LISC alongside the nonprofit stakeholders because it works primarily as a funder and not as a property owner in Overtown, and is more vested in developing affordable housing than attracting private developers and market-rate housing. There are also a large number of community development corporations in Overtown, somewhat complicating nonprofit stakeholder collaboration, but there is general recognition of the leadership of Dorothy Fields of the Black Archives and Kris Smith of LISC, who maintain an active partnership.[10] The challenge for Overtown nonprofit stakeholders is negotiating the opportunities as well as risks of collaborating with quasi-public stakeholders and private investment capital to try to jump-start an urban renewal process that has been somewhat stalled for the last two decades. There are also competing master plans in Overtown; nonprofit stakeholders speak in favor of the earlier DPZ-led master plan, but are willing to work with the Collins Center-led plan. Overtown is trying to overcome its image as an inner-city ghetto that is beset by crime, decline, and weed-strewn vacant lots. African Americans in Overtown are anxious that they don't mortgage away the future of their low-income community as they work and negotiate with private capital and the Miami urban growth machine to define the future of urban renewal and community development in their neighborhood.

The Cuban American community of Little Havana, by contrast, is led by a dynamic ethnic enclave economy of Cuban American entrepreneurs with links to co-ethnic politicians representing key positions in the urban growth machine. They have become adept at employing the standard tools of urban boosterism, such as "walks of fame," parades, and festivals, employed by Chambers of Commerce and public officials in other U.S. cities. Tourism in the Latin Quarter assists in the promoting of an image of Cuban Americans and other Latin American immigrants to the U.S. as "ethnic entrepreneurs" and "model minorities." Still, there are some indications of socioeconomic class divides and a clash between local and global interests as evidenced by the conflict between the luxury high-rise condominium market, which is aimed at affluent overseas Latin American buyers, and the Cuban American Freedom Tower in downtown Miami. In Little Havana, there are some anxieties that overseas investors may tip the balance and promote gentrification in the local property market, at the risk of displacing existing local residents and mom-and-pop businesses.

In Overtown, the mode of cultural localization centers more on principles of historic preservation through the planned reconstruction of a Folklife Village, although the Lyric Theater also presents opportunities to celebrate more contemporary black arts and culture. The grand re-opening of the Lyric Theater in March 2000, for instance, was held in conjunction with the Pan African Bookfest and Cultural Conference with the theme: "The Glory of Overtown: The Harlem Renaissance of the South." In Little Havana, preservation of the Tower Theater was an important early touchstone, but the current cultural thematics of community development actively celebrate the contemporary local ethnocultural arts and culinary scene and the Calle Ocho festival.

While tourism shows much promise as an engine of economic development, there are also many pitfalls associated with this economic sector. While tourism as an industry is less polluting, for instance, than the manufacturing sector, the service sector jobs in tourism offer wages generally far lower than in the manufacturing sector. The Service Employees International Union (SEIU) has been fighting to organize condominium workers in Miami, who suffer poor wages and working conditions (Yudice 2005). African Americans in Miami have also had a somewhat ambivalent relationship to the tourism industry in recent years. When South African political leader Nelson Mandela was snubbed by the City of Miami during his visit to the city for the convention of the American Federation of State, County, and Municipal Employees (AFSCME) in 1990 because of his public support of Fidel Castro, African Americans angrily organized a three-year boycott of tourist conventions and other tourism activities in Miami in retribution (Croucher 1997).

Still, there are some similarities and common best practices to be ascertained in both the neighborhood case studies. In both Little Havana and Overtown, there has been key emphasis placed on the opening of ethnic theaters or cultural centers that showcase the ethnic arts, music, and forms of cultural expression and performance, as a way of luring people dispersed into the suburbs back to inner-city neighborhoods in downtown Miami. Historic preservation of buildings and heritage preservation through archival and museum work are strategies for promoting collective memory and public history in both the African American and Cuban American communities. Ethnic tourism is increasingly seen as an engine of economic development in both neighborhoods, which have cooperated with the Greater Miami Convention and Visitors Bureau to attract visitors. Tourism, urban planning, and community development efforts in both neighborhoods have also relied on the creating and sustaining of attractive streetscapes and "ethnic village"-like settings that invite pedestrian activity as well as opportunities for civic interaction. Urban renewal in both neighborhoods has the potential to promote many of the principles of the New Urbanism architecture and urban planning movement insofar as there is an emphasis on human scale, heritage preservation, civic interaction, and mixed-use residential and commercial building projects.

Ethnic localization processes may also be understood from both spatial and temporal dimensions. Table 5.2 gives a comparison of

Table 5.2	Miami Ethnic Places in Space and Time	
	Overtown	*Little Havana*
Localization in Space		
Cultural centers	Lyric Theater	Tower Theater
		Little Havana Cultural Center
Historic buildings	Dorsey House	Freedom Tower**
	Cola Nip Bottling Company	
	Greater B.A.M.E. Church	
	Mt. Zion Baptist Church	
	St. John Baptist Church	
Artistic sidewalks	9th Street Pedestrian Mall	Calle Ocho Walk of Fame
	Jazz Walk of Fame*	
Monuments		Cuban Memorial Boulevard
		Plaza de la Cubanidad (Plaza of Cuban Patriots)
Parks		Maximo Gomez domino park
Museums		Bay of Pigs museum
Localization in Time		
Monthly events		Viernes Culturales (Cultural Fridays)
Seasonal events	Mother's Day events	Calle Ocho festival
	Family reunions	
Genealogical time	Black Archives	

* This is a proposed space not yet constructed.
** The Freedom Tower is located at the bayside downtown, but is included because it is a separate focus of Miami's Cuban American preservation movement and the location for a planned museum.

cultural localization projects in both space and time in Overtown and Little Havana. The process of spatial localization may be discerned through the establishing of ethnocultural theaters and community centers, the preservation of historic buildings, construction of artistic sidewalks and monuments, and creation of parks and museums. These trends signal the continuing salience of locality and place within the broader machinations of globalization in Miami. Ethnic practices in space provide a locational focus for the preservation of ethnic traditions and collective memories as well as the celebrating of local heroes and ethnic public history. Especially in Little Havana, these trends have also provided a platform for the emergence of an ethnic arts and culinary scene that draws coethnic audiences and visitors as well as non-Latin consumers and tourists. The Calle Ocho arts scene fosters ethnic creative capital as well as ethnic social capital through relationships of trust and reciprocity between the art galleries, restaurants, and retailers, who cooperate around weekly events like Cultural Fridays, and work to overcome challenges like street closures, parking, and crowd control. Nonprofit organizations like the Little Havana Cultural Center and the Black Archives promote local volunteerism and civic engagement among ethnic individuals and boards of directors that are scattered residentially throughout the metropolis.

The temporal dimensions of ethnocultural localization can be seen through weekly events (such as Viernes Culturales in Little Havana) and seasonal events such as Mother's Day events at the Lyric Theater and planned black family reunions. In Little Havana, the Calle Ocho street festival is now an annual event. In addition, the Black Archives fosters a sense of genealogical time on behalf of individuals tracing their ethnocultural roots. These are social practices of play and pilgrimage that promote a temporal sense of seasonality and life cycle that counter the hegemony of capitalist industrial clock-time; to wit, they revive a sense of the *gemeinschaft* within the *gesellschaft*.

6

REMOVAL AND RENEWAL OF LOS ANGELES CHINATOWN FROM THE FRONTIER PUEBLO TO THE GLOBAL CITY

Los Angeles Chinatown presents an intriguing case study of the removal and renewal of an ethnic enclave through changing historical stages of U.S. capitalism. The chapter comprises two main parts, a historical overview of the urban developmental experience of Los Angeles Chinatown, followed by an examination of the contemporary period. I distinguish three stages in the history of Los Angeles Chinatown, from the frontier era of the pueblo and imperialist drive-to-maturity period of industrialization, through the period of fordist industrialization and into the contemporary era of the global postfordist city. I found that Chinese Americans were subject to segregation and ethno-violence in the phase of westward expansion; then their community was subject to removal for the building of Union Station during the period of fordist urban renewal. Despite this oppression from white supremacists and eviction by the urban growth machine, the Chinese Americans regularly reached out to the general public through the prism of touristic cultural attractions, such as dragon parades and Lunar New Year parades. They built a New Chinatown and China City, complete with public plazas fringed by Chinese vernacular gateways, Chinese curio shops, and restaurants. Chinatown tourism has served both economic and political motives, at times serving as gestures of local cultural diplomacy to promote community interests, generate consent, and create public "good will" in the larger geopolitics of U.S.–Chinese relations.

This chapter then turns to the contemporary period to interpret the economic and cultural renewal currently taking place in Los Angeles Chinatown since the 1970s. Chinatown has expanded with the arrival of new Southeast Asian immigrant labor and capital flows after the end of the Vietnam War. New Chinese American business interests and place entrepreneurs comprise an ethnic growth machine that works in partnership with white developers and public governmental interests to boost cultural tourism and profitable redevelopment projects. The emergence of a Chinatown art scene especially along Chung King Road reflects the new transitional dynamics of a neighborhood where a declining number of family-run Chinese American curio shops co-exist with a growing number of hip and bohemian white gallery owners and designer boutiques. The opening of the new Gold Line rapid transit station in 2003 further boosts cultural tourism and the prospects for residential gentrification. While Chinatown was historically victimized by the white establishment and the urban growth machine, Chinese Americans are now part of the conspiracy of urban growth machine interests with a greater influence in determining their future.

I found stakeholders in the Chinese American heritage and arts community to be circumspect about the potential benefits of cultural tourism and the new arts scene. As guardians of the cultural heritage of the community, they are concerned with creating a kind of cultural tourism where visitors experience intercultural learning as opposed to be being lured by sensationalistic stereotypes and touristic kitsch. They reach out to second-generation Chinese American youth and students as well as overseas Chinese visitors. While there are clear economic benefits to tourism and growth, they are concerned about the displacement effects of gentrification and redevelopment.

During the course of research on this chapter, I conducted participatory action research as the director of an oral history project in Chinatown, leading Occidental College students in their interviews with a variety of community stakeholders. I was a volunteer at the Chinatown Heritage and Visitors Center and gave lectures to the Chinese Historical Society of Southern California. I also conducted archival historical research at the Chinatown Heritage and Visitors Center that is managed by the Chinese Historical Society of Southern California, the Huntington Library, the Los Angeles Public Library, and the Specialized Libraries and Archival Collections of the University of Southern California.

Table 6.1 presents a tabular overview of Los Angeles Chinatown through successive historical periods of urban development from the 1870s to the first decade of the twenty-first century. Los Angeles was comparatively delayed in its urban development, attracting a sparse settlement of western frontiersmen amidst the remnants of a Mexican pueblo until the arrival of the transcontinental railroad in the late 1880s, after which the metropolis entered a drive-to-maturity period of agro-industrial capitalism that included important regional industries like large-scale agriculture (most memorably the citrus industry), property development, oil, and Hollywood film. The prevailing race relations paradigm of this time period was imperialism and Anglo superiority, with the Manifest Destiny doctrine of westward expansion and Mexican conquest in 1848 representing important historical events in regional collective memory. The bloody Chinese massacre of 1871 was one of the seminal incidents of anti-foreign violence, an ethnic cleansing episode which compares with the lynching of southern blacks in American history.

During this time the Chinese immigrants were spatially and socially segregated in a sector of the city known as the Apablasa tract, through the force of anti-Chinese racism and violence, federal immigrant exclusion acts (especially the Chinese Exclusion Act, 1882–1943), and state-level Alien Land Acts that prohibited property ownership. The Chinese American community nevertheless reached out to connect in local acts of cultural diplomacy, through their participation with a dragon dance in the Fiesta de Los Angeles parade. The fiesta was comparable to other displays of ethnic exhibition and pageantry in the international expositions, world's fairs, festivals, and parades that were common in a spirit of lively competition among cities during the drive-to-maturity phase of U.S. imperialism. Corporate interests and policies of economic liberalism, including free trade, immigration, pursuit of foreign markets, and U.S. military intervention abroad, drove these urban social phenomena.

The end of World War I brought increasing restrictionism in U.S. immigration policy, through a succession of acts, including the Quota Act of 1921 and the National Origins Act of 1924. These restrictive quotas on immigration were not lifted until the 1965 Hart–Celler Immigration and Nationality Act. The prevailing mode of accumulation was the fordist or mass consumption stage of industrial capitalism, characterized by mass production methods and fordist collective bargaining agreements. Principles of modernization promoted an urban renewal policy in favor of slum clearance of transitional communities in favor of modern transportation infrastructure and public housing. The removal of Los Angeles Chinatown to make way for Union Station, in the years 1931 to 1938, is emblematic of the fordist urban renewal strategy. This period of protectionist restrictionism in immigration policy and relative retreat from foreign affairs was characterized by an easing of imperialistic doctrines in favor of assimilation policies, including Americanization programs that stressed English language acquisition and the gradual dissemination of a more tolerant "melting-pot" paradigm of cultural assimilation.

The Los Angeles Chinese made the best of their experience of urban removal, partnering with preservationist and municipal stakeholders to construct new settlements, China City, and New Chinatown. The walled courtyards and decorative gateways were built with Chinese vernacular architectural designs. There were antiques and curios from Hollywood stage sets. These were like the ethnic tourist villages in the westward expansion era of the world's fairs but rather than being disappearing relics of imperialist fascination, the Chinese were now represented by a bold new cadre of second-generation leaders and entrepreneurs born on U.S. soil with rights of citizenship and legal title to purchase real property. Chinatown thrived during the liberal Bowron administration of the 1930s and 1940s, spanning the New Deal years and wartime years of U.S.–China diplomatic cooperation against the Japanese. The Chinese Exclusion Act was lifted in 1943. The community became more patriotic and markedly anti-communist after the Chinese revolution of 1949, which played favorably during the McCarthy "red scare" climate of the 1950s under Mayor Poulson. Chinatown entered a period of decline, however, as postwar suburbanization fueled downtown disinvestment and the construction of urban expressways, notably the I-101, created a concrete chasm separating Chinatown from the central business district.

The 1960s and 1970s coincide with the "neoliberal" opening up of U.S. immigration controls with the Hart–Celler Immigration and Nationality Act of 1965, growing foreign direct investment, and the emergence of Los Angeles as a Pacific Rim gateway and corporate headquarters complex for transnational capitalism. Los Angeles Chinatown has expanded both demographically and economically in the global era, with the original Cantonese colony now augmented by other

Table 6.1 Historical Periods of Urban Development in Los Angeles Chinatown

	1870s to 1910s	*1920s to 1960s*	*1970s to present*
Mode of Production	Drive-to-maturity period of capitalism	Fordist period of capitalism	Postfordist period of global capitalism
Immigration Policy	Generally liberal immigration except exclusion of Chinese	Immigrant restriction	Neoliberal period of immigration with some restrictionism
Prevailing Race Relations Paradigm	Imperialism and Anglo superiority	Assimilation	Pluralism
Important National and Local Historical Events	Chinese massacre 1871 Fiesta de Los Angeles 1894–97	Quota Act 1921 Origins Act 1924 Hart–Celler Act 1965	Nixon to China 1972 L.A. Olympics 1984
Urban Experience of Los Angeles Chinatown	Segregation of Chinese immigrants at Calle de los Negros, then the Apablasa tract	Removal of Chinatown for Union Station and creation of China City and New Chinatown, 1931–38	Renewal of Chinatown with new panethnic diversity and emergence of local growth machine and arts scene

provinces of China as well as ethnic Chinese from Vietnam and other areas of Southeast Asia. The thriving Chinese ethnic enclave economy is indicative of the flexible specialization systems and niche marketing strategies of the postfordist regime of accumulation. Important historical events affecting Chinatown include President Nixon's visit to the People's Republic of China in 1972, which helped to create a new rapprochement between the U.S. and China and sparked a public interest in Chinese cuisine. The Los Angeles Olympics of 1984 did much to signal the city's rise as a global city of demographic diversity and cultural pluralism.

The stakeholders of Chinatown have new opportunities to present their cultural attractions for tourism and popular consumption in the era of the postfordist global city. New generations of Chinese American entrepreneurs, activists, and community leaders have more control than the communities of the past, as they work with power brokers of the City of Los Angeles and the downtown business elite. In the second part of this paper, I consider how these social actors and community institutions have negotiated the new landscape of race, space, and power in the metropolis of the global era.

Chinatown in the Frontier and Early Industrial Era

Los Angeles was founded in 1781 as an agricultural settlement, or *pueblo*, to play a supporting role to the system of missions and presidios established up the California coast by the Spanish crown in New Spain. Rule of the city passed to the newly established state of Mexico in 1822, then to the United States in 1847. Chinese immigrants disembarked initially through San Francisco as laborers with gold and silver mining and railroad companies, but began to arrive in Southern California by the 1850s through work with the wagon roads, the construction of the Southern Pacific Railroad, and the digging of the San Fernando Tunnel. The Burlingame Treaty of 1868 signed between China and the U.S. encouraged the flow of immigration.

Chinese immigrants faced increasing hostilities and competition with native labor after the completion of the transcontinental railroad in 1869, which enabled native workers from the East Coast a quicker and safer trip to the West Coast than the arduous journey over overland trail on foot or stagecoach. A notable incident was the Los Angeles "Chinese massacre" of October 24, 1871, in which 19 Chinese immigrants were publicly lynched or shot dead and their stores and residences looted.[1] The Chinese Exclusion Act of 1882 prohibited further immigration and excluded the Chinese from U.S. naturalization. For the rest of the exclusion era up until 1943, U.S. Chinatowns were "bachelor societies" of migratory men who lacked rights of citizenship and property ownership. The Los Angeles Chinatown still had a frontier "wild West" quality in the dusty streets area around the Plaza. The Chinese experienced numerous legal and economic barriers to the forming of a larger immigrant community for most of the nineteenth and early twentieth centuries. They were denied the right of purchasing property in Los Angeles through local restrictive covenants and state laws including California's 1913 Alien Land Act.

Figure 6.1 Stagecoach in front of old Chinatown, circa 1875. The long low building in the center background was the Coronel adobe, where the Chinese massacre started. "Nigger Alley," where Chinese resided among African Americans, runs back to the right. University of Southern California Libraries Special Collections.

Persisting despite these difficulties, the Chinese colony reached some 2,000 persons in the late 1880s in an area east of the old City Plaza dubbed locally "Calle de Los Negroes" or "Negro Alley."[2] This was a dim dead-end alley occupied by declining, sub-divided adobes undesired by the businessmen of the Anglo power elite who were pushing downtown development to the south and west of the original City Plaza. The Chinese leased space in the Coronel adobe. After the decline of mining and railroad employment, Chinese immigrants were settling into vegetable farming on agricultural land southwest of the city center, marketing their produce door to door from horse-drawn carts by 1880 and in 1890 at the first public market at the old City Plaza. Their operations were based in 50 small sheds, jutting out of old, wooden buildings on the east end of Apablasa Street. The Chinese made up 50 of the 60 peddlers licensed in L.A. in 1880. By 1894, there were 103 licensed Chinese wagons (Greenwood 1996: 37). In the days before refrigerated railroad cars, Chinese vegetable peddlers were the principal source of fresh produce in the City of Los Angeles.

The Chinese bachelor society sustained a market for unrespectable entertainments such as opium parlors, gambling houses and lotteries, and prostitution cribs. While Anglos operated similar establishments, the Chinese suffered greater public condemnation. The Chinese were seen to represent the deepest depths of degeneracy by the police, the press, and moral temperance organizations. Chinatown was seen as a threat to public morality because the district was seen as a temptation for wayward Anglos of deficient character. Anglos could be redeemed, it was believed, but the Chinese could not. The Chinese were also seen as dirty and unsanitary. In 1880, the City Council's Subcommittee on Chinese made an effort to remove the Chinese completely from the city limits. Chinatown was judged a health hazard under the Cubic Air Ordinance of 1870. The motion for removal of the Chinese was ruled invalid, however, by the city attorney, who said it violated the Burlingame Treaty and the 14th Amendment. In the 1880s, a Grand Jury was called to investigate reports of poor sanitation in Chinatown. The Chinese, however, were able to convince city officials and health inspectors that the garbage and dusty conditions in Chinatown were less their own making than the result of neglect of the district by city garbage collectors. The public criticism of the Chinese emboldened anti-Chinese activists. In the mid-1880s there were incidents of anti-Chinese violence in a number of western cities and towns. In Los Angeles, there were repeated incidents of arson in Negro Alley, and a major fire in July 1887 caused extensive damage, destroying major commercial stores, and several gambling houses, temples, and boarding houses (Lou 1982). The area was increasingly subject to abandonment by property owners and insurance companies. That same year, Negro Alley was condemned and cleared for the extension of Los Angeles Street to the Plaza (Greenwood 1996).

The Chinese were outraged and sought to sue the city for damages on account of negligence by the fire department. The Chinese Consul, Colonel Bee, came to Los Angeles from San Francisco seeking to find proof of arson or malfeasance. He was unsuccessful, but he became a leader in finding a new location for the Chinese. The majority of Chinese moved to the east of Alameda to the Apablasa tract, a parcel of ranching and agricultural vineyard land controlled by the descendants of the rancher Juan Apablasa. The Apablasa and adjoining tracts were situated in an undesirable area adjacent to railroad yards and gas works and the Los Angeles River. The land was subject to flooding by the river, such as in 1884 and 1886, when the river swept away orchards, vineyards, and homes below Alameda Street. The Chinese leased the land and dilapidated woodframe housing in this area and improved many of the buildings into more durable brick construction. Despite their efforts, the area was generally a site of municipal neglect by the City of Los Angeles and the utility and municipal services companies. While other neighborhoods were acquiring modern street lighting, drainage and water works, and street paving, Chinatown was ignored as an area of absentee property ownership. Property inspectors were lax in their housing code enforcement, even when they found conditions of squalor and ill health. Until the 1920s, there were only two paved streets in Chinatown, along with 13 dirt alleyways.

Many Chinese were engaged in the produce trade, but others were entering domestic work, or moving into independent proprietorship

Figure 6.2 Chinatown street, circa 1898. University of Southern California Libraries Special Collections.

operating laundries, restaurants, groceries, and curio shops. Many became small business owners working in the retail trade for produce, and some were moving into wholesale importation of a variety of demand goods from China including antiques and curios, jewelry, bamboo, rattan and ivory products, silk, lace, clothing, and food including canned fish, preserved fruit, tea and coffee, various oils, drugs, spices, herbs, and other items. The market included the growing middle-class Chinese immigrant community and also native Angelenos. The Apablasa–Marchessault area was perceived to be an exotic shopping district, with several shops offering "curios" of Chinese as well as Japanese origin. Several operated over the years in the old Lugo adobe (Greenwood 1996: 25–26).

Marchessault Street was Chinatown's restaurant row with some 15 restaurants in its heyday, though dineries also appeared in non-Chinese neighborhoods by the 1930s. Many Chinese restaurants began as tiny humble quarters serving simpler fare, but some opened up ornate restaurant lounges to serve middle-class Chinese and the American market. Chop suey, a California-Chinese creation, was devised for American palates. The Chinatown at the Apablasa tract occupied 200 buildings with some 3,000 people by 1910 in some 15 blocks and alleyways to the east of the Central Plaza. There were three temples, a Chinese opera house, a school, and a newspaper. The merchant elite maintained their offices within the Garnier Building at the old Plaza. News and notices were posted on a brick wall on Alameda Street that functioned as a communications center for the Chinese community until the establishment of a telephone exchange. Many lived in the back of stores or upstairs in congested residential quarters.

With the congestion of wagons, horses, and stables around China-town, in 1909, the Chinese American produce merchant Louie Gwan united Japanese, Russian, Italian, and Chinese farmers to promote a larger City Market at 9th and San Pedro. Some Chinese moved to this market area, but the majority of the population remained at the Central Plaza colony. Some continued to operate businesses in locations closer to the old Plaza, such as the Lugo adobe and the Garnier Building. The area around the Plaza was becoming increasingly multiethnic, with French and Italian colonies in Sonoratown, previously more uniformly Mexican. Frenchman Philip Garnier built the Garnier Building in 1910 and leased the building to the Chinese immigrant community. According to Chinese *feng shui* principles, the upper floors of the building were closer to heaven and thus more appropriate for locating temples, schools, or fraternal and social organizations, while commercial tenants occupied the ground floor and mezzanine.[3] Among the community organizations were the CCBA, an umbrella leadership organization, and the Chinese American Citizens Alliance (CACA), a civil rights organization, and the Chinese Chamber of Commerce. Lacking police protection and political representation in matters that affected their lives and work during the Chinese Exclusion, the community founded its own organizations for mutual aid and services. During the heyday of the exclusion era, Chinatown's community center or "town hall" was near the Plaza at the Garnier Building, while the focus of commercial and residential life was across Alameda Street in the Apablasa tract, with the City Market area forming a satellite location. All these locations together created "Greater Chinatown."[4]

In 1894, Los Angeles Merchants and Manufacturers Association (the M&M) with support from Chamber of Commerce and other boosters devised the idea of a parade, the Fiesta de Los Angeles, similar to the Mardi Gras in New Orleans and Pasadena's Tournament of Roses (an annual event without the football game yet, that had already been running for a dozen years). It was imagined as a combination of a carnival, pageant, parade, and fandango. The driving force was a downtown electrical fixtures merchant named Max Meyberg. To some degree the Fiesta distracted the public from labor strife connected with the 1894 Pullman railroad strike led by Eugene Debs. One roving reporter with the *Philadelphia Record* wrote that the fiesta marked LA's transformation from a "sleepy Mexican town" into the rising metropolis of the Pacific Coast (Deverell 2004: 58). The genius of La Fiesta was that it appropriated celebratory aspects of regional Mexican culture of the *pueblo* period for the boosterish and commercial purposes of white Los Angeles. During the ranchero period of the *Californios*, the Plaza had been the economic and cultural center of the Mexican American community, and there were a variety of religious and secular fiestas conducted annually in the streets and the Plaza (Castillo: 18). The past was choreographed as nostalgia by white organizers who whitewashed the unpleasant aspects of southern Californian history while scripting a narrative of ethnic peace and social progress (Deverell 2004: 61).

An invitation to the Chinese to assemble a float or dragon entry was initially met with some opposition among the parade organizers. It was only 20 years since the massacre of 1871, and some felt Chinese participation might cause a disturbance. The decision was made that there should be a wider ethnic participation of other groups in the parade to create an atmosphere of regional progress predicated on racial hierarchy. La Fiesta's Historical Day was organized as the grade finale of the week's events. It all began with a float of angels accompanying a pageant to the Spanish Mission period with the genocide of Native Americans obscured. The diversity of the city was represented through a moving sequential tableau of Native American, Mexican American, Chinese American, and African American participation. The Chinese initially balked at the idea of appearing at the second Fiesta because of the previous year's conflict, but Fiesta committee members now recognized that the touristic spectacle of the Chinese dragon dance was hugely popular with onlookers. By participating in the parade,

Figure 6.3 Spectators observing the Chinese dragon in a parade at the Los Angeles Fiesta of 1901. One parade marcher carries a stool on which the head of the dragon sits when at rest. University of Southern California Libraries Special Collections.

committee member J. M. Crawley argued that the Chinese would demonstrate that they were concerned for the welfare of Los Angeles. Charles Walton summed up the committee's sentiment by saying the Chinese merchants "had a chance to strike a blow for all their people by assisting their American fellow merchants in the celebration" (Lou 1982). In 1895, the Chinese obliged with a huge dragon 800 hundred feet long that took 150 men to operate.

The merriment increasingly drew the criticism of moral and temperance interests, such as the Catholic America Protective Association (APA) which found the La Fiesta to be uncivilized and degraded, encouraging public drunkenness, debauchery, and heathenism, especially during the All Fools Night event that took place at the end of the Fiesta. Masks were outlawed in 1896 unless participants were an organized part of the procession. Still there was support among the business interests, and Harrison Gray Otis of the *Los Angeles Times* adopted the Fiesta as a boosterist tool. In 1898, there was a more dramatic attack on the Fiesta by opponents who drew attention to the dangerous race-mixing tendencies of La Fiesta's supposed "multiculturalism." The parade was renamed Fiesta de los Flores in 1901 and became a more Americanized event, with "American" themes on the cover promotions. Intermittent Fiesta de los Flores events were held through the years of the Depression, more like flower festivals. They never matched the pageantry and exuberance of the late 1890s (Deverell 2004).

By 1913 discussions had arisen about demolishing Chinatown to build a railway terminal, but litigation tied up the plan for 20 years. The Apablasa family and the City of Los Angeles first tangled over who owned Chinatown's streets and the estate was awarded ownership since it had made all historic street improvements. The family then sold to a San Francisco entrepreneur, L. F. Hanchett, who initially proposed a new commercial district for the Chinese colony, but his demolition plan was thrown out of court when it was revealed he was secretly planning a railroad terminal. In 1928, the Southern Pacific Railroad bought the land and with the Union Pacific began planning a railroad terminal in earnest. On May 19, 1931, the California Supreme Court upheld a decision to condemn and demolish the land east of Alameda Street, including the heart of Chinatown, to construct the new Union Station (Cheng and Kwok 1988).

In the 1930s Chinatown figured in the Los Angeles press and popular imagination as a corrupt and shady place, particularly in the reports of investigative reporters and vice cops who worked in the Chinatown district.[5] Chinatown was popularly associated with the Mexican American barrio nearby, known as Sonoratown or "Dogtown." There was an urban legend popularized at the time that there was once a Chinese underground city, a network of catacombs that were the site of prostitution, opium, and other depraved immoralities and sins (Klein 1990). There was also an old vaudeville district on Main Street that had acquired the quality of a "red light district" littered with pawn shops, Filipino taxi-dance halls,[6] all-night picture houses, bars, and honky-tonks, which the Italian American author John Fante describes in his period novel, *Ask the Dust* ([1939] 1980). Fante champions the everyday heroism of the ordinary people of the Bunker Hill district and associated neighborhoods of downtown. They were flawed characters that had been dispossessed by the Depression, the hapless victims of a "sunshine" myth that had initially drawn them to Southern California but found themselves ultimately exiled by respectable society. The prevailing view, however, was that Chinatown, Sonoratown, Bunker Hill, and other neighborhoods of downtown were dilapidated and blighted slums in need of removal and redevelopment.

The Creation of New Chinatown and China City

While demolition of Chinatown for the construction of Union Station proceeded from 1933 to 1938, Chinatown was reborn as an assortment of different settlements. A special parade and formal ceremony were held in September 1934 marking the passing of Chinatown (Greenwood 1996: 38). A contingent of Chinese relocated to the satellite Chinatown in the neighborhood surrounding the new City Market area at 9th and San Pedro. Two newly constructed commercial districts emerged, "New Chinatown" and "China City," two Chinese-themed construction projects that infused the theatrics of the Hollywood stage lot with the historical romance of the emerging preservation movement. They were simulations of an original that no longer existed, social worlds that were destroyed by modernization but recreated as exhibitionary arcades like miniature "world's fairs." A carnival atmosphere pervaded China City that foreshadowed the theme parks of the postwar era. Out of the tragic destruction of old Chinatown there arose an economic opportunity for Chinese business leaders to make investments in the Chinatown of the future. These ethnic entrepreneurs furthermore took advantage of political opportunities, including the presence of a sympathetic mayor and downtown reform coalition, and a wartime rapprochement in diplomatic relations between the U.S. and China.

"China City" was the brainchild of Christine Sterling, a transplant turned Angeleno lured by the romance of the "mission myth" promulgated at the turn of the century around Helen Hunt Jackson's novel *Ramona* and the landmarks preservation work of editor Charles Fletcher Lummis of the *Los Angeles Times*, that had drawn idealized views of California's past, while seeking to preserve the Spanish missions. Sterling gained the support of Harry Chandler, publisher of the *Times*, and obtained civic as well as financial support to block the demolition of historic properties near the old City Plaza, especially the Avila house, Los Angeles' oldest extant building. The site was historically preserved as the Olvera Street marketplace, a Mexican theme market and heritage showplace for the pre-modern Los Angeles *pueblo* period of Mexican American romance and fiestas. China City was built a few blocks away from the Olvera Street market and offered a Hollywood-style simulacrum of Chinatown featuring stage sets and costumes used in the 1937 film *The Good Earth*, donated by the studio MGM, which had built an entire Chinese village stage lot while filming in the San Fernando Valley. Visitors rode rickshaws from the "Court of the Four Seasons" down the "Passage of One Hundred Surprises" and "Dragon Road" as they munched on "Chinaburgers." The streets and plazas were given romantic Chinese names like Court of Lotus Pools and Harbor of Whang Po. A "Great Wall" surrounded the touristic marketplace. The project drew the participation of some 70 Chinese merchants in various booths and stalls, but was destroyed by fire soon after its

Figure 6.4 Chinese rickshaw, circa 1938–58. China City pandered especially to ethnic stereotypes. University of Southern California Libraries Special Collections.

opening in 1938. It was rebuilt only to be burned a second time in 1948, and by the early 1950s was gone (Cheng and Kwok 1988, Poole and Ball 2002).

A second more lasting project was led by Peter SooHoo, a second-generation Chinese American born and raised in Chinatown who obtained an engineering degree at the University of Southern California and was the first Chinese American to join the Los Angeles Department of Water and Power. He moved easily between the immigrant and host society, and became spokesperson for the community with the press and liaison with the Los Angeles Chamber of Commerce. He assembled a New Chinatown Corporation comprising 28 Chinese American families and merchant associations.[7] They adapted a plan first put out in 1933 by George Eastman, a past Chamber of Commerce president, to relocate Chinatown and build a new central plaza surrounded by shops, restaurants, a temple, theater, gardens, all in a Chinese architectural style. The American architects worked to combine Chinese designs on modern concrete buildings working with economy and a limited budget. The buildings were more simple facsimiles rather than exacting authentic replicas of a typical *hutong*, a historic alley or lane common in Chinese cities such as Beijing. Chinese characters announcing each store and restaurant were translated into English with matching brushstrokes, and outlined in neon lights (Zeiger 2003).

A site was obtained in the North Broadway area that had been a storage yard area for the Santa Fe Railway, purchased for 75 cents a square foot and procured through the help of the sympathetic railway agent Herbert Lapham.[8] The "New Chinatown" opened to great fanfare on June 25, 1938, just three weeks after the debut of "China City." Paid advertisements or feature articles were carried in all the major Los Angeles newspapers announcing the grand opening. Chinese dignitaries, American politicians, and Chinese American movie stars

Figure 6.5 Family exits New Chinatown courtyard under ornate gateway, circa 1938–58. University of Southern California Libraries Special Collections.

presided at the parade and dedication ceremonies. The Chinese American actress Anna May Wong helped to plant a willow tree behind the "Wishing Well" in the Central Plaza. A decorative gate, or *pailou*, was built on both the east and west entrances to the Plaza on opposite ends of Gin Ling Way, the main pedestrian thoroughfare. Street names indicated the importance of the Nationalist movement in China, such as Mei Ling Way (named for the maiden name of Madame Chiang Kai-shek) and Sun Mun Way (for Sun Yat-sen's *Three Principles of the People*).

The next year, 1939, Union Station opened as the last major urban train terminal to be completed in the United States. A half a million Angelenos attended the dedication ceremony that included a parade down Alameda Street. Advertised as the most modern terminal of its time, the station was designed through a combination of the Streamline Moderne and Mission Revival architectural styles (Poole and Ball 2002). It was an impressive monument to the achievement of the public officials who helped unify the railroads and to the public who approved a bond issue to finance the construction. In many ways it was a monument to the end of an era. The railroad industry was in the midst of a general decline, experiencing losses in ridership and some employment lay-offs. Traffic increased dramatically during World War II with the flow of soldiers and war industry workers to the Pacific front, but dwindled after the 1950s, with the rapid proliferation of automobiles on the expanding freeway system. As a foreshadowing of what was to come, the Arroyo Seco Parkway was completed only a year after Union Station, in 1940. Later renamed the Pasadena Freeway, it was the first freeway completed in the American West.

China City and the New Chinatown in Los Angeles at mid-century evoked the sense of the urban international expositions, or as observed by Garding Lui, who gave this description in a 1948 book called *Inside Los Angeles Chinatown*:

"The Little World's Fair," it is called by strangers who see it for the first time, is in a very conspicuous location . . . When trains from the north and the east enter Los Angeles at night, children

on the west side of the coaches flatten their noses against the
windowpanes and say "Look at Fairyland!" The last thing that is
seen before the train gets into the new Union Depot, are the lights
of New Chinatown.

(1948: 20)

World's fairs were promulgated in European cities in the mid-
nineteenth century as a way of showcasing exhibits on industrial and
technological progress, promotions for manufacturers' products and
investment opportunities, and various entertainments to attract tourists
and visitors. They were a celebration of urban culture and society,
architectural spectacles created for fun, edification, and profit. The
penultimate U.S. fair of the nineteenth century was the Great
Columbian Exhibition of 1893 in Chicago, which was known for its
spectacular Beaux Arts architecture and monumental exhibition halls,
as well as the rowdy Midway Plaisance, which offered a range of raffish
carnival entertainments and international exhibits, including reproductions of Blarney Castle, a German and a Japanese village, a street
in Cairo and a Moorish palace. In 1939 the New York World's Fair
explored technological innovation and the World of Tomorrow,
especially the Futurama ride and exhibit sponsored by General Motors.
In the Amusement Zone, there was a recreation of old New York
from the 1890s, complete with a Chinatown cafe. The futurism of its
monumental Trylon and Perisphere and the elaborate amusement park
drew great renown at the time.[9] San Francisco also held its Golden Gate
International Exposition that celebrated California as the "Empire of
the West" and touted the benefits of trade with Latin America and the
Pacific Basin. Los Angeles produced two ill-fated plans for fairs that
were never held, the Pacific Mercado in 1940 and Exposition-Cabrillo
Fair in 1942.

Olvera Street, China City, and New Chinatown were idealized urban
spaces, places of spectacle and exhibition. They were reconstructions of
places that were slated for destruction. They pandered unabashedly
to ethnic stereotypes. They preserved the architectural integrity and
cultural heritage of the ethnic enclave while creating a new public space

for ethnic residents as well as touristic outsiders. The preservationist Christine Sterling and the ethnic entrepreneur Peter SooHoo raised the interest and support of Harry Chandler, influential scion of the *Los Angeles Times*, the Chamber of Commerce, and other downtown power brokers in sustaining business investment and commercial life in the central business district as a counterbalance to the ongoing decentralization of businesses to the West Side along Wilshire Boulevard, to the San Fernando Valley, and other locations. The late 1930s was also a period of political rapprochement between China and the U.S., which became diplomatic allies against the growing Japanese military threat in East Asia. In 1943, Madame Chiang Kai-shek, wife of the Nationalist Party leader in China, came to solicit American support for the Chinese war relief effort with appearances at the Hollywood Bowl and Los Angeles City Hall. She urged U.S. congressmen who were among the assembled to strike down the Chinese Exclusion Law. Her work proved helpful as the U.S. Congress thereafter responded with a repeal of the exclusion law and instating of the right to naturalized citizenship.

By the 1940s, the tourism trade was bringing prosperity to New Chinatown and China City. China City was a casting area for Chinese extras in Hollywood films. In her family history of Los Angeles Chinatown, *On Gold Mountain*, Lisa See recounts how her great grand-uncle Fong Yun became the first president of the China City Association. Among the visitors to China City were public figures and celebrities such as Eleanor Roosevelt, Gene Tierney, Anna May Wong, and Mae West. She discusses how Chinese American children both worked in China City as well as delighting as tourists in the magical, carnival atmosphere (1995: 221–23). Chinatown's finest restaurant, Man Jen Low (House of 10,000 Treasures), was renamed General Lee's Restaurant to appeal to outsiders and tourists. Located on Bamboo Lane, it had a piano bar and was a favorite of celebrities during the 1940s and 1950s such as Frank Sinatra, Judy Garland, and Spencer Tracey (Baum 2004). In 1950, New Chinatown was expanded with the construction of a West Side across Castelar Street (now Hill Street), with the addition of Chung King Road, named to signify the importance of Chungking in the war with Japan. As supporters of the Nationalist Party

(Kuomintang) of Chiang Kai-shek rather than the Communist Party of Mao Tse-Tung in China, the promoters of New Chinatown and China City enjoyed political favor during the McCarthy years in Los Angeles. Chinese Americans became more fervently pro-American and patriotic in the 1950s with the red scare, and the Korean War.

New Chinatown opened in 1938, the same year that Mayor Fletcher Bowron was voted into office as part of a reform coalition that took the initiative of obtaining federal funding through the Housing Act of 1937 (Wagner Act) to develop public housing projects comprising thousands of units over the next several years. The City Planning Commission began to study the redevelopment of Chavez Ravine for the Elysian Heights public housing project as the cornerstone for a humane and democratic citywide redevelopment program (Parson 2005: 165–67). The Bowron coalition was redbaited during the run-up to the election of 1953, however, by a pro-growth coalition given support by the *Los Angeles Times* that promoted Norris Poulson for mayor. In 1957, Poulson gave the Chavez Ravine site to Walter O'Malley, owner of the Brooklyn Dodgers baseball team, as part of an incentive package to move the team to Los Angeles. He employed the CRA, created in 1947, as his developmental tool, abandoning the "community modernism" of the public housing-friendly Bowron years in favor of a "corporate modernism" that sought to redevelop downtown as a corporate headquarters and elite residential and civic center complex at Bunker Hill. The displacement of Latinos from Chavez Ravine has become a real symbol of collective outrage within that racial–ethnic community. The muralist Judith Baca with support from the Social and Public Art Resource Center painted a giant mural called "Division of the Barrios" along the concretized Los Angeles River that commemorates the tragedy of community evisceration and dislocation caused by the freeways (Villa 2000).[10] Latino activists dubbed the CRA the "Chicano Removal Agency" in the 1960s (Parson 2005).

While New Chinatown was thriving, old Chinatown continued to decline. In 1949, the last vestige of old Chinatown, a block of 22 buildings between Sunset Boulevard and Los Angeles, Alameda, and Aliso Streets, was demolished to make way for the Hollywood Freeway

(I-101) and a park. The construction of the Hollywood Freeway served to divide and isolate Olvera Street and Chinatown from the rest of the downtown. The freeway still serves as a spatial as well as political divide that symbolizes the division between the city's power elite and their ethnic constituents (Ouroussoff 1999). The state park came about through the adoption of a general plan for the El Pueblo Historic Park in 1953 for redevelopment of the Olvera Street area along the lines of a multiethnic tourist district as first envisioned by Christine Sterling. The El Pueblo Historical Monument has done much to support the cultural and economic stability of the ethnic neighborhoods of downtown and help alleviate the spatial and cultural divide between downtown interest groups. El Pueblo and Olvera Street have become instrumental to cultural tourism efforts in the old Plaza in the era of the global city.

A Growing Chinatown in the Era of the Global City

The Hart–Celler Immigration and Nationality Act of 1965 overturned decades-long restrictions on the entry of Chinese and other immigrants to the United States. The advent of the Civil Rights Act of 1964 over-turned the constitutionality of a range of mortgage restrictions and racial covenants in homeowners and neighborhood associations that had operated to keep the Chinese segregated in Chinatown. The Chinese began to move into the suburbs like the majority of Angelenos, and established new residential and business enclaves in San Gabriel Valley cities such as Monterey Park and Alhambra. Chinatown in the post-exclusion era is more decentralized an ethnoburb emerging to compete with the older core Chinatown, just as the suburbs have sprouted new "edge cities" to compete with traditional downtowns (Garreau 1991). Yet many downtowns continue to persist through their function as advance corporate management and headquarters com-plexes for the emerging "global city" (Sassen 1988, Davis 1990). While traditional manufacturing centers such as Detroit and Buffalo suffered the negative consequences of globalization through the "deindustrial-ization" caused by "runaway shops" to cheaper overseas locations, immigrant gateway cities such as Los Angeles and New York have seen more positive effects through the emergence of ethnic enclaves that have revitalized declining industrial and retailing districts in the urban centers.

The Japanese were particularly active in the Los Angeles financial and property market of Los Angeles in the 1980s and 1990s, building bank and corporate office towers, hotels, and condominiums downtown as well as in Little Tokyo. In the downtown core Chinatown, there was a smaller-scale and more diverse assembly of local and overseas Chinese investors, especially from Southeast Asian sectors of the transnational Chinese diaspora. A number of new local Chinese American and overseas Chinese banks have established branch offices in Los Angeles Chinatown since the 1960s. The Cathay Bank was established in 1962, the first Chinese American bank in Southern California. The East West Bank (1973) is also Chinese American. There are several overseas Chinese banks operating in Chinatown, including Far East Bank, Bank of Canton of California, Bank of China, Bank of Taiwan, and Chang Hwa Commercial Bank. These banks have been involved in the development of a number of new shopping plazas in Chinatown since the 1970s. Mandarin Plaza, completed in the early 1970s, was the first to be built, and is across Broadway from the East Gate of the Chinatown Central Plaza.[11] Bamboo Plaza, just north of the Central Plaza, was completed in 1989. In the blocks to the south along lower Broadway and Hill Street, heading toward the central city, there have emerged several other new plazas, including Dragon Plaza, Saigon Plaza, Chinatown Plaza, Dynasty Center, Far East Plaza, BC Plaza, and Asian Center. The New Chinatown Central Plaza began a decline in the 1970s with the suburbanization of the Chinese population, as well as the market competition caused by the plethora of new malls. By 1984, the Vietnamese Chinese owned half of Chinatown's estimated 1400 businesses (Lew 1988).

The Vietnam War and its political and economic dislocations caused an influx of ethnic Chinese, especially of ethnic Chinese from Vietnam, Cambodia, and other areas of Southeast Asia. Members of the traditional business elite traveled to a Vietnamese refugee settlement in Camp Pendleton to encourage them to settle in Los Angeles

Chinatown. Quite visible is a colony of Teo Chew (also Chao Zhou) Chinese. The Teo Chew Association is a transnational network with centers in Southeast Asia, Europe, and North America. The Teo Chew Chinese in Los Angeles Chinatown came from Southeast Asia, but the diaspora originated in the Chao Zhou region of China. The members speak the Chao Zhou dialect or Cantonese. The Teo Chew Chinese spearheaded the Chinatown Gateway Project with a community pledge drive combined with public funds to complete the $500,000 structure in 1989. This is a 16-foot bridge that stretches over the North Broadway entrance to Chinatown at Cesar Chavez Avenue, with neon lighting and pagoda crown, and acts as a strong visual statement for visitors to Chinatown entering from the south. The business style of the more assimilated and established Cantonese-origin merchant community clashes with the plucky entrepreneurialism of the Teo Chew and other Southeast Asian Chinese, who operate sidewalk tables and open-air stalls, encourage bargaining and lopping off of the sales tax. Language acts as a divide, as the Teo Chew Chinese are just beginning to become members of such existing business associations as the Chinese Chamber of Commerce or the Los Angeles Chinatown Business Council, which hold their meetings in English. The arrival of Southeast Asian Chinese has helped to reverse some of the economic decline experienced in Chinatown between the 1950s and the 1970s, giving Chinatown the flavor of diasporic Chinese diversity as the ethnic enclave economy has expanded.

The Chinese Chamber of Commerce, created in 1955, was Chinatown's first nonprofit local development corporation. It superseded the efforts of such earlier business associations as the Consolidated Chinese Benevolent Association (or Six Companies, which dates from the late nineteenth century) and the business group led by Peter SooHoo to create the New Chinatown in the 1930s. It emulated the traditional booster business associations and chambers of commerce commonly found throughout the U.S., by encouraging local growth and civic engagement through such events as patriotic and ethnic parades and beauty pageants. The Lunar New Year parade and festival is the focal event, as well as the Miss Chinatown Beauty Pageant. The business leadership has grown even more diverse with the addition of Southeast Asian entrepreneurs and merchant associations since the 1970s. By the 1990s, the ethnic growth machine included white partners with the formation of the Chinatown Business Council, which began working to create a business improvement district.

In August 2000, a majority of Chinatown property owners voted 56–43 in favor of a business improvement district (BID), creating a special assessment to be levied on property owners. The money is used to pay for graffiti removal, private security patrols, sidewalk sweeping, tree and shrubbery planning to lure visitors to Chinatown and improve the area. Successful BIDs have been implemented in Santa Monica, Old Town Pasadena, and Hollywood. The Los Angeles Chinatown Business Council is the management entity for the BID. The Chinatown BID has published a slick and informative brochure, the Chinatown Visitor Map, with a streetmap and index of cultural landmarks, sites, and businesses in Chinatown, which has been distributed throughout the city. It sponsors periodic food festivals and "Chinatown Nights," events combining outdoor entertainment, merchandising, and restaurant promotion. The L.A. Chinatown Business Council offers walking tours, and a calendar of events through its website, www.chinatownla.com.

BID president Kim Benjamin is also president of Manhattan Beach-based Laeroc Partners, Inc., a real estate development company that also owns prominent parcels in Chinatown. As a white American, he and other non-Chinese members of the BID board of directors mark a growing trend of extra-ethnic, or outsider, investor and developer interest in Chinatown. The investment and redevelopmental boom began to accelerate with the opening of the Gold Line Metro station on Alameda Street in 2003, with investors converting old shopping malls and undertaking new construction in several condominium and commercial mixed-use development projects. Blossom Plaza, for instance, is a $150 million mixed-use project that includes two residential condominium towers as well as a cultural plaza, with retail and commercial uses. The City of Los Angeles provided $36 million in funding, negotiated by City Council member Ed P. Reyes, announced in January 2007. In April 2007, the CRA approved a five-story mixed-use project called Chinatown Gateway that converts previously commercial space to 280 residential condominiums with a pool and landscaped plaza along with retail uses.

An ethnic growth machine has emerged in Los Angeles Chinatown comprising a coalition of interests including the Chinese Chamber of Commerce, the Chinatown Business Council, Chinese developers, white developers, the City of Los Angeles, and the CRA. While many Chinatown residents, business owners, and community stakeholders recognize the benefits of economic development, there is also apprehension about displacement of established businesses and residents in the neighborhood. Gentrification also raises questions about cultural ownership and community identity.

Cultural heritage stakeholders in Chinatown are at a crossroads with the growth of tourism in the local economy. The Chinese Historical Society of Southern California (CHSSC) was founded in 1975 to pursue, preserve, and communicate knowledge of Chinese American history in the state. In 1995, the CHSSC moved into the two Victorian houses on Bernard Street, built in 1886 and 1888 by Philip Fritz, an immigrant from Alsace (on the German–French border), when the area was still Frenchtown. The site is now the location of the Chinatown Heritage and Visitors Center. In 1988, the Friends of the Museum of Chinese American History formed with representatives from El Pueblo, the Chinese Historical Society of Southern California, and the local community. This group worked for the next decade to raise public and private funds to establish a museum in the Garnier Building, which opened the Chinese American Museum of Los Angeles (CAMLA) in 2003. CAMLA is equipped with spacious exhibition spaces and attracts many visitors entering the community from the Olvera Street and old City Plaza area. The Chinatown Heritage and Visitors Center offers a significant archive and library, and is frequented by visitors entering Chinatown from the north who are visiting the New Chinatown Central Plaza. While local history was an original mission of both heritage museums, they also document the history of other Chinese settlements in California, as well as Chinese American history at large.

Figure 6.6 Staff in front of the Chinese American Museum of Los Angeles. Photo by Jan Lin.

While there is a strong local heritage movement in Los Angeles Chinatown, the Chinese cultural scene is limited by the lack of a first-class community theater or cultural center. The all-purpose room at Castelar Elementary School serves as a meeting and performance space for various cultural groups inviting speakers and performers, such as the CHSSC. Films and theatrical performances can be shown in adjoining neighborhoods, such as the David Henry Hwang Theater in Little Tokyo and the ImaginAsian Theater on South Main Street downtown.

The Emergence of the Chinatown Art Scene

In the late 1990s, the Chinatown art scene emerged as a part of a wider cultural phenomenon known as the Los Angeles East Side art scene that encompassed the adjoining communities of Boyle Heights, Echo Park, Highland Park, and Eagle Rock. The availability of low commercial rents and property values and the appeal of a bohemian and "edgy" neighborhood quality drew many artists and investors to open studios, galleries, and shops in these locales. While there are some Chinese artists associated with the Chinatown art scene, the majority of studios and galleries have been set up by outsiders who are renting or buying commercial and residential spaces being leased or sold by latter-generation Chinese American owners who inherited family properties, including antiquated Chinese art, furniture, and curio shops and other businesses that they were no longer interested in or were seen as unprofitable. The local market for Chinese art and furniture had gradually declined since the heyday of the 1940s when Hollywood studios often bought or leased objects for use in films demanding Oriental decor and arts for stage sets. The decline and disinvestment in the commercial plazas of New Chinatown were also correlated with the outmovement of Chinese Americans to the suburbs, especially the emerging "suburban Chinatown" or ethnoburb of the San Gabriel Valley.[12] Another factor was the normalization of U.S. diplomatic relations with the People's Republic of China (PRC) in 1973, followed by the gradual re-entry of the PRC into the world market with its transition from socialism to capitalism. This meant that consumers of Chinese art and culture could now go directly to the original source of Chinese cultural products rather than relying on local businesses as providers. Globalization had caused economic and cultural changes in local conditions, and many local owners decided to sell off their patrimony.

A succession of reporters has covered the hipster scene for the *Los Angeles Times* since 2000. The bohemian Chinatown art scene also drew reportage from the *New York Times* and comparisons to Manhattan's East Village. A visitor named Autumn de Wilde, 32, an invitation designer, said, "Los Feliz and Silver Lake got expensive and overrun, so we came to Chinatown. If it gets corrupted here, we'll find a new area" (Corcoran 2003). Even *Rolling Stone* covered the phenomenon, with writer Jonathan Craven (2001) reporting on a Saturday night opening when "a live unicorn hobnobbed with hundreds of revelers while Joel Mesler turned the basement of his Diannepruess Gallery into a speakeasy featuring live music (OK, it was just a white horse with a fiberglass horn)." The fashion publication, *W Magazine*, ran a feature by Kimberly Cutter (2001), who gushed of celebrity sightings in the crowds, such as actress Christine Ricci and musicians Gwen Stefani, Beck, and Iggy Pop. Alexandria Abramian-Mott (2003) covered the scene for *Sunset*, the travel, home and garden magazine of the West, with thoughtful interviews with the new gallery and shop owners. The hot Chinatown art scene is also listed now in the *Los Angeles Times*, as well as the alternative *L.A. Weekly* entertainment newspaper, and the glossy and upscale *Los Angeles* metropolitan arts and lifestyle magazine.

The Chinatown art scene is centered in Chung King Road, a quiet pedestrian alleyway that forms a west wing to the Chinatown Central Plaza on upper Broadway. Sleepy Chinese art and curio shops proliferated among first-floor business spaces before the gallery influx, while the second-floor spaces are still actively in use as residential apartments. UCLA painting professor Roger Herman and his associate Hubert Schmalix were the pioneers in 1998, when they bought the Black Dragon kung fu studio and transformed it into the district's first modern art gallery. Artists Steve Hanson and Giovanni Intra followed in 1999 with the opening of China Art Objects Galleries. Steve Hanson had been coming to Chinatown since the early 1980s when it was a haven for punk clubs such as the Hong Kong Cafe, and lives with his wife in Chinatown. Galleries began exhibiting the work of rising local talents such as Jorge Pardo, Laura Owens, Sharon Lockhart, Pae White, and Dave Muller. Jorge Pardo established a studio space in the main Chinatown plaza and eventually transformed it into the Mountain Bar with partners Hanson and Mark McManus, an architect. Other nightspots in the Central Plaza include the kitschy pagoda-style bar at Hop Louie restaurant, as well as the popular Grand Star jazz cafe and the Firecracker dance club upstairs.

Los Angeles Times writer David Pagel (2001) presents a thoughtful analysis of the Chinatown art scene, contending that the galleries are not guided as much by standards of profitability as the more established galleries in areas like Beverly Hills and Santa Monica. In Chinatown, many of the artists and gallery owners have day jobs separate from the art world. They are establishing innovative new relationships between art, lifestyle, and commerce. The atmosphere is communal,

Figure 6.7 Visitors on Chung King Road. The Jade Tree gift and antique store has been a fixture since 1947. The Black Dragon kung fu studio was converted to an art gallery in 1998, then sold to the Jancar Gallery in 2008. Photo by Jan Lin.

freewheeling, and intimate, with the spaces being part studio, part retail gallery, and part social hangout. The art exhibited is humorous, innovative, experimental, and often risky.

Said Jose Pardo in an interview with Kimberly Cutter (2001), "It used to be that the people who went to Cal Arts and Art Center would move to New York the minute they graduated because it was difficult to have an art career here, but increasingly, that is no longer the case." In the same article, artist Pae White commented,

> What's nice about the Chinatown galleries is that they're very organized. They're in the same part of town that the artists themselves actually live in and hang out in, so there's this sense of a whole community orbiting around them.

In an interview with Alexandria Abramian-Mott (2003), Mike McManus, an investor in the Mountain Bar, opined, "The normal cycle is that artists come, rents go up, artists leave. That's not going to happen here. The community here is about a reputation economy, not a money economy." Richard Liu, an architect who grew up in Chinatown, purchased an abandoned restaurant in 2002 and converted it into a gift shop called Realm. He commented to Abramian-Mott, "I want the area to have unified lighting, benches, and planters, as well as later business hours. But I want to avoid gentrification. It's all about the balance."

An article by Frances Anderton (2001) for the *New York Times*, however, suggests that the gentrification is already in progress. She quotes Sherwood Lee, who played on Chung King Road as a child, and whose mother rents space to China Art Objects: "This [scene] is very positive, but the only drawback is that Chinatown may lose its flavor through all these other businesses coming in." In the same article, Roger Herman, the owner of Black Dragon Society gallery, felt very wary of gentrification: "It was nice and quiet three years ago, but we are killing the goose, the charm has gone."

Throwing their support to the new art scene, the Los Angeles Chinatown Business Council launched a Chinatown Art Festival in July 2001 to celebrate the opening of the Hong Gallery, featuring 138 pictures of Chinatown painted the previous month by nearly 100 artists from the California Art Club. One empress in pink silk was pulled in on a rickshaw. Another empress sported a towering headdress adorned with pearls and feathers. Men dressed in embroidered robes and silk slippers escorted them in a procession through the Central Plaza. The fantastical costumes were reproductions of clothes from the Ming and Qing dynasty, and created by the designer Peter Lai, who has a boutique in San Marino (MacGregor 2001).

The new Chinatown arts scene has received the blessing of many property owners and business interests, but it is quite apparent that the gentrification process is under way. There is a rather uncertain balance between art scene and the traditional world of Chinatown. The two social worlds do not really mix. Says Cindy Suriyani, an artist who operates the Bamboo Lane Gallery, in a December 2005 field interview:

Figure 6.8 Cindy Suriyani, owner of Bamboo Lane Gallery, at a March 2005 art opening. Photo by Jan Lin.

There is a dichotomy in terms of where the two groups come from. There have been attempts to bridge the gap but there is not much continuing conversation. The business community has accepted the galleries; there is a realization from a business angle that the galleries bring people into Chinatown. But initially it wasn't so apparent because the gallery openings are at night and the Chinese businesses aren't open at night, but now the mom-and-pop shops have adjusted and are staying open at night.

There is a growing sector of people coming into Chinatown to look at art. It's good to have a certain number of galleries that make it appealing for visitors to come into Chinatown, a critical mass of galleries. More investors and buyers are coming in here, waiting in line, counter-bidding each other. Places are selling at twice the price of a few years ago. The investment environment is very competitive right now. In the long term the rental prices will go up and it will impact me. Traditional businesses are being bought up and replaced by businesses with a connection to the arts.

She contends that some galleries are beginning to become truly profitable in Chinatown, with some artists selling pieces regularly for thousands of dollars, to buyers that include transnational cosmopolitans from locations such as New York City and Europe. The growing speculative property market calls into question whether outsiders or Chinese Americans will control the Chinatown art scene.

The New Cultural Tourism and the Metro Gold Line

With the completion of the new Metro Gold Line transit stations at Chinatown and Union Station in 2003, a new era in cultural tourism has come to Los Angeles Chinatown. What this new cultural tourism means in terms of cultural ownership and the commercialization of Chinese culture is a continuing question. I interviewed several art gallery owners, as well as staff of the cultural preservation and heritage organizations in Los Angeles Chinatown, and asked them to reflect on the character and impact of the new cultural tourism and the Gold Line,

Figure 6.9 The Chinatown Gold Line transit station was completed in 2003. Photo by Jan Lin.

the new art scene, and gentrification trends in Chinatown. Says Eugene Moy, who is with the Chinese Historical Society of Southern California and also a volunteer with the Chinatown Heritage and Visitors Center:

> I think that people still come here but perhaps now with more of a strong interest in the arts, culture, and traditions of Chinatown. Maybe in the past, people came to the gift shops and the restaurants looking to be entertained, perhaps in a selfish or self-interested kind of way. The perception of the Chinese community was very stereotyped, and there was a self-mocking approach towards marketing by the business people of earlier generations. There were cheap gadgets available to shop for. But I think there is a lot more serious interest now in learning about the art and culture of China and Chinese Americans. I also meet families that are non-Chinese parents who have adopted children from China, who want to learn about classical Chinese history and culture so they can pass that on to their Chinese adopted children.
>
> I think there is a community of both the business people and residents who really want to promote the authenticity of the community. There is tremendous depth here. It is not this shallow facade that some of the businesses presented in the past, selling cheap toys for example. Perhaps it's partly the way we have been promoting ourselves. This is a 150-year-old Chinese community that has made tremendous contributions to the commercial and community development of Los Angeles and has contributed to the diverse economy. They have some very interesting stories to tell. We have families who have been here for four, five, or six generations. The experience of our Chinese American pioneers is of real interest to people these days. We have Chinese coming from affluent suburbs like South Pasadena. Their second-generation children who are college students are coming in searching out the history of [the] Chinese in America.

Suellen Cheng, interim executive director of CAMLA, is similarly optimistic about the prospects for cultural tourism in Chinatown:

I think that tourism is an important part of Chinatown's future, but this is a new cultural tourism, not the earlier days of curiosity of cultural stereotypes. It's more in-depth now, that when tourists come here they are not just thinking about buying a few souvenir items, but that they are really interested in Chinese American history. If there were more cultural institutions that people can understand, like classes in kung fu, tai chi, painting and art classes, even more people would be drawn to Chinatown. For CAMLA, we are trying to understand the background and history of Chinese Americans and understand how they have become a part of American society. When we first opened, a tourism company brought people from China and Hong Kong, and they said they were more interested in seeing America than a history of Chinese Americans. But after two years, the tour group leaders now point out specifically the merits of our museum. We're a part of their tours. I think because the products in the shops are increasingly not as unique but the Chinese American museum has become to be perceived as being more unique and worthwhile to visit than the shops.

Sonia Mak, curator at CAMLA, is more circumspect about the costs and benefits of the new cultural tourism:

Cultural tourism is increasing in Chinatown and the character of that cultural tourism has changed. Because the world is a smaller place and because everything is made in China, the mass-produced consumer goods and souvenirs that used to be only found only in Chinatown stores are less competitive in the changing market-place. Because of gentrification, white middle-class people are moving into what had traditionally been minority communities and adaptively reusing those spaces, fixing up storefronts, and changing the demographics of the tourists. Money is being spent on high art and the community experiences demographic and broader social and cultural changes. These are huge sweeping changes to the identity of the neighborhoods. Chinatown started in 1938 as an act of business activism in which the businessmen said that the City couldn't kick them out of this area, that this area would be ours. And now the community is changing and the terms in which the community is "ours" is changing. Some businessmen encourage this change, because of the economic stimulation that has resulted. It's an interesting kind of collision at gallery openings, where the audience is very diverse and multicultural.

The impact of gentrification on the elderly, the low-income residential community, and small businesses is a serious question in the current economic environment. Residents in Chinatown are generally poorer, less educated, less acculturated, and more recent immigrants than the Chinese as a whole in Southern California. The demand for housing in Chinatown outstrips the available supply, and many immigrants have moved into nearby areas such as Echo Park or across the Los Angeles River in Lincoln Heights (Allen and Turner 1997). The elderly population is especially challenged by the lack of affordable housing. When the CRA-subsidized Cathay Manor opened in the mid-1980s, there were ten times more applicants than units available. Low-income immigrants, the elderly, and small Chinese mom-and-pop businesses are threatened with displacement by the process of gentrification in Los Angeles Chinatown.

In the current period, Chinatown is entering an era of new possibilities, as ethnic places are increasingly a factor rather than a barrier to urban renewal. In postindustrial, global cities like Los Angeles, ethnic sites are linked to strategies attracting global investment capital and immigrant labor. After years of decline, downtown Los Angeles is experiencing a revival, and has been the focus of recurring attempts at renewal by public officials, downtown boosters, and the CRA. Beginning in the 1970s, there was a land rush of investment capital (much of it from overseas European, Middle Eastern, or Japanese sources) in the construction of downtown skyscrapers that did much to signify the ascendance of Los Angeles as a nodal "global city" of the Pacific Rim, an advanced headquarters and management complex for the global economy (Davis 1987, Sassen 1988). The CRA has been principal overseer to the emergence of an elite arts and civic center complex on Bunker Hill, especially along Grand Avenue, which includes the Music Center, California Plaza, the Museum of Contemporary Art (MOCA) and the Walt Disney Concert Hall, completed in 2003.

The challenge that confronts Los Angeles Chinatown in the contemporary era is how to refashion itself to the opportunities associated with the postindustrial city in the new global economy. Culture has become a growing sector of growth in our urban economies, replacing some of the losses associated with the decline of manufacturing. In the declining manufacturing and warehousing districts of downtown Los Angeles, we see the intersecting of two economic sectors, namely the ethnic enclave economies of Chinatown and Little Tokyo, and the growth of arts scenes and gallery districts. The completion of the Gold Line mass transit stations at Chinatown and Union Station has brought new opportunities to boost tourism in the ethnic enclave economies of Chinatown, Olvera Street, and Little Tokyo. The Metropolitan Transportation Authority (MTA) has also been boosting cultural tourism throughout Los Angeles through a website: www.experiencela.com. A Chinatown self-guided tourist brochure was published in 2003 to coincide with the opening of the Gold Line Chinatown station by Angels Walk(r) LA, a tourist booster organization that is active mainly in the Bunker Hill area (www.angelswalkla.org). The Angels Walk(r) LA guide to Chinatown was written by the author Lisa See, who wrote the autobiographical family memoir *On Gold Mountain*.

The coming of the Gold Line mass transit line to Chinatown and Union Station in the new millennium is a marked contrast to the destructive episode of "ethnic removal" that beset old Chinatown several decades ago with the completion of the original Union Station railroad depot. An ethnic growth machine has emerged in Los Angeles Chinatown through the coalition of ethnic entrepreneurs as well as nonethnic entrepreneurs. Rather than being victims of a conspiracy of interests in the early days of the Los Angeles growth machine, Chinatown is now part of the conspiracy of urban growth machine interests. There has emerged a new growth opportunity for Los Angeles Chinatown to

Figure 6.10 Chinatown tourism banner. Photo by Jan Lin.

service consumers and visitors from downtown Los Angeles as well as
the surrounding metropolis and outside visitors. In the global era of
Los Angeles Chinatown we find a delicate partnership between old
Cantonese American businesses, the new Southeast Asian Chinese
businesses, and a new bohemian arts economy working with the MTA,
the CRA, and other city agencies to link Chinatown with emerging
culture and tourism strategies. How it accomplishes renewal and growth
while preserving the social institutions and cultural integrity of its low-
income and elderly residential community will be a continuing question

as Chinatown moves into the future. There are risks as well as opportunities that come with globalization.

The current economic scenario in Los Angeles Chinatown is different from the stark socioeconomic polarization seen by Mike Davis (1987, 1990) between the high-security citadel of the transnational power elite and the homeless and dispossessed minorities of post-industrial Los Angeles. The new fortress city of transnational bank and corporate office towers, hotels, museums, and elite cultural facilities has arisen downtown and on Bunker Hill since the 1960s. Class polarization and spatial segregation can be seen also in Los Angeles Koreatown (Park and Kim 2005) where overseas capital has financed a landscape of hotels, department stores, and bank towers in a fortress environment. A similar class polarization can be seen between the low-income elderly residential community of Little Tokyo and the hotels, banks, and department stores financed by transnational Japanese banks since the 1970s. Class polarization in Los Angeles Chinatown may very well increase, however, if gentrification and redevelopment accelerate to the point of disrupting community stability. In the new "gold rush" to capitalize on the economic benefits brought by the Gold Line transit station, Los Angeles Chinatown may sell off the future of its low-income residential community if it moves too quickly to reap the benefits of cultural tourism in the new global economy.

7

PRESERVATION AND CULTURAL HERITAGE IN NEW YORK'S CHINATOWN AND LOWER EAST SIDE AND THE IMPACT OF THE 9/11 DISASTER

New York's Chinatown is a seminal case of the ethnic enclave economy, a dynamic motor of immigrant labor and capital that expanded from its initial core on the Lower East Side of Manhattan to encompass surrounding neighborhoods, as well as establishing satellite Chinatown locations in the outer boroughs of New York City, notably in Queens and Brooklyn.

New York's Chinatown was for decades frozen by the Chinese Exclusion Act in the status of a "bachelor society" of male immigrants without rights of naturalization and citizenship, until the liberalization of immigration law in 1965. Since then it has become the largest Chinatown in the U.S. with thousands of Chinese-owned enterprises encompassing distinct sectoral clusters including a banking sector of dozens of local and transnational banks, a manufacturing sector that includes hundreds of garment shops, and a trade and tourism zone that includes numerous restaurants, markets, and jewelry shops. The manufacturing and trade sector occupies an infrastructure of loft manufacturing buildings and there are dozens of blocks of residential "tenement" buildings that provide affordable housing and small business spaces for the working- and middle-class immigrant community.

As Chinatown has expanded from its bachelor society stage to become a more economically diversified and institutionally complete enclave economy, it has experienced major political and social transformations. The patronage power of traditional family, clan, and supra-regional associations such as the CCBA has given way to the brokerage power of new community-based organizations, such as the Chinatown Planning Council (CPC), Asian Americans for Equality (AAFE), Chinatown Staff and Workers Association (CSWA), which service the needs of the community in a diverse array of areas including health, social services, housing, legal assistance, and labor rights. There is a new leadership that can mobilize immigrants and broker the resources that can be obtained from the governmental and corporate establishments, foundations, and grassroots activism networks. The spirit of social change also sparked the exploration of ethnic cultural heritage. The New York Chinatown History Project (NYCHP) emerged to document Chinese American history and create a new sense of historical self-image for the community. The Tenement Museum has begun to document immigrant heritage in the adjoining neighborhood of the Lower East Side. These organizations form a key framework for creating new political and cultural representations to confront racism and prejudice. They also challenge persisting public images of Chinatown and other immigrant enclaves as overcrowded, dilapidated, and crime-ridden slums.

Thinking about New York's Chinatown as a globally sourced ethnic enclave economy of transnational flows of labor and capital was the subject of my first book, *Reconstructing Chinatown: Ethnic Enclave, Global Change* (1998c), where I found that everyday neighborhood-level urban and social changes were impacted by larger economic and cultural forces in the world context. I sought to explode false myths proliferated by the establishment and the media that Chinatown was a dangerous and unsanitary slum by presenting a picture of a community that was acquiring new political and social agency in labor struggles against exploitative bosses and landlords, and community battles against racial oppression from the police and the political establishment. Community self-identity was activated through mobilization in an overlapping network of urban social movements. The unifying sense of community through mobilization was enhanced by the perception of an external threat. Unification helped to combat internal factionalism, which is endemic in Chinatowns because of provincial differences among immigrants from China as well as geopolitical differences between the People's Republic of China and Taiwan. In the final analysis I saw community as an outgrowth of community building and social change, which would help to create a new sense of collective self-understanding. Community was furthermore not a static social phenomenon but a transformational social process of continuing adaptation to forces from the inside as well battles with the outside.

But the spirit of social change that created the new Chinatown also was confronted by broader local and global forces. There was a continuing outmovement of people and jobs in the ethnic enclave from the core Chinatown in Manhattan to satellite Chinatowns in the outer boroughs of Queens and Brooklyn, because of congestion and competition for limited residential and commercial space in the core. The low-income residential and small-business community in the Chinatown core was further threatened with displacement through gentrification by more affluent white residential inmovers as well as speculative redevelopmental high-rise construction funded by overseas Chinese investment interests. There were local and global forces affecting Chinatown from the inside as well as the outside. I believed that preservation of an affordable tenement housing inventory and favorable environment for small-business growth held the best prospects for sustaining the immigrant community into the future.

As my career has progressed since the mid-1990s, I increasingly see preservation as a set of ideas and practices that encompasses fields of design, urban planning, and social policy. Preservation of tenement buildings and their social histories carries forth architectural, historical, and cultural goals. There is a "power of place" (Hayden 1995) that comes with recognizing and protecting humble buildings and neighborhoods as historical sites and cultural memorials that are just as legitimate as the great national palaces, landmark museums, and world heritage sites that are the focal landmarks of preservationists. They foster public appreciation of immigrant ancestors that came from modest beginnings and struggled to adapt to a new society. Protecting the cultural spaces of Chinatown like tenement buildings, churches, and parks helps to create repositories of collective sentiment and memory that in turn encourage the preservation of ethnic and community identity in the future. I see history as a powerful weapon for fostering community identity and ethnic self-respect. At the same time, heritage workers have to adapt to the continuing dynamics of community change as well as to the wider forces of the political establishment and global capitalism.

I returned to New York's Chinatown in the summer of 2005 to interview community stakeholders on the challenges of historical preservation and community development with the continuing impacts of local and global social change. I was also interested in learning the specific economic and cultural impacts of the 9/11 disaster and how the community had responded to its consequences.

Tenement Preservation and Cultural Heritage in Chinatown and the Lower East Side

I acquired an interest in residential tenement preservation early in my graduate student career. Through my work with organizations such as the Joint Planning Council of the Lower East Side and It's Time (a housing and services organization in Chinatown), I was a proponent of preservation movements to rehabilitate residential tenement housing in New York City, which is a ubiquitous feature of Chinatown, the Lower East Side of Manhattan and many other New York City neighborhoods. Although the century-old building stock of walk-up brick residential apartment buildings had deteriorated through age and disinvestment, many community activists, architects, and housing experts saw their value as an affordable housing stock with historical and vernacular significance. If properly rehabilitated, they were a force in urban planning and housing policy for low- and middle-income New Yorkers, in contrast to the more upscale condominium towers that were a tool for gentrification by urban redevelopmental growth interests. In the 1970s and 1980s, New York City acquired about 100,000 units of abandoned, tax-delinquent properties. To promote rehabilitation of these properties, the city manager gave recognition to "squatters," homesteaders, and many community-based organizations that were renovating buildings.

Preservation of tenements was tied to the emergence of the cultural heritage movement in Chinatown. Community activists occupied a large tenement building at 70 Mulberry Street, a former Public School 23 (P.S. 23) that fell into city ownership. Chinatown stakeholders were able to procure public support for community use and a range of cultural and social service organizations were eventually housed, including Chen and Dancers, Young Lions dancers, United East Athletic Association, Chinatown Manpower Project, and the senior citizens center of the Chinese American Planning Council. Through the community engagement, the building was in time rehabilitated. As a walk-up tenement building typical of many found throughout the Lower East Side of Manhattan, P.S. 23 did not possess the kind of architectural distinctiveness characteristic of buildings championed by preservationists in other areas of the country, but the building elicited many sentimental feelings in the community. In 1984, the New York Chinatown History Project moved its headquarters into the building. The museum recognized the special qualities of tenement buildings through such exhibitions as "The Tenement: Place for Survival, Object of Reform," which was curated in 1988 by Sam Sue and Andrea Callard. The exhibition called our attention to the persisting importance of the humble walk-up brick-built tenement buildings, which for decades since the mid-nineteenth century had housed a succession of white ethnic European, then African, Caribbean, Latin American, and Asian immigrant groups through the portal of New York City. They tried to portray a sense of struggle and social agency on the part of immigrants different from the passive portraits of people in poverty that were common in the past.

Classic images of immigrants overcrowded in dilapidated tenement apartments were initially disseminated into the American popular imagination by photojournalists such as Jacob Riis in his 1890 book *How the Other Half Lives*. Although Riis and many other "muckraker" journalists at the turn of the century were guilty of fanning some racial–ethnic prejudice against immigrants, the popular outrage that they incited provided much positive impetus for tenement housing reform and regulation. In many respects, the images also fed public perceptions of immigrant neighborhoods as places of immorality, vice, and danger to public health that provided legitimacy for federal government programs of slum clearance and urban renewal. Designating tenement neighborhoods as "slums" and "blighted" areas gave the political and commercial establishment moral and political legitimacy to condemn them or acquire them under eminent domain.

Chinatown largely escaped these modernist slum clearance programs of the interwar and postwar period because the community was still a small bachelor enclave restricted in its growth by the Chinese Exclusion Act to an area near the Five Point neighborhood dubbed by local historians the "plow and harrow" site (named after a tavern). The adjacent neighborhood of Mulberry Bend, however, was demolished and stood vacant until pressure from community leaders including Jacob Riis led to its designation as a park, named after Christopher Columbus to recognize the Italian immigrant community that was displaced. Meanwhile, dozens of blocks of riverfront tenement buildings on the Lower East Side were demolished for construction of the East River Drive freeway arterial and for public housing. Condemnation, eviction, and demolition of buildings often were not followed by timely new construction, and properties lay derelict for decades, many becoming vacant lots. Slum clearance and urban renewal in New York's Lower East Side and many other U.S. urban neighborhoods was a very haphazard process that essentially replaced one problem with another problem, notably a reduction in affordable housing and the creation of disinvested communities. In the worst blocks along the East River, there is a quite stark geography of monotonous public housing slab tower blocks, disinvested tenement buildings, and weed-strewn vacant lots. The impression is familiar to many New York City residents walking in the Alphabet City area of the East Village from west to east, that the neighborhood steadily deteriorates as one walks from Avenue A to Avenue D. There were some model demonstration projects, however, such as First Houses (1936), which were actually tenement buildings rebuilt with bricks from condemned buildings, and the nicely landscaped Peter Cooper Village–Stuyvesant Town (1947) built for war veterans.

The contemporary movement for the preservation of tenements presents a more enlightened scenario of urban renewal that recognizes the viability of tenement buildings as an affordable housing stock for low- and middle-income New Yorkers. There is a connection to the preservation of cultural heritage with the emergence of community-based history organizations such as the New York Chinatown History Project, Henry Street Settlement, the Eldridge Street Synagogue, and the Lower East Side Tenement Museum. To cite architectural historian Dolores Hayden once more, these sites establish a "power of place" for cultural heritage exploration and story telling. These museums give new visibility and validation to the experiences of women, immigrants, and racial–ethnic minorities in America that were previously ignored, silenced, or marginalized. These projects contribute to the creating of a multicultural narrative of American experience. They preserve local vernacular architecture to serve as symbols of the immigrant experience of struggle, hope, and adaptation to life in America.

The New York Chinatown History Project was started in 1980 by Charlie Lai and John Kuo Wei Tchen. Charlie Lai had come from Hong Kong in 1968 with his parents and five siblings and grown up in Chinatown. Tchen was a Chinese American born in the U.S. who moved from Wisconsin to New York City in 1975 so he could work in an Asian American community. The two met through the Basement Workshop, a nonprofit Asian American resource center on Catherine Street. Charlie Lai said in an August 2005 interview with me:

> The changes of the 1960s, civil rights and immigration law change … All of those factors come into play … There was the anti-war movement and Vietnam, and there was a perception that they were Asian like us. We were situated in Chinatown, in the midst of turmoil, and a feeling of wanting to take the community back …

In the early days, there were not many books written, not much
doing of research, preserving of history.

As the story goes, the two turned their cultural activism to the streets
when they began to notice the treasure trove of community artifacts
that were being left on Chinatown sidewalks by older households and
commercial merchants making way for new immigrants. These included
very mundane household items like suitcases, house slippers, letters and
old newspapers. Tchen once found and saved a seven- by three-foot
sign that simply read "Chinese Laundry." When they moved into P.S.
23 in 1984, their first exhibition chronicled the quiet but heroic
struggles of the Chinese American laundry worker, a stock figure of
the bachelor society period (Kwon 2007). This exhibition had great
appeal with Chinatown seniors. Later there was an exhibition on
Chinese American garment workers that featured oral histories of
women immigrants who helped to make up the new Chinatown of the
post-1965 period.

When the NYCHP became the Museum of the Chinese in the
Americas, it decided to stay in P.S. 23 because according to Fay Chew,
it recognized the school building "as an artifact itself, meriting historical
preservation." The building was also a focal point for outreach to
community and former community residents with memories of
attending the school (Simpson 2001). A series of alumni reunions of
former students of P.S. 23 exhibition provided an opportunity for
reunion in the spirit of intercultural remembrance and dialogue while
also forming a collection of artifacts and stories that would subsequently
form the exhibition "What Did You Learn in School Today? P.S. 23,
1893–1976."

As the NYCHP continued to grow it tried to be more inclusive to
represent other segments of the Chinatown population, such as the
Fukienese (also Fujianese) Chinese immigrants that occupied the East
Broadway and Allen Street corridors in an area sometimes dubbed
"East Chinatown."[1] A 1996 exhibition, "The Art of the Golden
Venture Refugees," featured paper sculptures created by the Fukienese
immigrants held in federal detention after their rescue from the

grounded smuggling ship. The museum also sought to reach beyond its local historical scope to encompass a more global perspective on the Chinese diaspora. In 1995, the NYCHP changed its name to the Museum of the Chinese in the Americas (MoCA). A 1998–1999 exhibition, "Mi Familia, Mi Comunidad," brought together artifacts and stories from Chinese families in Cuba, Guatemala, and Peru, representing the historical Chinese diaspora in Latin America. Cynthia Lee, chief curator at MoCA, described in an August 2005 interview how the outreach experience helped to spark new perspectives on Chinese diasporic identity:

> Participants in the focus groups said things like, "you know, I never thought about myself as Chino-Latino until you asked me to come here." What came out of those interviews were different ideas about ethnicity and race. It seemed that in the Caribbean there was more a fluid notion of ethnicity. In South America the communities were more segregated and their Chinese identities were a little stronger ... They were astonished by the idea that there were other people having similar cultural and psychological issues.

The tasks of keeping things fresh and dynamic, of making history sensible to the whole spectrum of the Chinese American experience, from the local neighborhood to the global diaspora, have been an evolving experience over the years at the Museum of the Chinese in the Americas. Charlie Lai commented in August 2005:

> We have gone through several names changes, from the Chinatown History Project, the Chinatown History Museum, to the Museum of the Chinese in the Americas. We initially thought in the short term and eventually found the name confining. After more than ten years, people in the community wanted something that expressed who we really are, and we see that Chinatown is a metaphor for Chinese throughout the U.S. We want to create a sense of how Chinese are creating new communities—we think of our museum as a place for dialogue that is also about the

different nature of the city itself, where practically everybody comes through as a diaspora, and understand that Chinese come from everywhere.

MoCA also found its original space of 2,500 square feet in four rooms of P.S. 23 to be too confining for a museum experiencing growth and self-redefinition. Exhibitions were limited to two rooms and the office staff and archives were squeezed into cramped quarters. In the fall of 2009, the MoCA moved into a new 14,000-square-foot space at 211–215 Centre Street, on the western side of Chinatown bordering Soho. The old space will continue as an archival and research center, while the new quarters will have larger offices and exhibition space that can better accommodate educational visits. The experience of redefinition and relocation for MoCA suggests that the work of ethnic cultural preservation must be adaptable and transformational in order to represent both the local and global features of ethnicity and community in the contemporary context.

The Lower East Side Tenement Museum has also emerged to foster cultural preservation in both the local and global context. It has uniquely joined architectural and cultural heritage work through its central focus on preservation of tenement buildings that have been rehabilitated into exhibitionary living-history museums. It was founded in 1988 by Ruth Abrams, an M.A. in history and former social worker, with the assistance of a curator, Anita Jacobsen, after they acquired 97 Orchard Street, a tenement building originally built in 1863 that had held a succession of immigrant residents from some 20 countries since the mid-nineteenth century. The building had been boarded up from 1935 to 1987 and was like a time capsule with thousands of nineteenth- and twentieth-century artifacts including furniture, clothing, kitchenware, letters, and newspapers still intact. The artifacts have subsequently been restored, catalogued, and researched to reconstruct the migration history and family life of the building's immigrant residents and the social milieu in which they lived. Through guided tours, programs, and exhibitions, the museum staff are providing a window into the stories and lives of typical families among the several thousand people that lived in the building between 1863 and 1935. While the museum has acquired several other properties in the vicinity, 97 Orchard Street remains the centerpiece of their holdings. Some of the first multilingual tour guides were English language students working with the local University Settlement. Tour guides are versed in interpretation as well as role playing at the Tenement Museum. Many of the guides are amateur or professional actors who study archival recipes, songs, and letters to familiarize and better perform the roles of people who lived in the building (Sandrow 2001).

In an August 2005 interview with me, Ruth Abrams identified the originating mission of the Tenement Museum:

> We grew out of the social history movement, which says you cannot know the history of America without knowing the history

Figure 7.1 Tenement Museum tour group. Photo by Jan Lin.

of the poor and the working- and middle-class, that history is not just the history of the rich and famous . . . I came to believe that history had become a very powerful tool that was useful in my own transformation so I wanted to bring this possibility to other people.

In 1992, 97 Orchard Street became the first tenement building to earn recognition on the National Register of Historic Places. Ruth Abrams recalled how established preservationists initially scoffed at the idea of creating the Tenement Museum:

> People in the preservation movement initially did not think that tenements had any redeeming architectural value and didn't provide a lot of support at first. But the preservation movement has come around and we are now part of the National Trust for Historic Preservation and the National Park Service, all of who want their values represented in the Tenement Museum. We encountered a little resistance when we began, and foundations did not initially understand why we were teaching English or training housing inspectors, because that didn't seem like museum work.

The museum aims to promote social tolerance among the public through fostering an understanding of shared heritage. It seeks to think critically about the past rather than promote facile tropes of patriotic but uncritical national history. Ethnic identity is seen as a phenomenon that assists in adaptation to the new world and does not impede the assimilation process. The Tenement Museum pays special attention to the hardships of immigrant women and children, such as Nathalie Gumpertz from Prussia, a single mother who lived with her three children. She worked as a dressmaker and brought piecework home to make ends meet. There is also attention to immigrant children, such as Victoria Confino, a 13-year-old Sephardic Jew from Turkey. There is outreach to local schools to promote educational field trips to the museum. It also provides lesson plans for local history and social science teachers. The museum also provides services for new immigrants. There is a Teaching English through History program that uses diaries, letters, and memoirs of earlier immigrants to teach English to new immigrants. It publishes a multilingual immigrant resource guide to assist new immigrants with commonly asked questions and a resource directory of helpful organizations. It educates the public on housing code violations and provides training for people to do housing inspection. It founded a local coalition of community leaders to foster dialogue on local preservation. This is an important undertaking because gentrification is taking place on Orchard Street, with new upscale condominium residential buildings being constructed on vacant lots or after the demolition of condemned tenement buildings.

The Tenement Museum has also worked to build global networks in cultural heritage work. Ruth Abrams obtained a start-up grant from the Rockefeller Center to assemble leaders of a group of international museums devoted to social causes in meetings in Bellagio, Italy, from which they emerged as the International Coalition of the Sites of Conscience. The Coalition sponsors resource workshops, information exchanges, strategic advocacy, and civic engagement for a worldwide network of heritage sites documenting past struggles for justice and addressing contemporary legacies. These include sites memorializing slavery in Africa, state terrorism and concentration camps in Russia, the Holocaust in the Czech Republic, and civil rights and women's rights in the United States.

Liz Sevcenko is vice president of interpretation at the Tenement Museum, and secretary general of the International Coalition of the Sites of Conscience. In an August 2005 interview, she discussed the special qualities of the Tenement Museum as a site of conscience:

> This neighborhood is all about struggles for social justice, over immigration, sweatshops, child labor, housing rights and welfare rights. This neighborhood is famous for the number of grassroots struggles that were fought and won here.

She also reflected on their mandate for creating an international coalition, and on her vocational motives:

Our greatest challenge in the Sites of Conscience is to establish ourselves as a fundamental pillar of the international effort on human rights, to help contribute to easing the experience of people coming out of trauma or genocide. Like people establish schools and courts, we want these museums to become places of memory to address these issues. For international dramatic examples like Rwanda or our own communities at home in the U.S. There is a cumulative emerging notion that museums can take active roles in helping people to understand their society critically ... My whole understanding of what I needed to do as an individual is that the things I thought were fixed or unchangeable had been produced historically, that history had been fabricated. So my inspiration for change came from looking at the past.

While MoCA and the Tenement Museum help to mediate the experience of historical trauma in Chinatown and the Lower East Side, I was also interested to explore the impact of contemporary trauma through the experience of the 9/11 disaster in lower Manhattan.

The 9/11 Impact and the Rebuild Chinatown Initiative (RCI)

The September 11, 2001 disaster at the World Trade Center in New York City dealt a harsh blow to the infrastructure, economy, and social fabric of lower Manhattan. The residential neighborhood of Battery Park City, closest to the World Trade Center, was physically devastated by the attack, while adjoining neighborhoods such as Tribeca and Chinatown were crippled through street and subway station closures for months. Just six blocks from Ground Zero, many important streets and subway stations in Chinatown were in a "frozen zone" subject to extended closures after the disaster. Businesses could not make their deliveries, and people could not easily get to Chinatown to work or engage in buying and selling. In the four months after the tragedy, 42,000 people visited the Federal Emergency Management Agency (FEMA) relief center at 142 Worth Street in Chinatown (Gerog 2002). An economic impact study conducted by the Asian American Federation of New York (AAFNY), *Chinatown: One Year After September 11*, found that 75 percent of Chinatown's labor force became unemployed in the first two weeks after September 11, while 25 percent or nearly 8,000 remained unemployed three months later. The impact was most palpable in the garment industry, which lost nearly $500 million in revenues in the year following September 11, and was hit by the closure of over 25 percent of the 250 shops making up the Chinatown garment production zone. There were also declines throughout the restaurant industry, the jewelry trade, construction, and other small business sectors.

The public officials and other power brokers of lower Manhattan relatively ignored Chinatown in the months after the 9/11 disaster. City Councilman Alan Gerson led demonstrations of angry small business owners outside the headquarters of the Lower Manhattan Development Corporation. After this intensive lobbying, the original dividing line for the Liberty Zone (that is, the area that was eligible for relief) was extended northward from Chambers Street to Canal Street, thus qualifying Chinatown for public funds dedicated towards rebuilding.

The residents of Chinatown also experienced high levels of psychological dislocation, including shock, trauma, and ongoing mental illnesses such as post-traumatic stress disorder (PTSD). The low-income elderly population that is endemic in Chinatown suffered especially. Service providers had to contend with the phenomenon that many people in Chinatown consider mental health to be a taboo topic.

A major avenue of improvement emerged through the Rebuild Chinatown Initiative, a comprehensive community-planning project sponsored by AAFE. AAFE started as a political organization in 1974 that spearheaded community protests over minority hiring policies at the Confucius Plaza housing project (Chinatown's largest housing project with 762 mostly middle-income units), and was called Asian Americans for Equal Employment (AAFEE) at the time. AAFE was also involved in political conflicts over police brutality and electoral redistricting, as well as voter registration and education. One of AAFE's leaders, Margaret Chin, ran for City Council in the 1990s. Over the last 30 years, AAFE also moved into affordable housing development, raising over $50 million to build 500 units of residential housing for low-income and homeless individuals and families of New York, helped families obtain $150 million in mortgage financing to purchase homes, and provided legal support and counseling on fair housing law. AAFE is now arguably Chinatown's largest multi-service community development corporation. It continues to carry forward its political advocacy functions.

AAFE obtained an initial grant from the Freddie Mac Corporation to start up the initiative and subsequent grants from the Carnegie Corporation of New York, Deutsche Bank, and Rockefeller Brothers Fund. It obtained broad participation from a range of Chinatown leaders and stakeholders on the RCI advisory board and in the comprehensive planning process. AAFE had great legitimacy in the Chinese American community after three decades of work and endorsements from figures such as City Councilman Alan Gerson, Assembly Speaker Sheldon Silver, and City Planning Commissioner Amanda Burden added to the public legitimacy of the RCI.

In its first phase, the RCI carried out a research survey of 1800 residents and held community focus-group meetings that resulted in the publication of the report *Rebuild Chinatown Initiative: The Community Speaks* in November 2002. Prepared by Mourad, Warnke and Associates, the report identified sanitation, affordable housing, and employment and income generation as the main issues confronting Chinatown residents in the post-9/11 environment. The second phase of the RCI moved from assessment to planning and a steering committee of 30 community leaders undertook a series of workshops that eventually resulted in the release in April 2004 of *America's Chinatown: A Community Plan*, a report prepared by Phillips Preiss Shapiro Associates. This community recovery plan highlighted initiatives in eight action areas, namely: Historic Chinatown, Arts and Architecture, Jobs, the Waterfront, Linkages, Affordable Housing, Family Neighborhoods, and Business Districts. In its third phase, RCI moved on to implement some of its first planning initiatives, including Explore Chinatown, a tourism and marketing campaign, and the start-up of the new Chinatown Partnership Local Development Corporation.[2]

The Chinatown Partnership LDC has the active support of existing nonprofit community development corporations, such as AAFE, which works mainly in housing, and Renaissance Economic Development Corporation, which works in employment and business development. The decision to launch the tourism and marketing initiative Explore Chinatown immediately marks the importance of cultural heritage as a factor in the economic recovery. Ethnic tourism and niche marketing campaigns represent the postindustrial character of the postfordist period of contemporary capitalism. The designation of an Empire Zone in Chinatown by the New York State Assembly in January 2006 was a further step in neoliberal economic policy, establishing sales tax exemptions and local property tax abatements for qualified businesses for up to ten years. The tax-free urban investment zone and the new local development corporation are symptoms of economic neoliberalism insofar as they mark a retreat or devolution from public financing of urban infrastructure and services in favor of privatization and public–private partnerships. It is akin to the neoliberal economic strategies pursued by developing countries that invite foreign investment through tax holidays and free trade zones. This has created an opportunity space for local economic and cultural stakeholders insofar as they can control the pace of privatization and balance local interests and global market imperatives. AAFE has altered the dynamics of economic and cultural change in Chinatown by moving from the practice of community development to the business of economic development.

Explore Chinatown: Marketing an Ethnic Theme Park?

In its first two years, the Explore Chinatown tourism and marketing campaign was funded through the joint efforts of the Lower Manhattan Development Corporation ($1 million) and the September 11 Fund ($1.7 million). In its third year, Explore Chinatown will be incorporated into the emerging Chinatown Partnership LDC. Explore Chinatown undertook an extensive marketing campaign to market Chinatown through advertisements in subways, newspapers and magazines, and the radio. Traditional events such as the Lunar New Year and the Autumn Moon festival were boosted, as well as a new biannual campaign, the Taste of Chinatown, held in October and April. A tourist kiosk was erected and opened in December 2004 on a triangle of open land at the intersection of Baxter, Canal, and Walker Streets. The impetus for the kiosk came out of the RCI as well as the AAFNY study.

The logos on the side of the kiosk, promotional brochures, and the website of Explore Chinatown (explorechinatown.com) include NYC and Company (the city's official tourism and convention marketing organization), the New York City Department of Transportation and Department of City Planning, New York City Art Commission, the September 11th Fund, the Lower Manhattan Development Corporation, and the U.S. Department of Housing and Urban Development. Coupon books offer discounts to local restaurants and gift shops. The world of corporate branding meets with strategies familiar to local chambers of commerce in the effort to market the ethnic community in the new era of public–private partnership.

Explore Chinatown provides core services of public relations, promotion, and marketing of events and sites in Chinatown. A variety of advertising and marketing companies responded to the request for proposals for tourism contracts, and a team of firms was eventually

Figure 7.2 Explore Chinatown tourist kiosk. Photo by Jan Lin.

funded, including M. Silver, Dentsu Communications, and Asian Women in Business, with NYC and Company responsible for overall management. Explore Chinatown created a user-friendly web page (www.explorechinatown.com) to help tourists orient themselves online. The tourist kiosk involves multi-agency coordination with a range of public agencies including the New York City Arts Commission, the Department of City Planning, and the Department of Transportation.

Explore Chinatown also created slick brochures offering detailed maps identifying transit stations, cultural sites and landmarks, and commercial shopping streets for tourists and visitors. Asian Women in Business, directed by Bonnie Wong, created a Chinatown guidebook with coupons that describe the full array of regional Chinese and pan-Asian cuisines available, including Cantonese, Shanghai, Fuzhou, Vietnamese, Malaysian, and Thai. The guidebook also spotlights the Chinatown jewelry district and cultural sites, as well as offering more discount coupons for shopping in Chinatown's many retail trade establishments. Asian Women in Business also collaborates with Explore Chinatown to sponsor biannual "Taste of Chinatown" outdoor food festivals, in April and October, in addition to the traditional Lunar New Year celebrations usually in February.

I believe the Explore Chinatown tourist kiosk and marketing campaign exhibit features of "McDonaldization," to evoke George Ritzer's provocative thesis in *The McDonaldization of Society* (2008, 5th edition, first published 1993), in which he argues that American life, especially in fast food and other consumer industries, is increasingly marked by features of bureaucracy, efficiency, control, and predictability. Ritzer's idea of McDonaldization updates German sociologist Max Weber's thesis on "rationalization" and the growth of the "iron cage of rationality" in modern society. The Chinatown kiosk is like an "iron cage" that regularizes and standardizes the cultural heritage of the Chinese American community for tourism and popular consumption. The online marketing campaign could be seen as a "digital cage" of rationalization. In many ways, Explore Chinatown also represents a trend of "Disneyfication" although in this case this is a real living and breathing community and not a formulaic "ethnic theme park" that is fabricated by mass media programmers or corporate "imagineers" for popular consumption.

Since Explore Chinatown is not directly controlled by a corporation or the governmental establishment, representing instead a public–private partnership controlled by Chinatown place entrepreneurs and other stakeholders, I believe that Explore Chinatown borrows the structures of bureaucratic rationality to present an ethnic theme park without the superstructure of a large corporation. While the Explore Chinatown campaign and Chinatown Partnership Local Development Corporation have the broad support of respected community stakeholders and the leadership of AAFE in the aftermath of economic and social dislocation, I found these stakeholders to be somewhat apprehensive about the negative consequences of commercialization and economic growth.

Mapping Chinatown: Where is Chinatown?

The difficulty of mapping Chinatown locations led to a concern of the RCI, namely the problem of "wayfinding" in the maze of narrow intersecting streets and wide boulevards often congested with traffic that constitutes greater Chinatown. There are plans to improve signage and lighting in Chinatown to assist pedestrians, shoppers, and tourists in orienting themselves and finding their destinations. Lighting is important to enhance the nocturnal pedestrian environment, and the report proposed the creation of an open-air "night market" similar to those found in Singapore, Hong Kong, and San Francisco's Chinatown. Wayfinding for tourists is associated with a "place making" project identifying and promoting important historical and cultural sites to create a Chinatown Heritage Trail along the model of the Lowell, Massachusetts heritage trail and the Sun-Yat-Sen interpretive trail in Hong Kong. The Chinatown Heritage Trail could link with heritage trails in the Lower East Side and Lower Manhattan. There is a proposal to improve Chinatown's link to the Lower East Side and sites such as the Tenement Museum through a redesigning and improvement of Allen Street as an "Avenue of the Immigrants." There is another proposal to improve transportation linkages with City Hall and Wall Street through improved street alignments. Chatham Square is a main focus because it is a nexus point for several streets and major boulevards, and acts as something of a gateway between the historically Cantonese population of Mott-Pell-Doyer Streets and the Fukienese population of East Broadway. High-rise residential buildings such as Chatham Green, Chatham Towers, and Confucius Towers give it an anchor as one of the best addresses to live in Chinatown. Statuary and memorials also mark the public symbolic importance of Chatham Square.

These challenges of wayfinding and place making reveal the complex challenges faced by planners and community stakeholders working to revitalize the economy and cultural life of New York's Chinatown. The tourist kiosk does not mark the center of the community, but the nexus point of a transportation hub for immigrants in transit to other locations on the East Coast. It sits on an inconspicuous intersection of streets amidst the throng of tourists, shoppers, immigrants, workers, and commuters. It helps to orient the visitor to a Chinatown that has no central geographical location, but rather exists as a nexus of commercial thoroughfares and scattered sites across the residential tenement and commercial loft-manufacturing building infrastructure of

Figure 7.3 Explore Chinatown banner on Mott Street. Photo by Jan Lin.

lower Manhattan. There are several candidates for central locations, of community and commercial importance in Chinatown, including the playgrounds and picnic tables at Columbus Park where many residents congregate and recreate, the statues and monuments at Chatham Square, the old Cantonese commercial district on Mott and Mulberry Street, the new Fujianese commercial district on East Broadway, and the Grand Street produce market. These are important locations for local Chinese American residents but many non-Chinese tourists and shoppers enter Chinatown along the commercial artery of Canal Street, which pulsates with cross-town traffic and trucks heavy with goods. The sidewalks are jammed with pedestrians jostling for ground among stalls and mini-malls bursting with cheap imported goods. This is one of the premier cheap "knockoff" markets in New York City, a raffish street bazaar that offers shoppers and tourists the chance to find bargain counterfeit knockoffs of items like Rolex watches from sidewalk vendors and shopping arcades.

Sub-ethnic factionalism between the Cantonese and the Fujianese is a distinct phenomenon among the residents and stakeholders of China-town, with geopolitical origins. The old Cantonese group historically supported the government of the Republic of China in Taiwan, while the Fujianese community is affiliated with the People's Republic of China on the mainland. While the Cantonese-speaking Chinese dominate in the original core Chinatown, the Fuzhouese-speaking Chinese from Fujian Province have established a new commercial corridor as well as immigrant association offices along East Broadway. The two factions sponsor parades on differing dates marking the political independence of Taiwan and China. Subethnic differences also reflect the transnational dimensions of the overseas Chinese diaspora, which has brought ethnic Chinese immigrants from other nations such as Vietnam and Thailand.

Chinatown has a variety of important community and sub-community sites but no real central location. Where is Chinatown? Chinatown is a gateway for immigrant flows of labor and capital in the twentieth-century metropolis. The kiosk tries to map locations for a Chinese American community that is more diasporic, highly dispersed and on the move. Chinese Americans in the greater metropolis of New York do not just live, work, and shop only in Manhattan's Chinatown, but are scattered in satellite outer-borough Chinatowns in Brooklyn and Queens as well as residential concentrations in outer-lying suburban communities in New Jersey, Long Island, upstate New York and Connecticut. Amy Chin, interim executive director of the Chinatown Partnership LDC, reflects on the decreasing centrality of Chinatown as a place for buying and selling in the new era of online commerce:

> I was traveling with a Chinese folk dance outfit for a while throughout the country, sometimes in small towns. People made one trip a year to an urban Chinatown and stocked up on provisions. But there is no longer any need for that anymore with the Internet where you can get provisions delivered to you from all over the world. There's no need for the pilgrimages your parents used to make to Chinatown. There is Chinese television that you can watch from your home in suburban New Jersey. These kinds of things are not place-centered anymore. You don't need to go someplace to achieve them.

John Leo, Chinatown Liaison for the Lower Manhattan Development Corporation, agrees that Chinese Americans are becoming more geographically dispersed, but points to the continuing salience of Manhattan's Chinatown as a focal site for cultural activities and collective sentiments:

> People still come to Chinatown because this is where the family associations are, and they feel more at home. The language is still Chinese. People like to come back to Chinatown for weddings, banquets, holidays, and also to find work with the family associations. Chinatown is transient like a transportation hub, but it's still a focus for holidays.

Deflected Immigration

Mr. Leo draws attention to the growing number of local, regional, and interstate travel companies and van companies operating in New

York's Chinatown. There are van and bus services from satellite China-towns in Brooklyn and Queens to Manhattan, and interstate services between different cities such as Boston, New York, Philadelphia, and Washington, D.C. These services are popular among the latest immigrants from Fujian Province, who may be undocumented and afraid of traveling in regular transportation. There are various locations for pick-up on Canal Street, the Bowery, and Forsyth Street, with Forsyth Street being a special focus. There are some locations designated by the New York City Department of Transportation (DOT) for bus and van layover. DOT has found enforcement a challenging situation, with some violence occurring between bus companies competing for customers. Many of the companies operate informally, with people selling bus tickets right along the street. Others have storefronts and websites.

Thomas Yu, a Project Manager at Asian Americans for Equality, agrees that regional and interstate transportation companies are doing a thriving business. The Sunset Park Chinatown in Brooklyn, he asserts, was assisted in its development by the availability of a van service that used to stop at Confucius Plaza and Canal Street. The price was cheaper than a subway token. Chinese American passengers feel safer in these vans than on the subways, where they feel they can be the target of robberies or harassment. He reports that the interstate buses are popular with Asian American college students along the East Coast. He began

Figure 7.4 Flushing–Chinatown van service. Photo by Jan Lin.

using the buses about 1999 while enrolled as a student at Harvard University, in order to commute between Boston and his home in New York's Lower East Side. The Fung Wah bus line, he reports, offered a $20 roundtrip bus fare from Boston to New York, compared with an $80 roundtrip fare with Greyhound bus line.

The Washington Post reports that the bus routes are popular with Asian restaurant workers seeking employment in Chinatowns in other cities. The competition among rival bus lines can be cutthroat. The New York police department investigated reports that a turf war between competing bargain bus lines and possible participation of organized crime may have been to blame for two killings, an assault, and two bus fires.[3] *The Wall Street Journal* reports that other Chinese bus lines named Lucky Star and Boston Deluxe were offering $10 or $15 fares between Boston and New York in the first months of 2005. The price competition has even forced the industry giants, Greyhound and Peter Pan, to lower prices on their competing routes. Taking a tip from discount airline companies such as JetBlue, the Chinese travel operators have become very savvy entrepreneurs. Some are advertising on the Internet and appealing to travelers beyond the Chinese American community. One popular website is www.ivymedia.com, launched in 2002 by Jimmy Chen, who came to the U.S. from Shanghai for a computer science doctorate. His inspiration was Internet travel service companies like Expedia.[4] The phenomenon of Chinese immigrants being deflected from New York's Chinatown is comparable to that found by Ivan Light (2006) among Mexican immigrants being deflected from Los Angeles into peripheral metropolitan regions and neighboring southwestern states in search of employment and affordable housing. In New York Chinatown, Chinese immigrants contended with the economic and social dislocations caused by the 9/11 disaster. They likely will continue to be deflected as New York's Chinatown is hurt by economic recession that beset the nation in 2007.

The Dispersal of Chinese Americans to the Suburbs

Geographic mobility is also tied to cultural mobility with the phenomenon of Chinese Americans moving into the suburbs. Geographic mobility out of Manhattan's Chinatown into the outer-borough "satellite" Chinatowns of Queens and Brooklyn and the outer-lying suburbs of Long Island and New Jersey is often correlated with a move into home ownership, access to better schools, and upward social mobility into the middle class. Many of these Chinese Americans, particularly in the suburbs, are often more culturally assimilated than the residents of the core Chinatown. The second-, third-, and fourth-generation Chinese Americans growing up in the suburbs of New Jersey, Long Island, upstate New York, and Connecticut carry different values and interests. These generational, cultural, and social differences are a challenge to the Chinese American heritage and arts organizations working in Manhattan's Chinatown. These issues actively confront the staff of MoCA. As Executive Director Charlie Lai reflects in an August 2005 interview:

> People need to understand that Chinatown is only a metaphor of community development that somehow has expanded beyond four initial square blocks to the entire Lower East Side, encompassing the Cantonese, Toishanese, Fukienese, and mainlanders. Do they all need to come into Chinatown? Absolutely not. They are self-contained; they do not need to come into Chinatown to shop or for services. So we are trying to figure out what connection they still have to Chinatown? We are trying to reach out to Chinese of the second, third, and fourth generation, to see if they are part of the Chinese American issues. They live in Long Island and Connecticut and we need to tell their story of the population from 1950s to 2000. If what we do does not resonate with these other members of the community then we better change our rhetoric.

Deputy Director of Programs Cynthia Ai-Fen Lee reflected on their planned move from a site on Mulberry Street in the historical core of Chinatown to a new location on the border of Soho and Chinatown:

> This will address a tension in different audience constituents. There are Chinese Americans that don't have an association with

Chinatown. New York is an important site to look at the issues, in treating the immigration history of Chinese Americans, and the diasporic perspective. We're excited about the location because we will be able to reach out to two spectrums. There is the constituency interested in the laundry stories, the labor and social history and interest in modest beginnings. There is another spectrum of people that have no connection to that history, who immigrated with more educated backgrounds and have possibly suburban and middle-class experiences.

Amy Chin, interim executive director of the Chinatown Partnership LDC, is very upbeat on what she feels is a capacity for the performing arts to help bridge generational and cultural differences within the broader Chinese American community. She says in an August 2005 interview:

I think that culture, performing arts are so powerful, even more than television. Culturally unique performances are some of the last things place-oriented. I come from a performing arts background, and you can see audiences really coming together. Prior to coming to this job, I was the executive director of the New York Chinese Cultural Center, which was a community school of arts and also home to the Chinese Folk Dance Company. I was seeing second-generation Chinese American families bringing their children to class to learn culturally specific art that was relevant to their culture. But there was also this new network of non-Chinese parents who had adopted children from China who would come to connect to other people to build a community around the art. And there were immigrant parents too with their children. I saw a true integration in our community between the ABCs [American-born Chinese] and the foreign-born. People developed friendships then. It was really a miraculous kind of experience. On the subway people do not interact at a deep level. But when you are engaged in the arts, you interact at a very deep level. It's not a forced reaction, it's a very natural integration, and very cross-generational. People do not easily talk across generations, but in teaching the arts, you encourage a level of interaction beyond language.

Telly Wong, Program Manager with the Explore Chinatown campaign, is a second-generation Chinese American who spent his first several years in Chinatown, then moved with his family to a white neighborhood in Brooklyn, and later attended New York University. Like many second-generation Chinese Americans, he tended to suppress his cultural identity while growing up, with a later reawakening at college. He got exposed to Chinese culture again through exploring vegetarian restaurants in Chinatown. With his new interest in Chinese culture, he began getting part-time jobs and volunteer internships in Chinatown. He saw that there was a lack of cultural facilities for second-generation youth in Chinatown, and set out to create a viable venue in partnership with Mr. Choi, the owner of the Silk Road Cafe at 30 Mott Street. He has created a popular subcultural scene called the Tea Bag Open Mike, every Friday night. They have expanded to music shows on Saturdays and jazz on Monday nights. Telly Wong reflects in an August 2005 interview:

> The original idea was to put together a forum for self-expression among Asian Americans. We started getting artists, performers, spoken word poets and comedians from different walks of life. We are the only weekly entertainment in Chinatown, and all perform in English. Our performers are Black, Latino, Gay, White, and Asian. This is for the youth of the community. They would otherwise be standing around outside smoking cigarettes, in the parks. There are not enough after-school programs for youth to help cultivate them to be leaders that care about the community. Chinatown is a transient community, with people coming in and out, rather than being stable with several generations of people living here that feel some kind of ownership in the area. Without that, the community is weak, does not have roots. What we do is very participatory; we get the audience involved. Anyone can be on stage. I hope that we are building bridges in audiences.

Planning a Chinatown Cultural Center

While heritage and arts organizations work to forge a lively cultural scene bridging generational and urban–suburban divides, there are growing efforts to create a world-class cultural and performing arts center in Chinatown. The idea has been floating around for years, but re-emerged through focus group discussion in the RCI-organized community workshops. City Councilperson Alan Gerson gave major support to the cultural affairs strategy and his director of constituent concerns, Tammy To, served as first president of the Committee to Revitalize and Enrich the Arts in Tomorrow's Economy in Chinatown (CREATE). A member of CREATE, Amy Chin wrote in a December 2004 issue of *Downtown Express*:

> Few will dispute New York's standing as an arts capital. Recognizing the vital role of the arts in enlivening surrounding neighborhoods and spurring economic growth, planners charged with re-envisioning the World Trade Center site incorporated a major complex of cultural spaces in the master plan. In downtown Brooklyn, the creation of cultural spaces is a cornerstone of the neighborhood's revitalization strategy. Chinatown needs to be part of this "cultural revolution" and the Lower Manhattan Development Corporation's recent funding of a feasibility study is an important first step in this direction.

Amy Chin eventually assumed the role of acting director at the Chinatown Partnership LDC, until the hiring of a permanent executive director, and did much to obtain funding and advance feasibility studies for a cultural center.

John Leo of the Lower Manhattan Development Corporation also gives his support to the cultural center initiative:

> At stake is the image of Asian Americans. We want to promote the cultural richness of Asian Americans, not the cheap stuff we sell in the streets. We have so many arts and culture in Chinatown and no place to showcase the talent. I think that cultural richness

can link with economic development . . . The cultural center could be the glue that holds the community together. When the Chinese opera performs, they are always sold out. We don't have much to offer in cultural entertainment in Chinatown. We have DVDs from Hong Kong, but there is no central gathering place in Chinatown.

Tom Healy, president of the Lower Manhattan Cultural Council, is an ardent supporter of a new cultural center in Chinatown:

If there is an international hub, if there is a way that Lower Manhattan is a site into which people come, where there are arts groups based, then Chinatown could do this as well. Where there are international Chinese artists, or Chinese American artists from other cities, they would come to New York to perform, if there are venues and opportunities for them to come through China-town. Right now there are none: no theaters, no auditoria, those sorts of things that create a cultural community. How would you draw back the people from throughout the tri-state area? If they were never going to live in Chinatown again, if they would say, let's go in on a Sunday, why not go around to the restaurants and food markets and maybe see some cultural activities. Right now a Chinese film festival might happen at Lincoln Center instead. The Japanese American community in Los Angeles does have a thriving cultural center right in the middle of the city and it becomes an important cultural gathering center for the Japanese community even if they don't live there.

Tourism, Authenticity, and Cultural Ownership

While the cultural heritage and arts sector works to bridge generational and cultural differences in the Chinese American community, the presentation of ethnic culture for tourism and consumption by outsiders also raises fundamental issues of authenticity and cultural ownership. Tourism initiatives have been a major focus in rebuilding efforts in New York's Chinatown, but tourism is not a panacea, and many community stakeholders express caution or outright skepticism about the potential impact of these efforts on the cultural life of Chinatown. At stake are such issues as authenticity and ownership. Frank Lang, director of planning and development at AAFE, warns that the cultural integrity of the people of Chinatown is at risk:

> I think the mandate coming out of the Rebuild Chinatown Initiative discussions was mainly tourism, and I think we need to respond effectively to move it forward from here. The reason why AAFE is involved is to try to temper it and make sure the effort does not "Orientalize" Chinatown and not sell off the authenticity of the culture and the people at heart. For the community-based arts organizations participating in CREATE, the situation here is that they come into the process with certain expectations about working with government. The challenge is to bring competing and disjointed interests and ideas into focus. There could be one cultural center built, or multiple centers. The Tenement Museum has created a cultural coalition of organizations in the Lower East Side area, but could benefit from more local partners. I think that some CREATE members have spoken of having two different clusters, one around the Tenement Museum and another around MoCA.

Charlie Lai of the Museum of the Chinese in the Americas comments about tourism in Chinatown:

> As someone who grew up in Chinatown I hated tourists who come into my community, looking at the ducks hanging in windows and blocking streets. They often don't spend much money and carry away a more affirmed stereotype of Chinatown. This was my impression in the early days . . . Over time I think we have moved from dependency to self-sufficiency, and can document the history ourselves. There is more room for education and I no longer frown upon tourists, but seek to educate the media at large as well as the Chinese media . . . The Chinatown press and New York

media come to MoCA for clarity on the historical past as well as a more accurate portrayal of what we are as Chinese Americans ... Readers outside of Chinatown now have a new curiosity about Chinatown, not about the stereotypes, but want to learn about the reality ... Tourists come with less tainted lenses and we benefit from that, the museum and the community. We see ourselves as having a very pivotal role in marketing Chinatown, in correcting the guidebooks that look at the Chinatown gangs or the Buddhist temples. That's not what people should be coming for. There is a lot more the community can offer, and in that sense we are serving as a cultural anchor in the tourism trade ... as a museum we have a responsibility not to sell stereotypes, and we believe that we have other cultural assets that are in the long term much more beneficial to all of us.

Charlie Lai articulates the sense of tourism as a double-edged sword, an economic tool that generates pitfalls and promises. A preponderance of the tourist traffic coming to New York's Chinatown is drawn to the low-cost bazaar of budget merchandise such as sunglasses, t-shirts, hats, purses, ties, jewelry, and electronic goods. As discussed earlier, especially popular are discount counterfeit knockoffs of coveted designer goods, such as Prada or Dolce and Gabbana handbags.[5] On any given day, Canal Street is swollen with throngs of tourists in search of bargains. These tourists are also drawn to gawk at the barbecued ducks and suckling pigs hanging in the windows of many noodle-houses and restaurants, as well as the groceries, curio shops, and martial arts stores on nearby streets. These tourists may generate revenues for the retailers of Chinatown, but often depart with an ingrained perception of Chinatown as a place of cheap amusements and a pervasive underground economy.

Thomas Yu, Project Manager at AAFE, doubts that tourism can generate jobs that realize the human potential of Chinatown's workers, pay a truly living wage, and provide opportunities for social mobility:

Our concern at AAFE is that if you boost tourism, make sure that the residents benefit from the upswing and beautify streets

without displacing low-income residents. There has to be balance
... you need capital coming from the outside in tourism. But
what happens to the women workers in the garment shops, what
happens to them in a tourism-based economy? We need to
continue to make productive use of their labor value. We say that
you still need manufacturing employment and have proximity to
Soho and warehouse loft space. There has been discussion of a
vertical incubator within a loft manufacturing building. The
French Culinary Institute approached AAFE about using their
building, and AAFE responded by asking what about offering
hospitality training for waiters, and English-speaking skills?
Chinatown needs to evolve from beyond the "corner takeout"
kind of restaurant to businesses that guarantee better wages for
more advanced skills. I think that job training and education are
of key importance to economic growth in Chinatown . . . Tourism
is a stopgap. Chinatown will shrink unless we can really redefine
our job base to attract the next generation to come back. Or
Chinatown will become instead like an old "hull" of a neighborhood, like a touristic leftover. We are still vibrant here, with an
authenticity of cultures.

Despite many apprehensions and varying levels of support, the nonprofit
community stakeholders that I interviewed in New York's Chinatown
were generally committed to the outcome of the RCI community-
planning process in which tourism and marketing played a leading role
among a range of other economic, residential, and community development arenas. They expressed support for the Explore Chinatown
marketing campaign as well as the Chinatown Partnership Local
Development Corporation. They discussed how both RCI and the
Chinatown Partnership LDC were supported by a wide diversity of
community stakeholders as well as actively endorsed by AAFE, one of
Chinatown's most influential nonprofit stakeholders. They addressed
how tourism and culture-based initiatives could bring suburban and
latter-generation Chinese American interest back to the recovery effort
at the core.

Preservation of Affordable Housing

The locational dispersal from the core to the periphery has confronted AAFE in its efforts to rehabilitate and build affordable housing for the Asian American community. Over the last 30 years, AAFE has rehabilitated or constructed 35 buildings and now manages some 400 units of low-income housing, mainly in the Lower East Side, where Chinese immigrants have sought housing outside of the traditional Chinatown neighborhood. In the 1970s and 1980s, a large inventory of "in-rem" housing abandoned by tax-delinquent landlords had accumulated in the Lower East Side and other neighborhoods and come under the ownership of the City of New York. AAFE moved to take advantage of City interest in developing these properties for affordable housing. It began its work with the 60-unit Equality Houses at 176 and 180 Eldridge Street, two blocks from a site of a building fire that killed two people and displaced 125 residents. The Equality Houses were the first New York City housing project to take advantage of the U.S. Low-Income Housing Tax Credit, which provides a write-off of about 90 percent of the construction costs for investors that provide financing to develop housing for families with incomes 60 percent below the median income in a given metropolitan area. In a *New York Times* article, Bill Frey, senior vice president of the Enterprise Foundation, which acted as syndicator on the project, called Equality Houses the breakthrough project that provided the model for affordable housing development with 85 other nonprofits throughout the City of New York, ultimately leading to the creation of about 13,000 units.[6]

AAFE is the major CDC in New York City that focuses primarily on housing for the Asian American community. As such AAFE is ethnic-based versus place-based, since it serves and manages housing for Asian Americans outside of Chinatown in the Lower East Side (LES) as well as in outer-borough locations. AAFE operates an office in the outer-borough Chinatown of Flushing, Queens. Director of Planning and Development, Frank Lang, reflects on the growth of the nonplace-based CDCs in other cities:

> In other parts of the country the paradigm is the place-based CDC. In many places that is still appropriate but as the population of a

neighborhood changes the CDC doesn't necessarily evolve along with the population . . . You have groups like New Economics for Women, Los Angeles, which started in one neighborhood but is now L.A.-wide dealing with the problems of Latina women and children. Little Tokyo Services Center works with Japanese Americans throughout the L.A. metropolitan area. The dynamic is that we are neighborhood-based, but we are pushing and educating our funders to understand that community development corporations address the "community" and the immigrant community is not necessarily only in one place . . . AAFE was never only in Chinatown, and always addressed the broader context, even if most Chinese Americans were in Chinatown in 1974. Now 30 years later, Chinatown is not the center for the Asian American community because they are in every borough. After several years of advocacy, we started created housing because we found there were abandoned buildings in neighboring areas like the LES. And the groups rehabilitating housing in these areas were essentially excluding the Chinese because they were not targeting those residents with Chinese language materials, etc. And every group in the affordable housing arena must legally meet federal equal access guidelines. And then we decided why couldn't we create community-controlled assets rather than letting those assets be controlled and determined by others?

The AAFE strategy of ethnic-based versus place-based community development addresses the challenges of working with a Chinese American population that is increasingly spatially dispersed across the New York metropolitan area. AAFE addresses the rights of Chinese immigrants to equal access housing by meeting their special language needs. As such, the AAFE strategy represents a fusing of identity politics and community politics applied to the mission of community development in a low-income community. It adapts to the vagaries of a population that is increasingly geographically dispersed, a community without propinquity.

The construction and rehabilitation of affordable housing in Chinatown and the Lower East Side are also integral to creating a stable residential environment in the face of mounting gentrification. A real estate bust in the 1980s, followed by an investment and construction boom in the 1990s, has spread the gentrification process from the East Village into Alphabet City and the Lower East Side where AAFE currently operates.

Conclusion

This chapter sheds light on the linkages between architectural preservation of tenement buildings and cultural preservation of immigrant heritage in New York's Chinatown and the Lower East Side. The Museum of the Chinese in the Americas and the Tenement Museum have established a "power of place" for the legacy of working-class immigrants, women and children in the annals of American history. These contemporary museums give more poignancy and social agency to the subaltern subjects of U.S. history than the stark images of the "huddled masses" presented by photojournalist Jacob Riis and other social reformers at the turn of the twentieth century. They are the creation of a new leadership in ethnic communities and historical circles that have helped transform the fields of preservation, museum work, and public history in America. Their exhibitions, walking tours, and cultural events are opportunities for educational outreach to children, families, and senior citizens in the communities they work in as well as tourists. They promote social tolerance through anti-racist dialogues, coalition work in the local community, and international networking among social justice organizations. As they have grown, the museums have continued to evolve their goals in order to adapt to the changing interests of the community.

While Chinese will continue to disperse throughout the greater New York City metropolitan area and outer-lying suburban locations, the core Chinatown retains its importance as a place of symbolic and spiritual attachment, of visits to church or temple, visits to restaurants for rites of passage and reunions, and festival celebrations of seasonal holidays. The core Chinatown retains its significance across the spatial as well as the temporal dimension. Chinatown is a focus for collective sentiment, despite the presence of numerous linguistic, sub-ethnic, generational, and socioeconomic class differences within the Chinese American population. The power of collective sentiment is of immense utility to any city or community recovering from war, disaster, decline, or dislocation. Collective sentiment can be mobilized in the service of community development.

The work of community-based organizations such as AAFE in political advocacy and affordable housing rehabilitation suggests a new paradigm of community development that is ethnic-based as much as it is place-based. Extending the stock of affordable housing in Chinatown and the Lower East Side through tenement preservation has brought some residential stability to the low-income community of Chinese Americans. An affordable housing strategy is place-based insofar as it preserves the residential integrity of low-income minority neighborhoods. But AAFE is very ethnic-based in the way it has adjusted to the geographic dispersal of Chinese by establishing offices in satellite Chinatowns such as Flushing, Queens and taking applications for their housing projects from residents throughout the metropolitan region. In the area of political advocacy, AAFE maintains a dedication to identity-based political issues confronting the Asian American community, such as anti-Chinese violence, bilingual balloting

Figure 7.5 Morning Chinese fan dance exercises in Columbus Park. Photo by Jan Lin.

and voter education, and discrimination in the workplace, housing markets, as well as government procurement and contracting.

In the wake of the 9/11 disaster, boosting tourism in Chinatown has become a focus of economic recovery efforts with the launching of the Explore Chinatown campaign and the Chinatown Partnership Local Development Corporation. While tourism campaigns boost the opportunities for cultural heritage organizations working in Chinatown and the Lower East Side, the participation of the corporate and governmental establishment has also brought qualities of commercial "branding" and "bureaucratic rationality" as symbolized through the erection of the Chinatown tourist kiosk. The growing use of public–private partnership and the touristic commercialization of culture is a portent of McDonaldization and Disneyfication of Chinatown, but community stakeholders like the Museum of the Chinese in the Americas and the Tenement Museum have greater power to present a cultural heritage that is authentic, heterogeneous, diverse, and dynamically evolving rather than formulaic, standardized, or homogenized. Explore Chinatown is not a corporate-produced global monoculture, but a locally sourced global culture.

Community stakeholders hope also to boost cultural solidarity and place attachment through the construction of a world-class performing arts center in Chinatown that can bridge generational and subcultural factions in the Chinese American community as well as attracting suburban audiences back to the city. A Chinatown cultural center can attract local as well as global artists to help make the past invigorate the present and create a fresh and evolving cultural heritage that appeals to the younger generations and helps to imagine the future of the Chinese American community. Cultural heritage and arts organizations can help to promote community development in a Chinatown suffering economic and social dislocation in the wake of the 9/11 disaster. They help our communities to recover from historical as well as contemporary trauma.

8

THE DEATH AND LIFE OF
URBAN ETHNIC PLACES

Ethnic heritage places are increasingly visible in U.S. cities through the founding of ethnic history museums, the restoration of historic buildings, the preservation and creation of other sites and monuments of cultural distinctness. They can be found in a variety of urban ethnic neighborhoods, including Chinatown, Little Havana, and African American districts. Some sites like Manhattan's Lower East Side Tenement Museum explore a succession of ethnic groups through a historic portal of immigration. Some people may criticize these ethnic places as subculturally clannish, socially fragmenting, and a challenge to our larger collective sense of national heritage. My book seeks to convince critics that the growth of ethnic heritage sites represents a multicultural retooling as opposed to a culture war against the nation state that offers opportunities for boosting education, the arts, local economic development, and community life. The sense of economic and cultural retooling is associated with the tendency for ethnic heritage preservation to be linked with tourism and the livelihood of ethnic enclaves and small business sectors in our immigration gateway cities. The growth of ethnic enclaves has helped to counterbalance much of the urban decline in the postfordist city that resulted from the outmovement of jobs and people to the suburbs, and deindustrialization caused by corporate global sourcing of manufacturing to offshore

244 THE DEATH AND LIFE OF URBAN ETHNIC PLACES

production sites. Ethnic enclaves and cultural heritage places can be harnessed as tools for neighborhood preservation. They offer a roadmap for local economic development.

The preservation of ethnic heritage and restoration of disinvested urban neighborhoods by ethnic enclaves in the current era presents a stark contrast to earlier historical episodes of slum clearance and removal of racial–ethnic minority communities when ethnic culture was devalued by our society. My critique of urban renewal as racial–ethnic removal draws much from the spirit of Jane Jacobs, the tenacious community activist and urbanist author who in the 1950s and 1960s spearheaded the defense of Greenwich Village and Washington Square Park from the bulldozers of New York City's master planning czar Robert Moses and his planned Lower Manhattan Expressway. She also railed against the social destructiveness and blunt design ethos of modernistic urban renewal as an editor of *Architectural Forum*. In her landmark book *The Death and Life of Great American Cities* (1961), she champions the vitality of urban street life and the importance of preserving dense, small-scale, walkable neighborhoods rather than the modernistic housing towers, freeways, and suburban tract housing that were favored in the postwar era. She looked behind the messiness and apparent social disorder of urban neighborhoods often labeled slums to reveal that there were eyes on the street and community networks that promoted social intimacy and public safety. She sought to liberate and empower the natural organs of local self-government, anticipating the community organizing and urban social movements of the 1960s and 1970s. Her counter-modernism and celebration of mixed-use neighborhoods presaged the neotraditional design and planning movement known as New Urbanism.[1]

Many white lower- and middle-class communities were able to organize local social movements against the master planners, public officials, and redevelopment authorities that were condemning and clearing their neighborhoods in the postwar era. Some racial–ethnic minority communities were acquiring increasing political power through the civil rights movement, but many still lacked the organization and the clout to challenge the local political establishment successfully, and their neighborhoods were often demolished and depopulated. Jacobs' indictment of (fordist) modernist urban renewal has great relevance to the new cadre of racial–ethnic minority and feminist preservationists and community activists who are now working to rehabilitate and culturally restore neighborhoods destroyed by urban removal and disinvestment. These new minority, ethnic, and subcultural actors are bringing new life to American cities where fordist modernism had earlier brought death in the form of disinvestment and decay. It is these new generations of architects, historians, artists, educators, community activists, business owners, and political leaders that represent the power of ethnic places in U.S. cities in the twenty-first century. They are the same voices that spoke in Chapter 1 that were in the Los Angeles Chinatown Oral History Project. Through their neighborhood-based efforts to preserve ethnic cultural heritage, they have created new sentimental focal sites for community memory and collective imagination that also form an emerging toolkit for local economic and community development.

The Political Economy of the Cases

I make a summary comparison and contrast of the cases through an exploration of the urban political economy. Table 8.1 compares the cases by urban history. In my case studies I have found a distinct contrast between urban dynamics of disinvestment in black communities and reinvestment in Asian and Latin American immigrant enclaves. The African American interests of Houston and Miami endured more destructive historical legacies of racial removal connected with urban renewal and freeway construction that left their original neighborhoods depopulated, disinvested, and plagued by vacant properties and vacant lots. Historic preservation and community development campaigns in Houston's Fourth Ward and Miami's Overtown have been huge obstacles to overcome when compared with efforts in New York and Los Angeles Chinatowns and Miami's Little Havana, which were not as dramatically impacted by slum clearance and urban disinvestment. There are fewer historical buildings to save and fewer people populating the most devastated and socially isolated black ghettos, and it is harder to attract governmental and nonprofit funders, corporate investors, and ethnic residents and small business owners to campaigns of preservation and community revitalization. New flows of Asian and Latin American immigration, by contrast, invigorate older immigrant enclaves or create new ethnic enclaves with new stocks of labor and capital.

While I generally identify ethnic enclaves as connected to patterns of neighborhood reinvestment, I recognize that immigrant entrepreneurs and workers typically occupy lower-rent districts of the city that have filtered down from the previous small-business and residential population that joined the outward movement of jobs and people to the suburbs. They often proliferate in the areas surrounding the central business district identified by the Chicago School of Sociology as the "zone-in-transition." Immigrant entrepreneurs find opportunity in the wake of urban decline, and their efforts to revalorize urban commercial zones and neighborhoods are still challenged by ongoing trends of decentralization to the outer city. Reinvestment takes place in the urban zone-in-transition in the wake of earlier disinvestment, but the disinvestment in ethnic enclaves was not as marked as in many racial–ethnic ghettos. African Americans suffered some of the greatest degree of disinvestment through forced removal during the decades of urban renewal policy. Urban renewal was sometimes dubbed "Negro removal." The heart of the black community in Miami's Overtown was divided by the "concrete monster" of Interstate I-95, which stoked disinvestment, absentee ownership, and the growth of vacant lots. Mexican Americans similarly endured urban renewal as "Chicano removal" from their downtown neighborhoods. A tragic episode in Chicano history in Chavez Ravine, Los Angeles, is popularly memorialized as the "Division of the Barrios" by leading mural artist Judith Baca. Mexican American neighborhoods in downtown San Diego experienced a similar fate (Villa 2000).

Ethnic enclaves are also confronted by deflected investment to other metropolitan and suburban locations. Deflected immigration is a phenomenon affecting many larger immigration gateways in the first decade of the twenty-first century such as Los Angeles with the growth of tight housing markets and declining labor markets (Light 2006), exacerbated by the sharp economic downturn at the end of the decade. The recent incidence of immigrant deflection to outer-borough

Table 8.1 Cases Compared by Urban History

Disinvestment (Ghetto)	Reinvestment (Ethnic Enclave)
Miami Overtown (African American)	New York Chinatown and Lower East Side
Houston Fourth Ward (African American)	Miami Little Havana
	Houston Third Ward (African American), East End (Mexican American), and Chinatown
	Los Angeles Chinatown

Chinatowns and other regional Chinatowns has been noticeable in New York's Chinatown, which experienced economic and cultural trauma in the wake of the 9/11 disaster. Deflected immigration also affects Los Angeles Chinatown, which has been largely superseded since the 1970s by the emergence of an expansive commercial and residential Chinese ethnoburb in Monterey Park and adjoining cities of the San Gabriel Valley (Li 2009). The downtown Los Angeles Chinatown made up for this attrition by attracting a flow of Southeast Asian immigrant labor and capital in the wake of the Vietnam War, which since the 1970s shares the downtown space with the older Cantonese community. Houston's Chinatown and Mexican American East End contend with declining interest in their downtown area neighborhoods with the continuing expansion of new immigrants into newer suburban areas in the northern and western reaches of the metropolitan area. Miami's Little Havana works to attract the interest of Cubans that are resettled in the suburbs.

The distinction between black ghetto and ethnic enclave should not be seen as a sharp divide but more a continuum where there are intermediary cases such as Houston's Third Ward, which is a reinvesting African American neighborhood that historically absorbed displaced blacks from the Fourth Ward. There are strong educational institutions in the Third Ward like the University of Houston and Texas Southern University, and the growth of a strong preservation and community development movement around Project Row Houses that helps to promote neighborhood stability. Project Row Houses has helped to stimulate a "back-to-the-city" movement by making it fashionable to rehabilitate vernacular design row housing in Houston and create a hip and chic focal point for the arts, civic volunteerism, and charitable giving among suburban middle-class blacks.

Table 8.2 classifies my case studies through the political perspective of community power structure. I offer three different paradigms of local community power structure around three different types of stakeholder partnership. One set of cases clusters around the paradigm of "private–public partnership" which I dub the "ethnic growth machine" because it emulates the larger urban "growth machine" (Logan and Molotch 1987) that grows from the nexus of corporate, developer, and governmental interests that boosts the process of urban development and redevelopment after decline. The Houston Chinatown Council, Houston East End Chamber of Commerce (Mexican American) and the Los Angeles Chinatown Business Council all represent coalitions of ethnic business leaders and place entrepreneurs that work closely with public governmental and redevelopment agency interests to promote local growth, especially through linking with tourism and convention interests. Los Angeles Chinatown Business Council operates one of the pioneering BIDs in Los Angeles, a common tool in other U.S. urban redevelopmental districts. A white developer, Kim Benjamin, leads the Los Angeles BID, working in coalition with Chinese American leaders and place entrepreneurs, while the seafood merchant turned developer Dan Nip has led the Houston Chinatown Council for decades. Nonprofit community stakeholders are not well connected in these growth coalitions that are more interested in spurring new tourists, new investment, and redevelopmental gentrification than nonprofit causes of heritage preservation and community development.

A second cluster of cases exhibit characteristics of nonprofit–public partnership as the paradigm of community power structure. A nonprofit community development organization, the Asian Americans for Equality, leads the Rebuild Chinatown Initiative, an economic recovery effort in New York's Chinatown in the wake of the 9/11 disaster. It has worked closely with an array of public agencies and quasi-public authorities to rebuild New York's Chinatown without losing sight of

Table 8.2 Cases Compared by Community Power Structure

Private–Public Partnership (Ethnic Growth Machine)	Nonprofit–Public Partnership	Nonprofit–Private Partnership
Houston Chinatown	New York Chinatown and Lower East Side	Miami Overtown (African American)
Houston East End (Mexican American)	New York Chinatown and Lower East Side	
Los Angeles Chinatown	Miami Little Havana	
	Houston Third Ward and Fourth Ward (African American)	

social priorities such as preserving affordable housing, workforce development, parks, and community development. The AAFE-led coalition has condoned the use of new economic development tools, such as a landmark tourist kiosk, a slick Explore Chinatown marketing campaign, a new Chinatown Partnership Local Development Corporation, as well as a Chinatown BID in its efforts. Nonprofit stakeholders include CREATE, a group that hopes to leverage new investment towards the creation of a world-class cultural center in New York's Chinatown. The Tenement Museum of the Lower East Side has furthermore worked with the public governmental and nonprofit foundation sector to promote heritage tourism while leading a local coalition in neighborhood preservation, and an international network of museums working for social tolerance.

In Miami's Little Havana, nonprofit stakeholders such as the Kiwanis Club and the Latin Quarter Cultural Center have worked closely with the Miami Planning Department for over two decades in a nonprofit–public partnership that began with the preservation of the historic Tower Theater. The City of Miami Office of Cultural Affairs now regularly works with the Latin Quarter Cultural Center to produce and manage open-air art showings and musical events, including the weekly Viernes Culturales (Cultural Fridays) and the annual Calle Ocho festival/Miami Carnival mega-event. Miami-Dade College brings an educational linkage in programming lectures, classes, and symposia at the Tower Theater. Houston's black Third and Fourth Wards also represent partnerships of nonprofit stakeholders doing heritage preservation and arts promotion in the service of community development.

I put Miami's Overtown in a category of its own as a nonprofit–private partnership. The nonprofit Black Archives, with the Local Initiatives Support Corporation, has the support of an array of church-based community development corporations. They work in a partnership with the quasi-public–private Knight Foundation/Collins Center, which seeks to broker the entrance of a larger developer, Crosswinds, for a mixed-income residential condominium mega-project that is clearly more entrepreneurial than nonprofit. While many in the community are apprehensive about gentrification, there is also the long-simmering belief that action needs to take place in a community hurt by disinvestment. The stakes are high in this more volatile partnership that has been through two decades of negotiation in which public officials and the Miami Community Redevelopment Agency have played an intermediary brokering role and the New Urbanist planners, Duany Plater-Zyberk, have worked to compromise the high-rise residential towers with preservational design aesthetics.

I believe the nonprofit–public partnership is the most productive paradigm for heritage preservation and community development, where nonprofit community development corporations play the leading role rather than place entrepreneurs, who are more interested in rapid returns on investment through redevelopmental change and gentrification, versus one premised more on preservation of affordable housing and community development priorities.

Model Projects and Best Practices

I identify some demonstration projects and best practices that came through my studies of ethnic heritage preservation in U.S. cities. These model projects and strategies can be of particular interest to the architectural design and urban planning sector, public officials, and community development interests. Ethnic cultural heritage interests can form productive partnerships with the arts and educational sector.

Ethnic and Vernacular Heritage Museums

The Tenement Museum of the Lower East Side and Project Row Houses in the Third Ward of Houston both stood out as model projects in the way they architecturally rehabilitated and culturally redeemed vernacular building types, residential tenements, and row houses that had previously drawn public outrage and stigmatization as slums and harbingers of residential overcrowding, vice, and immorality. These projects have joined historic preservation work with contemporary story telling in converting residential buildings to exhibitionary museums and gallery spaces. The Tenement Museum brings history to life through educational dialogue with students and visiting tourists. It has established an international network of museums working to increase social tolerance through its International Coalition of Sites of Conscience program. Project Row Houses rehabilitates "shotgun shacks" into artistic incubators that make artists think more deeply about social issues, as well as giving poor families new hope in transitional housing through the Young Mother's Residential Program.

Historic Theaters

A best practice emerging from the Miami case studies is the preserving of historical landmark theaters, including the Tower Theater in Little Havana and the Lyric Theater in Overtown. Saving and rehabilitating these theaters were initial focal campaigns in both neighborhoods that became anchors for broader strategies to establish ethnic cultural districts. The Tower Theater was well known among local Cuban Americans through nostalgic memories of Americanization, as the place where the exile and immigrant community was first introduced to English-language American films. The Lyric Theater of Overtown recalls an earlier heyday of economic affluence in the African American community when the lively entertainment district of "Little Broadway" showcased nationally prominent black performers to audiences throughout the South.

Streets, Sidewalks and Street Festivals

Street and sidewalk improvements with artistic and ethno-historical designs are significant features of some of my case studies. Two cases in African American neighborhoods involve preservation or renovation of artistic street intersections using African-origin symbols. Preservationists in Houston's Fourth Ward are working to rehabilitate Andrews Street with a cross-point brick pattern laid originally according to the BaKongo religion of West Africa. In Miami's Overtown, a new sidewalk was created altogether at the 9th Street pedestrian mall with brick inlay in multicolored African kente design. In Los Angeles' Little Tokyo, an artistic sidewalk lines the shop fronts of 1st Street with symbols to evoke the neighborhood's historical experience of Japanese forced relocation and internment. In Miami's Little Havana, the Calle Ocho (Latin Quarter) Walk of Fame invites pedestrians to follow a trail of Latin American stars and performers. The Latin Quarter also has artistic programs and musical street festivals on a monthly and annual basis that further enhance the place identity of the ethnic cultural district. The Chinatowns featured regular street festivals surrounding events like the Chinese New Year and the Autumn Moon Festival.

Churches

Churches are important landmarks for historical preservation as well as being a focus for community development activities in both the African American Fourth Ward of Houston and the Overtown community of Miami. In Miami's Overtown, there are three historically protected churches. Two of them, the Greater B.A.M.E. Church and St. John Baptist Church, also function in affordable housing development, workforce training, and other community development areas. These churches attract congregations which are often scattered in the suburbs, back to their ancestral neighborhoods. Followers make weekly pilgrimages to pay their respects. Churches are central foci of preservation and faith-based community development in the black communities to a degree I didn't find comparable in the Chinese American community.

Arts Partnerships

Working with artists is a useful linkage to ethnic preservation and cultural heritage interests. Fine artists, musicians, dancers, and theatrical artists all have a part to play in the interpretation of culture and the sustaining of ethnic heritage in the present and into the future. Miami's Little Havana has been particularly active in forging these arts partnerships. The Tenement Museum, Museum of the Chinese in the Americas, Project Row Houses, and Chinese American Museum of Los Angeles maintain lively relationships with artists in the community.

Educational Partnerships

Partnerships with primary and secondary schools, colleges and universities help to popularize the work of ethnic museums and theaters and sustain their public relevance in an atmosphere of civic engagement. While school children represent a civic audience, college and university students and faculty are important human resources to help conduct oral histories, do archival research, and work as volunteers, interns, and advisory board members. The Tower Theater in Miami's Little Havana contracts with Miami-Dade College to provide educational and cultural programming. The Museum of the Chinese in the Americas, the Tenement Museum, Project Row Houses, and the Chinese Museum of Los Angeles also maintain close ties with local schools.

Ethnic New Urbanism or Ethnic Theme Parks?

The growth of ethnic heritage preservation and the creation of ethnic cultural districts are phenomena that integrate with the urban design and planning movement known as New Urbanism. Duany Plater-Zyberk and Company, Architects and Town Planners, are leaders in the National Congress of the New Urbanism. They are headquartered in Miami's Little Havana and are leading Miami 21, the comprehensive master planning project for the City of Miami. They have been consultants to the Black Archives and its collaborators in Overtown, leading community meetings and a 1998 master planning charrette that created a blueprint endorsed by the Black Archives for a rehabilitated and reconstructed Overtown Folklife Village. The creating of ethnic heritage districts works well with New Urbanist principles of promoting neotraditional and vernacular architectural design elements, pedestrian walkability, green space, and public interaction in a civic environment that promotes local history and culture. Elite landmark neotraditional planned communities associated with New Urbanist design and planning firms have drawn social criticism. Seaside on the Florida Panhandle was caricaturized in Peter Weir's 1998 film *The Truman Show* as a place where the facade of perfect small-town life was revealed to be under the control of reality film programmers. Celebration, built by the Disney Corporation near Orlando, drew sociological criticism, such as from Andrew Ross (2000), who lived in the community for a year.

The sociological critique of the New Urbanist design and planning movement stems from the perception that the creating of a perfect neotraditional small-town community is for all intents and purposes a variation of the contemporary theme park. Attention to these trends of predictability and routinization of social life connects with the critique that George Ritzer ([1993] 2008) makes in applying Max Weber's ([1905] 2003) notion of the "iron cage of rationality" to the phenomenon of McDonald's restaurants. In our fast-food consumption society, he argues, corporate systems have increasingly entrapped us in production assembly lines and bureaucratic management structures for the sake of capitalist profit, technological efficiency, and social control. The critique of rationalization is also implicit in the mass culture critique of American culture promoted by "Frankfurt School" thinkers such as Max Horkheimer and Theodor Adorno ([1947] 2002) who argued that the large mass media companies created films and other cultural products through an assembly-line system of formulaic genres and reproducible themes that stunted artistic creativity and cultural originality.

I make a similar critical interpretation of the erection of a tourist information kiosk in December 2004 in New York's Chinatown in the wake of the 9/11 disaster. The kiosk is a red painted iron cage crowned by a dragon, situated at a crossroads in the confusing warren of arteries and streets that make up Chinatown, a node in the bureaucratic–rational New York City transportation system. New York's Chinatown is a geographically challenging and visually intoxicating bazaar that sprawls over several dozen blocks and can be entered from several subway stations and gateway surface streets. It has no real public center or central subway stop like 42nd Street/Times Square. It works with a

printed and online tourist and marketing campaign, Explore Chinatown, to regularize and standardize the many cultural locations,
shopping opportunities, and culinary offerings of New York's Chinatown on maps, calendars, and coupon books for popular tourism and
consumption.

The iron cage operating in New York's Chinatown imposes a
different cultural effect than the iron cage of McDonaldization in our
society. The Chinatown tourist kiosk and marketing campaign have
adjusted the bureaucratic system of rationalization to the dynamics of
a postfordist, more globally integrated U.S. marketplace marked by the
growing power of diversified ethnic, subcultural, and niche markets. This
contrasts to the mass marketplace that was the emphasis of American
corporate and governmental life in the postwar era. Subcultural and
ethnic marketing strategies signal a change in the way urban capitalism
works in an era of "globalization," where local culture is a factor rather
than a hindrance to modernization, as compared with the fordist
modernist period after World War II, when assimilation was the
prevailing practice for creating a nationally integrated mass society. This
reiterates my discussion in Chapter 2 concerning the intertwining of
global and local processes and the phenomenon of "glocalization" in
business practices. New Urbanism, it can be said, similarly integrates
neotraditional, vernacular, local cultural and heritage elements into
architectural design and planning practice, thus promoting "localization" as an integrated process of comprehensive master planning in the
cosmopolitan "world city."

New Urbanism can be linked to the legacy of Jane Jacobs and her
defending of neighborhood integrity and street life vitality from the
threat of modernist urban renewal. New Urbanism carries many
principles of counter-modernism in its faithfulness to principles of
neotraditional and vernacular design, local heritage and culture. I
comprehend New Urbanism not as a perfect antidote to the capitalist
city, but as a socially aware design and planning movement to make
cities more livable within a capitalist society. In its best ambitions, New
Urbanism is a socially progressive trend in urban planning that opposes
the techno-bureaucratic rationalism of modernist urban renewal and

suburban sprawl, to promote more mixed-use "smart growth," a more "livable" city that celebrates communal life in neighborhood and public spaces, and the preservation of heritage and the natural environment. It has also earned adherents among advocates of preservation and community-based planning such as in Miami's Overtown. New Urbanism is also gaining traction for environmentally sensitive planning through promoting urban greening and use of sustainable building materials.

While DPZ and other firms in the New Urbanist movement have earned social credibility for creating a progressive planning movement, they are also for-profit tools of corporate capitalism and the governmental establishment. This idea of working within capitalism to create a more livable city similarly confronts ethnic heritage preservation and community development interests when they cooperate with tourist promotion strategies that open their communities to popular consumption. As I discussed above, nonprofit partnership with the public sector such as seen in Miami's Little Havana helps control the scale and pace of urban revitalization. Private–public partnerships such as in Los Angeles Chinatown, where place entrepreneurs are leaders in partnership with government, by contrast, promote more of a process of gentrification and redevelopment. The low-income residents and small businesses that are the foundation of economic and social life in the ethnic neighborhood are threatened by displacement by higher-income residents and corporate business interests.

Authenticity and Folk Revival

I turn finally to the question of cultural authenticity. The anthropologist Dean MacCannell ([1976] 1989) gives some insights on the effects of the spread of tourism through the concept of "staged authenticity." He borrows the sociologist Erving Goffman's concept of life as a theater of symbolic interactions, and the differentiation between "front stages" and "back stages." He sees tourist attractions as "stage sets" that protect tourees, the subjects of tourism, from the intrusions of tourists. They are "back regions" that become "front regions" in order to stimulate and satisfy the tourist's interest in getting "behind the scenes" to experience the aura of the authentic. Ethnic tourist places are different from the traditional back stages of our society that are generally regarded as the spaces of authentic ethnic identity. They are instead, in MacCannell's terms, like "staged back regions" or living museums of cultural performance ([1976] 1989: 99). The phenomenon of the educational guided tour of the urban ethnic communities such as Chinatown, Little Italy, or Little Haiti creates a new kind of social space for outsiders, who are given access into the internal operation of an ethnic community. These spaces reproduce for the touristic outsider a sense of discovery, intimacy, and a sense of reattachment with what Ferdinand Tonnies called the "gemeinschaft" or "folk society" that people have lost with participation in the "gesellschaft" of the urbanized world. They expand the indeterminate space between the "traditional" and the "modern," giving us a more complex understanding of the dynamics of social change and disrupting the traditional notion of a dichotomous continuum between the folk society and the modern society.

The "staged authenticity" of ethnic tourism includes practices of restoration, preservation, and performance by ethnic actors in urban spaces like exhibitionary villages or theme parks, composed of ethnic history museums, monuments, and other historical sites, arts and cultural centers, as well as restaurants and retail marketplaces. Ethnic tourism exists for the benefit of ethnic insiders as well as touristic outsiders. Successful ethnic tourism and heritage preservation rely upon the efforts of a generative cluster of ethnic community leaders, business entrepreneurs, and institutional stakeholders, including artists, historians, museum curators, restaurant owners, tourism promoters, and community-based organizations. The staging of ethnic tourism in U.S. cities promotes greater public consumption of ethnic foods, culture, and heritage for a general cultural audience as well for ethnic audiences. The conversion of the "back regions" of ethnic neighborhoods and business enclaves into staged "front regions" of ethnic tourism involves a valorization of authentic ethnic traditions. At the same time, some of the authenticity of ethnic culture is degraded and denatured, through the commercial aspects of ethnic tourism and the creation of kitsch. The aura of authenticity may be annihilated by the technology of mass production methods and bureaucratic rationality. At the same time, there is an emancipatory potential in ethnic tourism in liberating our society from the hegemony of selective traditions and official history.

The growth of ethnic tourism inserts some interesting new dimensions into the dynamics of the pre-existing structure of racial–ethnic social relationships. The presence of tourists promotes the emergence of local middlemen specifically catering to the tourist market. Tourism can thus accelerate economic development, leading to broader social changes. Tourism can accommodate the acculturation and assimilation of marginal groups into the national society. The rise in ethnic tourism and commerce can also lead to the revival of native cultures or to the invention of new cultures that are not "traditional" or "modern." Tourism can debase and destroy what it touches but tourism can also be a profound stimulus for cultural transformation and renewal. As Pierre van den Berghe has discussed (1994: 17), the staged authenticity of tourism can become the authentic stage of cultural revival. Ethnic tourism is not categorically good or bad but is more complex than generally supposed. In studies of ethnic tourism in the town of San Cristobal in the Chiapas region of Mexico, he found new opportunities created for indigenous peoples, especially the Chamula group, to earn a livelihood in the production and trade of ethnic textiles, arts and crafts, foods, and other cultural goods. The status of women has been transformed as extensive participation in the ethnic tourism trade has boosted their economic independence. As Indian crafts and culture have become increasingly subject to popular consumption, there grew a touristic desire and popular fashion for "authentic" crafts markets, guided tours, and tourist hotels in San Cristobal. As Indians became a marketable commodity, the images of them as uncivilized beasts of burden and peasants made way to a representation of a respected culture and producer of valuable arts and crafts (1994: 143). Indigenous entrepreneurs have made inroads in the market for ethnic tourism, but middlemen, *ladinos* (Mexican nationals) and foreigners, have appropriated much of the revenue from ethnic tourism through their superior access to investment capital, language ability, and education.

Guidebooks like the Australian-origin *Lonely Planet* have fueled the phenomenon of the low-budget "backpacker tourist" who journeys to exotic and inaccessible places such as Chiapas in quest of the real experiences of untouched indigenous societies. Tour companies provide itineraries such as the "Maya circuit" through indigenous communities in a number of different Central American communities. A *National Geographic* article by Garrett and Garrett in 1989, "La Ruta Maya," did much to spread popular interest in this kind of ethnic heritage tourism. This kind of ethnic tourism constitutes the latest wave of capitalist expansion into the last remote peripheries of the capitalist world system, the final remnants of a planet not yet exploited. This ethnic tourism produces the local for export; it provides an arena for the revival of indigenous traditions that were previously suppressed.

The growth of an "ethnic circuit" of cultural and heritage tourism in U.S. cities thus parallels the emergence of a "global circuit" of indigenous cultural heritage sites. The ethnic circuit in American cities is also associated with the phenomenon of folk and vernacular revival that can be seen in the growing popularity of folk music and "folk festivals." Examples of folk festivals include Native American powwows, bluegrass festivals, fiddlers' conventions, and other indigenous, regional, or vernacular celebrations. The living quality of folk music, dancing, ritual practices, and foods can become canonized through repetition. Folkloric troupes often operate in the middle ground between the exotic and the familiar. Ethnic performances offer cultural content for ethnic identity. Explorations of past traditions and ethnic heritage lay a foundation for a "folklore" that is fundamental to the politics of culture. The preservation of cultural traditions and heritage by ethnic history museums and folkloric troupes helps bolster claims to cultural legitimacy.

Folk festivals epitomize some of the characteristics of "staged authenticity" insofar as the back stages of a vernacular oral culture normally transmitted only by face-to-face interaction between insiders in certain traditional contexts are now performed and displayed on the front stages of urban public life for the benefit of outsiders. These front stages include urban ethnic tourist enclaves as well as state and regional folklife festivals, such as the first National Folk Festival organized by

Sarah Gertrude Knott in St. Louis in 1934, which incorporated performances by Native Americans, African Americans, Appalachian musicians, cowboys, Mexican Americans, Sacred Harp singers, and costumed dancers of different ethnic origins. During the early years, folk festivals championed the culture of working peoples as a way of questioning the status quo, during the political unrest and economic dislocation of the Depression. The national venue for display and performance of American folk life has become regularized as the Smithsonian Festival of American Folklife, which has been held annually on the mall in Washington, D.C. since 1967.

The question of authenticity becomes of vital concern to heritage and festival curators who must distinguish between "authentic" folk artists who are cultural insiders, and outside artists who are involved with the revival of authentic folk art. This tension was for instance expressed at the Newport Folk Festival in the 1950s and 1960s, when traditional folk musicians shared the stage with popular folksong revivalists, or "folksingers," such as Bob Dylan and Joan Baez, who emulated the work of earlier figures like Woody Guthrie. The mixing of "survival" and "revival" performers joined much of the dignity and depth of the culture of everyday farmers and working people to the spirit of protest and social change (Wilson and Udall 1982: 8). The progressive character of cultural mixing in folk revival contrasts with the general tendency towards commercialization of folk art, where folk icons are converted to touristic kitsch and cheap imitations. Folk icons such as Davy Crockett, Billy the Kid, and Pocahontas have been appropriated for television and Disney Corporation films. Folklife festivals are carefully managed to produce the effect of education rather than entertainment. Heritage is a new mode in cultural production that produces something new in the present with recourse to the past (Kirshenblatt-Gimblett 1998: 149). The organizers and curators of the Smithsonian Folklife Festival are careful to regulate the authenticity of their displays and performances by controlling excessive use of ethnic costume beyond what is typical use in the traditional context.

The Smithsonian Folklife Festival is representative of the great transformation that has occurred at the Smithsonian Institution and other public history museums since the days of international expositions and world's fairs that proliferated around the world during the heyday of Victorian-era imperialism. In the great U.S. expositions of the time, such as the Columbian Exposition of 1893 in Chicago or the Louisiana Purchase Exposition in St. Louis of 1904, foreign "savages" and ethnic cultures were put on display in ethnographic "living villages" that resembled human zoos and exotic carnival sideshows. The Smithsonian Institution was extensively involved in the procuring, loaning, and curating of ethnographic objects and indigenous subjects for display in exhibitions and cultural performances. The people were put on stages of display and performance in "barbaric" states of relative undress or "exotic" environments that emphasized their "foreign" or "Oriental" character. By presenting them as objects of backwardness and "difference," they helped justify larger ideologies and practices of racial hierarchy, national progress, Manifest Destiny, imperialist hegemony and colonization abroad. It presented these dioramic spectacles of disappearing primitives amidst the grandiose environments of triumphant and beautiful Beaux Arts exhibition hall architecture. These exhibitionary spectacles helped to promote the City Beautiful urban planning movement while celebrating the fruits of world empire.

The annual Smithsonian Folklife Festival, by contrast, is a more democratic and socially inclusive exhibition of folk and international culture that is documented and staged by an institution that has been transformed by the social movements of the 1960s and works increasingly to represent the cultures of subaltern minorities. While the Smithsonian Folklife Festival is like a living museum exhibited on the national stage of the National Mall in Washington, D.C., the urban ethnic heritage places I have examined in this book are like local, neighborhood-level living museums. These local ethnic actors have new powers of self-representation, especially in the context of our multicultural global cities. While urban tourism threatens to accommodate the representation and consumption of ethnic culture to the standards of bureaucratic rationality or "Disneyfication," it is up to these ethnic and social historians, curators, artists, and community leaders to create a multicultural heritage that is authentic and legitimate and resists the tendency to formulaic themes and commercial kitsch. They can make history more relevant and sustain interest into the future through outreach and working partnerships with the educational sector, including primary and secondary schools, colleges and universities. They can grow their audience and enlarge the social infrastructure of ethnic culture and heritage through forming relationships with the arts.

The establishing of ethnic cultural heritage places should ideally create opportunities for visitors to explore ethnic self-identity and collective memory, in an atmosphere of civic engagement rather than the atmosphere of cheap amusement and popular entertainment of the theme park or the package tour. People can make cultural pilgrimages to ethnic museums, theaters, and street festivals to connect with their family ancestors and cultural roots. The broader public has an oppor-tunity to learn about ethnic heritage through educational consumption. Civic engagement helps to bridge generational, subcultural, and urban–suburban differences in the community. The nonprofit heritage sector of museums, theaters, and cultural centers promotes trust, volunteerism, and civic engagement in a way similar to churches, which especially in African American neighborhoods are important factors in themselves in heritage preservation and community development. Churches establish a more transcendental kind of collective spirit and community that is evident in weekly congregations and religious pilgrimages to sacred heritage sites. Ethnic heritage places do not possess this kind of sacred importance, but have a similar power to promote the sense of belonging for individuals in the sentimental life of the community.

As an actor in the educational sector who works with the ethnic and social heritage and arts sector, I bear my own responsibility to help create a multicultural heritage that offers a critical view of social history and guards the authenticity of culture from the drift towards pandering to stereotypes and commercialization. Getting students and youth involved in oral history and the public arts helps to make history more relevant to the life of the community. The creation of a multicultural heritage can help to replenish our sense of local and national community in the uncertain economic and social environment of the contemporary global era.

NOTES

Chapter 1

1   See *Driven Out: The Forgotten War Against Chinese Americans* by Jean Pfaelzer (New York: Random House, 2007), the new definitive history of anti-Chinese violence on the West Coast. Earlier work includes *The Indispensable Enemy: Labor and the Anti-Chinese Movement in California* by Alexander Saxton (Berkeley: University of California Press, 1975) and *The Anti-Chinese Movement in California* by Elmer Sandermeyer (University of Illinois Press, 1991).

2   I chart the historical development and contemporary expansion of New York's Chinatown in my first book, *Reconstructing Chinatown: Ethnic Enclave, Global Change*.

3   In 1978, the novelist and folklorist Harold Courlander brought forth a lawsuit alleging that Haley had plagiarized Courlander's historical novel, *The African* [1967] 1993. New York: Henry Holt and Co., which also depicts the capture and transport of a slave from Africa to the U.S. Haley made an out-of-court settlement with Courlander.

4   The Chinatown oral history project report comprises 15 oral histories. Copies are available for consultation at the Chinese Historical Society of Southern California, the Chinese American Museum of Los Angeles, the Chinatown branch of the Los Angeles Public Library, and Occidental College library. Additional copies can be obtained from sociology professor Jan Lin at Occidental College. I directed the project with assistance from Elizabeth Chang. We followed Occidental College Institutional Review Board procedures and all participants signed a consent form for the interviews and the copyright is in the public domain.

5   See William Wei's definitive history, *The Asian American Movement* (Philadelphia: Temple University Press, 1993). The book primarily covers activities in the San Francisco Bay area and New York City. There is less coverage of developments in the Los Angeles area.

6   Suellen Cheng's oral history was conducted by Claudia Castillo and Jason Ellinwood.

7   Ella Yee Quan's oral history was conducted by Kristen Bonilla and Cristina Franco.

8   Munson Kwok's oral history was conducted by Peter Ringold and Amy Unger.

9   Don Toy's oral history was conducted by Philip Arsenis and Colin Englesberg.

10 These archival histories, along with digital art exhibitions, U.S. census and data reports, and other technical reports can be viewed on www.nelanet.org, a community website created by our project, the Northeast Los Angeles Community Outreach Partnership

Center. This webpage was under repair at the time of writing but was intended to be publicly available again shortly.

11 See http://www.sparcmurals.org/sparcone/ for documentation, galleries, and contact information about the Social and Public Art Resource Center.

Chapter 2

1 I employ the term "world city" while noting the considerable debate surrounding the comparative relevance and analytical utility of both the term "world city" and the related concept of the global city (which is essentially a world city with first-order command functions in the global hierarchy of cities). See *Urban Affairs Review* (33, 4, March 1998) for a trenchant exchange between James W. White, Saskia Sassen, and Michael Peter Smith on the global city concept, particularly regarding the incidence of class and racial–ethnic polarization, and the question of political variables. I continue to deploy the world city concept because of its utility in linking urbanization to global processes. I downplay the aspect of socioeconomic polarization while retaining a sense that globalization is a problematical process that may raise contradictory social and economic consequences in the urban milieu. On the matter of political variables, my argument accounts for the significant role of community contenders as well as local state actors in affecting the pace and direction of globalization and the revalorizing of ethnic places.

2 Christopher Mele's (2000) study of the Lower East Side of New York similarly offers an incisive analysis of the artistic and countercultural pioneers who culturally revalorized the neighborhood, only to be subsequently displaced via gentrification and subcultural appropriation by corporate agents of the global cultural economy.

3 Along with sites such as the Los Angeles Memorial Coliseum and the Watts Tower, the Little Tokyo National Historic Landmark became the 15th in Los Angeles County and the 2,147th in the nation. The designation compels an official review if federal funds or permits are involved in substantial alterations of the landmark but does not absolutely protect the district from future demolition (Gordon 1994).

4 These were the words of the artist at Little Tokyo dedication ceremonies on August 8, 1996. Sheila Levrant de Brettville also designed "Biddy Mason: Time and Place," a commemorative wall documenting the struggles of a freed African American slave woman who journeyed the overland trails to Los Angeles and started a career as a midwife. This is part of an ensemble of public arts and architectural preservation projects called "The Power of Place" (which landmark sites of racial–ethnic, women's, and labor struggle), led by Dolores Hayden of the UCLA program in Architecture and Urban Planning (Hayden 1995).

5 As interpreted by Suellen Cheng and William Estrada, curators with El Pueblo de Los Angeles Historical Monument, in August 1996 field interviews. Acuna (1996: 26–30) gives a perspective of greater intergroup conflict during the negotiations. Museum director Jean Bruce Poole also gave some comments on the history of El Pueblo.

6 The Calle Ocho festival was the brainchild of Leslie Pantin, a Cuban American attorney, who (with partners) borrowed the idea of the Calle Ocho "Open House" from the New Orleans Mardi Gras and Philadelphia ethnic festivals of the 1970s. Wildly successful from its first year, the event has become integrated with a broader "Carnival Miami" festival staged throughout the city, which culminates on its second weekend with the Calle Ocho street festival.

7 The New Otani became the object of a vociferous labor struggle in 1996 when the Hotel Employees and Restaurant Employees Union launched a nationwide boycott of the hotel after management fired three union leaders of a campaign targeting the hotel for labor law abuses.

8 As related by Bruce Kaji, first president of the Little Tokyo Redevelopment Association in the 1960s and founding president of the Japanese-American National Museum in the 1980s, in an August 1996 interview.

9 As discussed by Dan Nip, a Houston Chinatown seafood wholesaler and head of the Houston Chinatown Council, in an August 1992 interview.

10 I suggest also two excellent documentary films that chronicle the interaction of arts communities and gentrification trends. *Division + Western* (2002), by Rachel Rinaldi while she was a graduate student in sociology at the University of Chicago, concerns the experience of Wicker Park. *Boom! The Sound of Eviction* examines these issues in the Mission District of San Francisco (2001).

Chapter 3

1 The concept of fordism was initially coined by Antonio Gramsci. 1971. "Americanism and Fordism," in *Selections from the Prison Notebooks*. New York: International Publishers. The theory of fordism as a "mode of regulation" was subsequently developed by French thinkers, such as M. Aglietta. 1979. *A Theory of Capitalist Regulation*. London: New Left Books, as well as Alain Lipietz. 1982. "Towards Global Fordism?" *New Left Review* 132: 33–47, and "New Tendencies in the International Division of Labor: Regimes of Accumulation and Modes of Regulation." In Scott, A. and M. Storper, eds. 1986. *Production, Work and Territory: The Geographical Anatomy of Industrial Capitalism*. London: Allen and Unwin.

2 Rydell (1993), Chapter 6. He cites oral histories conducted by the Missouri Historical Society that reported that fairgoers were transfixed by the Filipino exhibition.

3 See *Genthe's Photographs of San Francisco's Old Chinatown*, 1984, by Arnold Genthe and John Kuo Wei Tchen. New York: Dover Publications.

4 Bartholdi's other inspiration was reportedly a robed female Egyptian peasant, a *falaha*, with light beaming out from both a headband and a torch thrust dramatically upward into the skies. Its theme was "Progress" or "Egypt Carrying the Light to Asia." It was conceived as a design in a bid for a commission to Egyptian King Isma'il Pasha, in 1867, for a monument to accompany the completion of the Suez Canal. The sculptor envisioned a giant lighthouse standing beside the entrance that would convey the giant magnitude of a canal that pierced the desert from the Mediterranean to the Red Sea. It would be patterned after the Roman goddess Libertas, and twice the size of the Sphinx. But the project was never commissioned.

5 See the link on history on the Statue of Liberty on this webpage of the American Park Network: http://www.americanparknetwork.com/parkinfo/sl/history/liberty.html. The history indicates that Pulitzer raised the subscription of *The World* by 50,000 during the course of the fundraising effort.

6 John Higham. 1975. "Transformation of the Statue of Liberty," in *Send These To Me: Jews and Other Immigrants in Urban America*. New York: Atheneum, pp. 78–87.

7 There was also an amusements area with a rollercoaster, a parachute jump, and a variety of carnival sideshows. The amusement park rides, along with the presence of theme exhibition areas (transportation, communications, etc.) and displays of vernacular culture and architecture, are said to have given Walt Disney inspiration for the Disneyland theme park that he created in the 1950s.

Chapter 4

1 One hundred years later, in 1936, construction began on the San Jacinto Monument, financed partially with federal money. Though taller than the Washington Monument,

this major civic landmark stands alone as somewhat of a historical footnote in the tangle
of refineries, pipelines, and oil field equipment that has sprawled over the vast eastern
sector of the metropolis since oil became its main source of livelihood in the twentieth
century.

2 The "strip" was much vaunted by architect Robert Venturi (Venturi, Brown and Izenour
1972) as the apotheosis of the twentieth-century American urban landscape. The
continuing development of Las Vegas since 1972 has been explored by Alan Hess (1993).

3 This compares with the brooding, sinister, "noir" atmosphere associated with Los
Angeles in the novels of Raymond Chandler and the writing of Mike Davis (1990).

4 Although McMurtry is arguably Houston's best known, nationally-prominent author,
his depiction of a transient place culture might reflect the fact that he personally was
never committed to the city, experiencing only a temporary stay as a member of the
academic and literary community surrounding Rice University.

5 The "Eighth Wonder of the World," gushed Judge Roy Hofheinz, with some Texan
bravado, as promoter and builder of the Astrodome. Artificial grass, or "Astroturf," was
invented and installed on the playing field a year later when it was found that lack of
sunlight hampered the growth of natural grass (American Institute of Architects, 1990).

6 The East End Chamber of Commerce has an Anglo director, but its constituency
includes many Latino business owners.

7 Allens Landing Park commemorates the embarkation point of the Allen brothers, the
original city founders.

8 As discussed with Dan Nip, Chinatown seafood wholesaler and head of the Houston
Chinatown Council.

9 San Felipe Courts was initially inhabited by white defense workers. Lawsuits by the
National Association for Advancement of Colored People (NAACP) in the 1950s
eventually led to the integration of Allen Parkway Village in 1964. By the 1970s, the
housing project was primarily African American.

10 Opponents cried: "Warehousing!"

11 American General turned its investment interest to master-planned development
projects on Houston's exurban western fringe.

12 Personal communication from Sharon Zukin.

13 Houston has been described as a "growth machine" and "free enterprise city" as
compared with Los Angeles as a "dream factory" (Suttles 1984), "city of simulacra"
(Baudrillard 1983), or "theme park city" (Sorkin 1992).

14 Denzin (1992: 19–20) has issued such a call for a "merger," in which postmodernist
cultural studies would be seen as "supplementing—but not replacing," the works of the
classic symbolic interactionists. By the same token, adherents to postmodernism and
cultural studies would gain immensely from a careful reading of symbolic interactionism.

Chapter 5

1 The Jackie Gleason show shifted its filming location from New York City to Miami
Beach in the mid-1960s. Gleason enthusiastically promoted Miami as the "sun and fun
capital of the world" on camera. Gleason boosted tourism for the Florida economy.

2 The Freedomtown detention center did not actually exist. Immigrants under suspicion
of criminal backgrounds were held in Miami's Krome detention center, while the tent
city under the I-95 did not hold prisoners.

3 The Atlantis Condominium, completed in 1982, is a 20-story building with a glass facade
and pastel color scheme. A five-story palm court is cut out of the building that features
a red spiral staircase, Jacuzzi and palm tree.

4 Architect Clyde Judson in a June 2007 interview I conducted with him reported this. Lucas Lechuga, P.A., a real estate professional who maintains a website called miamicondoinvestments.com, in a July 21, 2007 blog entitled, "How Bad Can Things Get for the Miami Condo Market?" concurs.

5 DPZ was co-founded by Elizabeth Plater-Zyberk and her husband, Andres Duany. Elizabeth Plater-Zyberk is also dean of the University of Miami School of Architecture.

6 An interesting fact is that Andres Duany and his wife Elizabeth Plater-Zyberk were initially among the founders of Arquitectonica, along with Bernardo Fort-Brescia and his wife, Laurinda Hope Spear, in 1977, when it started as an experimental studio working in postmodern architecture, interior design, and urban planning. After DPZ was founded in 1980, it began to diverge from the path taken by Arquitectonica, which is now an international leader in the market for high-tech modern skyscrapers.

7 Another source I used here was the exhibit "100 Years of Architecture in Miami," a Centennial Exhibition displayed at the Miami Main Branch Library, June 15 to September 15, 1996.

8 There is also a middle-class Nicaraguan American neighborhood in Sweetwater on the western fringes of Dade County.

9 This information was taken from two articles by Karen Hochman, entitled, "Calle Ocho Walk of Fame" and "The Celebrities of the Walk of Fame," which are published on this website: http://www.education.miami.edu/ep/LittleHavana/index.html. Karen Hochman was a student in a Learning Community Project called "Exploring the Culture of Little Havana," taught at the School of Education, the College of Arts and Science and Eaton Residential College, University of Miami by Professors Eugene F. Provenzo, Jr. and Rafael Montes. The student papers, which incorporated newspaper and library research as well as interviews, are published on the website.

10 Kris Smith was previously an employee of the Black Archives. When he subsequently moved to LISC, Irby McKnight of the Empowerment Trust reported that this shifted his impression of LISC in a more positive direction.

Chapter 6

1 See Chapter 2 of Jean Pfaelzer's book, *Driven Out: The Forgotten War Against Chinese Americans* (New York: Random House, 2007) for an excellent review of the incident.

2 Many maps and historical sources list the racial epithet "Nigger Alley" as the name of the district.

3 See historical description and photographs at http://www.camla.org/garnier/garnier.htm, a website operated by CAMLA.

4 A residential and commercial satellite of the City Market settlement would eventually emerge further south, near the intersection of East Adams and San Pedro. This was also a multiethnic neighborhood, with Chinese and non-Chinese blocks, and is explored during its heyday from the 1930s to the 1950s, in the documentary film *East Adams Revisited*, created by Will Gow and Jennifer Cho.

5 "It's Chinatown, Jake," says the vice cop at the end of the film *Chinatown* (1973, directed by Roman Polanski), implying that crime and sin in Chinatown can never be cleaned up. Chinatown is implicated in the film as a symbol of the moral corruption that lies in the heart of the metropolis. The film draws from real historical incidents in the first two decades of the twentieth century, surrounding the diversion of water from the Owens Valley of the Sierra Nevada to Los Angeles through an aqueduct plan led by William Mulholland, chief of the Department of Water and Power. Screenwriter Robert Towne fictionalized the events and moved the setting to the 1930s, contributing to the *film noir* quality of the movie.

6 The taxi-dance hall was an establishment of the early twentieth century where dancers (usually women) were paid a commission to dance with patrons (typically men). The sociologist Paul Cressey published an ethnographic study of the phenomenon, *The Taxi-Dance Hall: A Sociological Study in Commercialized Recreation and City Life*. Chicago: University of Chicago Press, 1932.

7 The corporation was formed through the U.S.-born children of these founding families and associations, who were American citizens. The parents were prohibited from naturalized citizenship and property ownership because of the Chinese Exclusion Act, 1882 and the Alien Land Law, 1913.

8 The site was near an old bullring that was active before the 1850s, when the area was the Mexican settlement of Sonoratown. The district then became Frenchtown, and Little Italy, successively (Ling 2001).

9 The many amusement rides and stage-set representations of vernacular architecture at the 1939 New York World's Fair are said to have inspired Walt Disney when he created Disneyland in the 1950s.

10 See this webpage for an image and description of the mural: http://www.sparcmurals.org/present/cmt/jb.html.

11 When Mandarin Plaza opened, the major tenant was China Native Products, the first retail store to bring in goods from the People's Republic of China (PRC), which previously the Chinese had avoided because of the political conflict between Taiwan and the PRC. The early 1970s were a time of normalization of relations between the PRC and U.S. Many of the Southeast Asian migrants and other dialect groups began to arrive and Chinatown began to really diversify. Eugene Moy, a member of the Chinese Historical Society of Southern California in a November 2005 interview, made these points.

12 See Timothy Fong (1994) for the rise of suburban Chinatown of Monterey Park, and Wei Li (1999) on the expansion of the Chinese "ethnoburb" into adjoining San Gabriel cities.

Chapter 7

1 Thomas Yu of Asian Americans for Equality coined this term in an August 2005 interview.

2 The work of the Rebuild Chinatown Initiative can be found on the webpage: www.rebuildchinatown.org.

3 See Associated Press, "Bus Battle Might Be Behind Crime," *The Washington Post*, November 30, 2003, p. A11.

4 Barry Newman. "Street Smarts: On the East Coast, Chinese Buses Give Greyhound a Run," *The Wall Street Journal*, January 28, 2005, p. A1.

5 See Adam Fifield, "The Knockoff Squad," *The New York Times*, June 23, 2002, for a report of police investigation against the counterfeit and trademark infringement trade in New York's Chinatown, p. 14.1.

6 Dennis Hevesi. 2003. "Chinatown Journey: From Protesters to Developers," *The New York Times*, January 12, Real Estate, Section 11, p. 11.1.

Chapter 8

1 See *City and Community*, 5, 3, September 2006 for a retrospective symposium of essays on the legacy of Jane Jacobs on the occasion of her death in 2006, including contributions by Herbert J. Gans, Barry Wellman, Sharon Zukin, Peter Dreier, Philip Kasinitz, and David Halle.

BIBLIOGRAPHY

Abramian-Mott, Alexandria. 2003. "Orient Express: Once Sleepy, Now Hot, L.A.'s Chinatown Strives for a Balance between Newfound Prosperity and Artistic Soul," *Sunset* (October), pp. 34–38.

Abu-Lughod, Janet. 1994. *From Urban Village to East Village: The Battle for New York's Lower East Side*. Oxford, UK: Blackwell Publishers.

——. 1995. "Comparing Chicago, New York, and Los Angeles: Testing Some World Cities Hypotheses." In *World Cities in World-System*, edited by P. L. Knox and P. J. Taylor. Cambridge: Cambridge University Press, pp. 171–91.

Acuna, R. 1996. *Anything but Mexican: Chicanos in Contemporary Los Angeles*. New York: Verso.

Adams, Marilyn. 2005. "Condo Development on Miami Coast is Hot, Hotter, Hottest," *USA Today*, April 20, Section Money, p. B2.

Aguilar-San Juan, Karin. 2005. "Staying Vietnamese: Community and Place in Orange County and Boston," *City and Community* 4, 1 (March): 37–65.

——. 2009. *Staying Vietnamese: Community and Place in Orange County and Boston*. Minneapolis: University of Minnesota Press.

Allen, James P. and Eugene Turner. 1997. *The Ethnic Quilt: Population Diversity in Southern California*. Northridge, CA: California State University, the Center for Geographical Studies.

Alliance for the Arts. 2003. *Culture Builds New York: The Economic Impact of Capital Construction at New York City Cultural Institutions*. New York: Alliance of the Arts.

Alonso, Gastón. 2007. "Selling Miami: Tourism Promotion and Immigrant Neighborhoods in the Capital of Latin America." In *Tourism, Ethnic Diversity and the City*, edited by Jan Rath. New York: Routledge, pp. 164–80.

American Institute of Architects. 1972. *Houston: An Architectural Guide*. Houston: American Institute of Architects.

——. 1990. *Houston: Architectural Guide*. Houston: American Institute of Architects and Herring Press.

Anderton, Frances. 2001. "Chinatown Reborn as a Bohemian Outpost," *New York Times*, June 3, Section 9, p. 7.

Appadurai, Arjun. 1990. "Disjuncture and Difference in the Global Cultural Economy," *Public Culture* 2, 2: 1–21.

Arthur, Lisa. 2006. "Overtown Residents Celebrate First Homes," *Miami Herald*, September 25. Available online at http://www.floridacdc.org/articles/060925-1.html. Retrieved July 1, 2009.

Asian American Federation of New York. 2002. *Chinatown One Year after September 11th: An Economic Impact Study*. New York: Asian American Federation of New York.

Barber, Benjamin. 1995. *Jihad vs. McWorld: How Globalism and Tribalism are Reshaping the World*. New York: Random House.

Barna, Joel W. 1992. *The See-Through Years*. Houston: Rice University Press.

Baudrillard, Jean. 1983. *Simulations*. New York: Semiotext(e).

Baum, Geraldine. 2004. "Chinese History is on the Menu in NYC: A Museum Tells the Story of the Immigrant Diaspora through an Old L.A. Restaurant," *Los Angeles Times*, March 14, p. A20.

Beauregard, Robert. 2003. *Voices of Decline: The Postwar Fate of U.S. Cities* (2nd edition). New York: Routledge.

Berkowitz, Michael. 2001. "A 'New Deal' for Leisure: Making Mass Tourism during the Great Depression." In *Being Elsewhere: Tourism, Consumer Culture, and Identity in Modern Europe and North America*, edited by Shelley Baranowski and Ellen Furlough. Ann Arbor: University of Michigan Press, pp. 185–212.

Berman, Marshall. 1983. *All That is Solid Melts into Air*. New York: Verso.

Bhabha, Homi K. 1994. *The Location of Culture*. London: Routledge.

Bodnar, John. 1992. *Remaking America: Public Memory, Commemoration, and Patriotism in the Twentieth Century*. Princeton: Princeton University Press.

Booth, Cathy. 1993. "Miami: The Capital of Latin America," *Time* 142, 21 (Fall): 82–86.

Borrup, Tom. 2003. "Creative Organizations: Putting Culture to Work in Community Development," a report on The Role of Arts and Culture in the Community Development Initiative of "Active Public Space," part of the Ford Foundation Asset Building and Community Development Program. Reprinted by the Community Arts Network at http://www.communityarts.net/readingroom/archivefiles/2004/01/creative_organi.php.

Bourdieu, Pierre. 1984. *Distinction: A Social Critique of the Judgment of Taste*. Translated by Richard Nice. Cambridge, MA: Harvard University Press.

Bowles, Samuel and Herbert Gintis. 1976. *Schooling in Capitalist America*. London: Routledge.

Boyer, M. Christine. 1994. *The City of Collective Memory: Its Historical Imagery and Architectural Entertainments*. Cambridge, MA: MIT Press.

Bullard, Robert. 1987. *Invisible Houston: The Black Experience in Boom and Bust*. College Station: Texas A&M University Press.

Burawoy, Michael. 2007. "For Public Sociology." In *Public Sociology: Fifteen Eminent Sociologists Debate Politics and the Profession in the Twenty-First Century*, edited by Dan Clawson, Robert Zussman, Joya Misra, and Naomi Gerstel. Berkeley: University of California Press, pp. 23–66.

Burgess, Ernest. [1925] 1967. "The Growth of the City: An Introduction to a Research Project." In *The City*, edited by R. E. Park, Ernest Burgess, and Roderick McKenzie. Chicago: University of Chicago Press, pp. 47–62.

Bush, Gregory W. 1999. "'Playground of the USA': Miami and the Promotion of Spectacle," *Pacific Historical Review* 68, 2: 153–72.

Buttenweiser, Ann L. 1987. *Manhattan Water-Bound: Planning and Developing Manhattan's Waterfront from the Seventeenth Century to the Present.* New York: New York University Press.

Caro, Robert. 1975. *The Power Broker: Robert Moses and the Fall of New York.* New York: Vintage Books.

Cash, Stephanie and David Ebony. 2005. "Bloomberg's Gift to NYC," *Art in America* 93, 8 (September): 176.

Center for an Urban Future. 2002. "The Creative Engine: How Arts and Culture in Fueling Economic Growth in New York City Neighborhoods." New York: Center for an Urban Future, November. Available online at www.nycfuture.org. Retrieved July 1, 2009.

Cheng, Suellen and Munson Kwok. 1988. "The Golden Years of Los Angeles Chinatown: The Beginning." In *Los Angeles Chinatown: The Golden Years, 1938–1988.* Los Angeles: Los Angeles Chamber of Commerce, pp. 39–47.

Chin, Amy. 2004. "Cultural Center Will Build on Chinatown's Strengths," *Downtown Express* 16, 43 (March 26–April 1). Available online at http://www.downtownexpress.com/de_46/culturalcenterwill.html. Retrieved July 1, 2009.

Clark, Terry Nichols, ed. 2004. *The City as an Entertainment Machine*, a special issue of *Research in Urban Policy*, Vol. 19. Oxford, UK: Elsevier Ltd.

Cocks, Catherine. 2001a. *Doing the Town: The Rise of Urban Tourism in the United States, 1850–1915.* Berkeley: University of California Press.

——. 2001b. "The Chamber of Commerce's Carnival: City Festivals and Urban Tourism in the United States, 1890–1915." In *Being Elsewhere: Tourism, Consumer Culture, and Identity in Modern Europe and North America*, edited by Shelley Baranowski and Ellen Furlough. Ann Arbor: University of Michigan Press, pp. 89–107.

Conforti, J. 1996. "Ghettos as Tourism Attractions," *Annals of Tourism Research* 23, 4: 830–42.

Congress for the New Urbanism. 1999. In Leccese, Michael and Kathleen McCormick, eds. *Charter of the New Urbanism.* New York: McGraw-Hill Professional.

Corcoran, Monica. 2003. "In Chinatown, Bohemia," *New York Times*, July 27, Section 9, p. 7.

Corkern, Milton. 2004. "Heritage Tourism: Where Public and Private History Don't Always Meet," *American Studies International* 42, 2/3 (July/Oct): 7–17.

Corral, Oscar. 2004. "$150 Million Development Project Eyed for Overtown," *Miami Herald*, May 17. Available online at http://www.floridacdc.org/articles/040517-1.htm. Retrieved July 1, 2009.

Craven, Jonathan. 2001. "Hot Art Scene: Chung King Road," *Rolling Stone*, August 30, Issue 876, p. 78.

Croucher, Sheila L. 1997. *Imagining Miami: Ethnic Politics in a Postmodern World.* Charlottesville: University Press of Virginia.

Cuff, Dana. 1989. "Mirrors of Power: Reflective Professionals in the Neighborhood." In *The Power of Geography*, edited by Jennifer Wolch and Michael Dear. Boston: Unwin Hyman, pp. 331–50.

Cutter, Kimberly. 2001. "East Side Story: Once a Wasteland of Stripmalls and Auto Shops, L.A.'s East Side is Emerging as a Fertile Ground for Artists." *W Magazine*, September, pp. 204–09.

Dávila, Arlene. 2001. *Latinos, Inc.: The Marketing and Making of a People.* Berkeley, CA: University of California Press.

Dávila, Arlene. 2004. *Barrio Dreams: Puerto Ricans, Latinos, and the Neoliberal City*. Berkeley, CA: University of California Press.

Davis, Mike. 1985. "Urban Renaissance and the Spirit of Postmodernism." *New Left Review* 151 (May/June): 106–13.

———. 1987. "Chinatown Part Two? The 'Internationalization' of Downtown Los Angeles." *New Left Review* 164: 65–86.

———. 1990. *City of Quartz: Excavating the Future in Los Angeles*. London: Verso.

Davis, Susan G. 1986. *Parades and Power: Street Theatre in Nineteenth Century Philadelphia*. Philadelphia: Temple University Press.

Dear, Michael. 1986. "Postmodernism and Planning," *Environment and Planning D: Society and Space* 4: 367–84.

De Leon, Arnoldo. 1989. *Ethnicity in the Sunbelt: A History of Mexican Americans in Houston*. Houston: University of Houston Press.

Del Campo, Deserae. 2006. "Miami Issues $12 Million Grant, Permit for Overtown Project," *Miami Herald*, November 2. Available online at www.miamitodaynews.com. Retrieved July 1, 2009.

Denzin, Norman. 1992. *Symbolic Interactionism and Cultural Studies: The Politics of Interpretation*. Cambridge: Blackwell Publishers.

Deverell, William. 2004. *Whitewashed Adobe: The Rise of Los Angeles and the Remaking of Its Mexican Past*. Berkeley: University of California Press.

Di Justo, Patrick. 2006. "Manhattan Projects," *Wired* 14, 12 (December): 52–54.

Dietsch, Deborah K. 2000. "Blast From the Past: Return of the Shotgun," *The Washington Post*, July 29, Design section, p. C2.

Dixon, Terrell. 1979. "Houston, Houston, Houston: McMurtry's View of the City," *The Houston Review: History and Culture of the Gulf Coast* 1, 2 (Fall): 91–102.

Durkheim, Emile. [1912] 2008. *The Elementary Forms of the Religious Life*. Translated by Joseph Ward Swain. Mineola, NY: Dover Publications.

Espiritu, Y. L. 1992. *Asian American Panethnicity*. Philadelphia: Temple University Press.

Esser, Josef and Joachim Hirsch. 1989. "The Crisis of Fordism and the Dimensions of a 'Postfordist' Regional and Urban Structure," *International Journal of Urban and Regional Research* 13, 3 (September): 117–437.

Evans, Graeme. 2003. "Hard-Branding the Cultural City—From Prado to Prada," *International Journal of Urban and Regional Research* 27, 2 (June): 417–41.

Fainstein, S. S., N. I. Fainstein, R. C. Hill, D. Judd, and M. P. Smith. 1986. *Restructuring the City: The Political Economy of Urban Redevelopment* (revised edition). New York: Longman.

Fante, John. [1939] 1980. *Ask the Dust*. Santa Barbara, CA: Black Sparrow Press.

Feagin, Joe R. 1988. *Free Enterprise City*. New Brunswick, N.J.: Rutgers University Press.

Fields, Dorothy Jenkins. 1998. "Tracing Overtown's Vernacular Architectecture," *Journal of Decorative and Propaganda Arts* 23 (Florida Theme Issue): 323–32.

Fifield, Adam. 2002. "The Knockoff Squad," *New York Times*, June 23, p. 14.

Firey, Walter. 1945. "Sentiment and Symbolism as Ecological Variables," *American Sociological Review* 10 (April): 140–48.

Fisher, Robert. 1989. "Urban Policy in Houston, Texas," *Urban Studies* 26: 144–54.

Florida, Richard. 2002. *The Rise of the Creative Class*. New York: Basic Books.

Florida, Richard and A. Jonas. 1991. "U.S. Urban Policy: The Postwar State and Capitalist Regulation," *Antipode: A Journal of Radical Geography* 23, 4: 349–84.

Fong, Timothy. 1994. *The First Suburban Chinatown: The Remaking of Monterey Park, California*. Philadelphia: Temple University Press.

Friedmann, J. and G. Wolff. 1982. "World City Formation: An Agenda for Research and Action," *International Journal of Urban and Regional Research* 6, 3: 309–44.

Gabaccia, Donna. 1998. *We Are What We Eat: Ethnic Food and the Making of Americans*. Cambridge, MA: Harvard University Press.

Gans, Herbert. 1962. *The Urban Villagers: Group and Class in the Life of Italian-Americans*. New York: Free Press.

——. 1979. "Symbolic Ethnicity: The Future of Ethnic Groups and Cultures in America," *Ethnic and Racial Studies* 2, 1: 1–20.

Garreau, Joel. 1991. *Edge City*. New York: Doubleday.

Garrett, Wilbur E. and Kenneth Garrett. 1989. "La Ruta Maya," *National Geographic* (October): 424–79.

George, Paul S. 1991. *The Dr. Paul George Walking Tour of East Little Havana*. Miami, FL: Historical Museum of South Florida.

Gerog, Tomio. 2002. "Rebuilding Chinatown: New York City Activists Call Out for More," *Asian Week* 23, 22 (January 23): 18+.

Gillis, John R. 1994. "Introduction." In *Commemorations: The Politics of National Identity*, edited by John R. Gillis. Princeton: Princeton University Press, pp. 3–24.

Glassberg, David. 2003. "Rethinking the Statue of Liberty: Old Meanings, New Contexts." A paper prepared December, Department of History, University of Massachusetts, Amherst.

Glazer, N. and D. P. Moynihan. 1963. *Beyond the Melting Pot*. Cambridge: MIT Press.

Gordon, Larry. 1994. "A First-Class Landmark," *Los Angeles Times*, June 17, p. B1.

Gordon, Milton M. 1964. *Assimilation in American Life: The Role of Race, Religion and National Origins*. New York: Oxford University Press.

Gotham, Kevin Fox. 2007. *Authentic New Orleans: Tourism, Culture, and Race in the Big Easy*. New York: New York University Press.

Gottdiener, Mark and Joe R. Feagin. 1988. "The Paradigm Shift in Urban Sociology," *Urban Affairs Quarterly* 24, 2 (December): 163–87.

Greenwood, Roberta S. 1996. *Down by the Station: Los Angeles Chinatown, 1880–1933*. Los Angeles: UCLA Institute of Archaeology.

Greer, Scott. 1965. *Urban Renewal and American Cities*. New York: Bobbs-Merrill Company, Inc.

Grosfoguel, Ramon. 1995. "Global Logics in the Caribbean City System: The Case of Miami." In *World Cities in a World-System*, edited by Paul L. Knox and Peter J. Taylor. Cambridge: Cambridge University Press, pp. 156–170.

Hagan, Jacqueline and Nestor Rodriguez. 1992. "Recent Economic Restructuring and Evolving Intergroup Relations in Houston." In *Structuring Diversity: Ethnographic Perspectives on the New Immigration*, edited by Louise Lamphere. Chicago: University of Chicago Press, pp. 145–71.

Haley, Alex. 1976. *Roots: The Saga of an American Family*. New York: Doubleday.

Harkinson, Josh. 2004. "Hitting the Bricks: Preservationists Try to Keep the Pavers from a Fourth Ward Legacy, Brick Streets," *Houston Press*, August 8. Available online at http://www.houstonpress.com/2004-08-12/news/hitting-the-bricks/. Retrieved July 1, 2009.

Harvey, David. 1989. *The Condition of Postmodernity*. Oxford: Basil Blackwell.

Hayden, Dolores. 1995. *The Power of Place: Urban Landscapes as Public History*. Cambridge, MA: MIT Press.

Heldke, Lisa. 2003. *Exotic Appetites: Ruminations of a Food Adventurer*. New York: Routledge.

Hess, Alan. 1993. *Viva Las Vegas: After-Hours Architecture*. San Francisco: Chronicle Books.

Hevesi, Dennis. 2003. "Chinatown Journey: From Protesters to Developers," *New York Times*, January 12, Real Estate, Section 11, p. 11.

Hewison, R. 1987. *The Heritage Industry: Britain in a Climate of Decline*. Methuen: London.

Hobsbawm, Eric and Terence Ranger, eds. 1983. *The Invention of Tradition*. Cambridge: Cambridge University Press.

Hoffman, Lily M. 2003. "The Marketing of Diversity in the Inner City: Tourism and Regulation in Harlem," *International Journal of Urban and Regional Research* 27, 2 (June): 286–99.

hooks, bell. 1992. *Black Looks: Race and Representation*. Boston: South End Press.

Horkheimer, Max and Theodor Adorno. [1947] 2002. *Dialectic of Enlightenment*. Translated by Gunzelin Schmid Noerr. Stanford: Stanford University Press.

Hummon, David M. 1988. "Tourist Worlds: Tourist Advertising, Ritual and American Culture," *Sociological Quarterly* 29, 2 (July): 179–202.

Huxtable, Ada Louise. 1976. *Kicked a Building Lately?* New York: Quadrangle Books.

Ivry, Bob. 2007. "Miami Condo Glut Pushes Florida's Economy to Brink of Recession," Bloomberg.com, July 20.

Jacobs, Jane. 1961. *The Death and Life of Great American Cities*. New York: Vintage.

Jameson, Fredric. 1984. "Postmodernism, or the Cultural Logic of Late Capitalism," *New Left Review* 146 (July/August): 43–92.

Judd, Dennis R. and Todd Swanstrom. 1994. *City Politics: Private Power and Public Policy*. New York: HarperCollins.

Kaplan, Jay. 1996/97. "New York, New York: Cultural Life and Civic Experience in the Global City," *World Policy Journal* 13, 4 (Winter): 53–60.

Kershaw, S. 1997. "The 99 cent American Dream: Pakistani Immigrants Find a Niche in Discount Stores." *New York Times*, January 23, p. B1.

Kim, Elaine H. 2003. "Interstitial Subjects: Asian American Visual Art as a Site for New Cultural Conversations." In *Fresh Talk/Daring Gazes: Conversations on Asian American Art*, edited by Elaine H. Kim, Margo Machida, and Sharon Mizota. Berkeley: University of California Press, pp. 1–50.

Kirshenblatt-Gimblett, Barbara. 1998. *Destination Culture: Tourism, Museums, and Heritage*. Berkeley: University of California Press.

Klein, Norman. 1990. "The Sunshine Strategy: Buying and Selling the Fantasy of Los Angeles." In *Twentieth Century Los Angeles: Power, Promotion, and Social Conflict*, edited by Norman M. Klein and Martin J. Schiesl. Claremont, CA: Regina Books, pp. 1–38.

——. 2004. "Three Chinatowns," an essay in a brochure to accompany a performance piece by Jane Mulfinger, *The Fictive City and Its Real Estate: The Tale of the Transcontinental Railroad*. Los Angeles: Chinese Historical Society of Southern California.

Knox, Paul. 1993. *The Restless Urban Landscape*. Englewood Cliffs, N.J.: Prentice Hall.

Kofman, Jeffrey. 2007. "Miami Condo Boom Goes Bust: Once Hot Real Estate Market Begins to Sag," *ABC News: Frontline*. February 16. Available online at http://abcnews.go.com/Nightline/Business/story?id=2882620&page=1. Retrieved July 1, 2009.

Kotkin, Joel. 2001. *The New Geography*. New York: Random House.

Krase, Jerome. 1999. "The Present/Future of Little Italies," *Brooklyn Journal of Social Semiotics Research* 1, 1 (Spring): 1–22.

Kwon, Beth. 2007. "A Museum Grows in Chinatown," *Columbia Magazine: The Alumni Magazine of Columbia University* (September). Available online at http://www.columbia. edu/cu/alumni/Magazine/Spring2007/MuseumChinatown.html. Retrieved July 1, 2009.

Law, C. M. 1993. *Urban Tourism*. London: Mansell.

Lesh, Carla L. (2003). "Round 18. Project Row Houses." *The Public Historian* 25, 4 (Fall): 116–18.

Lessinger, J. 1995. *From the Ganges to the Hudson: Indian Immigrants in New York City*. Needham Heights, MA: Allyn & Bacon.

Levitt, Peggy. 2001. *The Transnational Villagers*. Berkeley: University of California Press.

Lew, Karen. 1988. "Chinatown: The Present." In commemorative booklet *Chinatown Los Angeles: The Golden Years 1938–1988*. Los Angeles: Chinese Chamber of Commerce, pp. 59, 63.

Li, Wei. 1999. "Building Ethnoburbia: The Emergence and Manifestation of the Chinese Ethnoburb in Los Angeles' San Gabriel Valley," *Journal of Asian American Studies* 2, 1: 1–28.

———. 2009. *Ethnoburb: The New Ethnic Community in Urban America*. Honolulu: University of Hawaii Press.

Light, Ivan. 2006. *Deflecting Immigration: Networks, Markets, and Regulation in Los Angeles*. New York: Russell Sage Foundation.

Lin, Jan. 1995. "Ethnic Places, Postmodernism and Urban Change in Houston," *Sociological Quarterly* 36, 4 (Fall): 501–19.

———. 1998a. "The Reclaiming of Asian Places in Downtown Los Angeles," *Hitting Critical Mass: Journal of Asian American Cultural Criticism* 5, 1 (Spring): 65–87.

———. 1998b. "Globalization and the Revalorizing of Ethnic Places in Immigration Gateway Cities," *Urban Affairs Review* 34, 2 (November): 313–39.

———. 1998c. *Reconstructing Chinatown: Ethnic Enclave, Global Change*. Minneapolis: University of Minnesota Press.

Ling, Susie. 2001. "Our Legacy: History of Chinese Americans in Southern California." In *Bridging the Centuries: History of Chinese Americans in Southern California*. Los Angeles: Chinese Historical Society of Southern California.

Lloyd, Richard. 2006. *Neo-Bohemia: Art and Commerce in the Postindustrial City*. New York: Routledge.

Lofland, Lyn H. 1991. "History, the City, and the Interactionist: Anselm Strauss, City Imagery, and Urban Sociology," *Symbolic Interaction* 14 (2): 205–23.

Logan, John R. and Harvey Molotch. 1987. *Urban Fortunes: The Political Economy of Place*. Berkeley: University of California Press.

Lopate, Phillip. 2000. "Deep in the Heart of Houston," *New York Times*, Sunday Magazine, February 27, p. 20.

Lou, Raymond. 1982. "The Chinese American Community of Los Angeles, 1870–1900: A Case of Resistance, Organization, and Participation." A dissertation in Comparative Culture at the University of California, Irvine.

Luckhurst, Kenneth W. 1951. *The Story of Exhibitions*. New York: The Studio Publications.

Lui, Garding. 1948. *Inside Los Angeles Chinatown*. Los Angeles: Published by Author.

MacCannell, Dean. [1976] 1989. *The Tourist: A New Theory of the Leisure Class* (new edition). New York: Schoken Books.

MacGregor, Hilary. 2001. "L.A. at Large; Visions in Silk; A 'Royal' Procession Adorned in Imperial Costumes Opens the Chinatown Art Festival with Pizzazz," *Los Angeles Times*, June 25, p. E2.

Maines, David R. and Jeffrey C. Bridger. 1992. "Narratives, Community and Land Use Decisions," *Social Science Journal* 29 (4): 363–80.

Matthews, Fred. H. 1977. *The Quest for an American Sociology: Robert E. Park and the Chicago School*. Montreal: McGill-Queen's University Press.

McWilliams, Carey. [1946] 1995. *Southern California: An Island on the Land*. Salt Lake City: Peregrine Smith Books.

Meethan, Kevin. 2004. "To Stand in the Shoes of My Ancestors: Tourism and Genealogy." In *Tourism, Diasporas and Space*. London: Routledge, pp. 139–50.

Mele, Christopher. 1996. "Globalization, Culture, and Neighborhood Change: Reinventing the Lower East Side of New York," *Urban Affairs Review* 32, 1 (September): 3–22.

——. 2000. *Selling the Lower East Side: Culture, Real Estate, and Resistance in New York City*. Minneapolis: University of Minnesota Press.

Mills, C. Wright. [1959] 2000. *The Sociological Imagination* (with afterward by Todd Gitlin). Oxford: Oxford University Press.

Min, Pyong Gap. 1996. *Caught in the Middle: Korean Communities in New York and Los Angeles*. Berkeley: University of California Press.

Mohl, Raymond A. 1993a. "Race and Space in the Modern City: Interstate-95 and the Black Community in Miami." In *Urban Policy in Twentieth-Century America*, edited by Arnold R. Hirsch and Raymond A. Mohl. New Brunswick, NJ: Rutgers University Press, pp. 100–58.

——. 1993b. "Blacks and Hispanics in Multicultural America: A Miami Case Study." In *The Making of Urban America* (2nd edition), edited by Raymond A. Mohl. Wilmington, DE: SR Books, pp. 283–308.

Moore, D. D. 1994. *To the Golden Cities: Pursuing the American Jewish Dream in Miami and L.A.* New York: Free Press.

Mourad, Warnke and Associates. 2002. *Rebuild Chinatown Initiative: The Community Speaks One Year After September 11, 2001*. Consultant's report, convened by Asian Americans for Equality.

Muller, T. 1993. *Immigrants and the American City*. New York: New York University Press.

Mumford, L. 1961. *The City in History*. New York: Harcourt, Brace & World.

Newman, Barry. 2005. "Street Smarts: On the East Coast, Chinese Buses Give Greyhound a Run," *Wall Street Journal*, January 28, p. A1.

Nijman, Jan. 2000. "The Paradigmatic City," *Annals of the Association of American Geographers* 90, 1: 135–45.

Norkunas, Martha K. 1993. *The Politics of Public Memory: Tourism, History, and Ethnicity in Monterey, California*. Albany, NY: State University of New York Press.

——. 2002. *Monuments and Memory: History and Representation in Lowell, Massachusetts*. Washington, D.C.: Smithsonian Institution Press.

Obama, Barack. 1995. *Dreams from My Father: A Story of Race and Inheritance*. New York: Times Books.

Olalquiaga, Celesta. 1992. *Megalopolis: Contemporary Cultural Sensibilities*. Minneapolis: University of Minnesota Press.

Ouroussoff, Nicolai. 1999. "Art and Architecture: Bridging L.A.'s Cultural Divide," *Los Angeles Times*, June 10, p. 47.

Pagel, David. 2001. "Storefront Galleries: In Some Low-Rent Neighborhoods, Art is a Home-Grown Highlight," *Los Angeles Times*, November 11, p. F7.

Park, Kyeyoung and Jessica Kim. 2005. "The Contested Nexus of Los Angeles Koreatown: Capital Restructuring, Gentrification and Displacement," *Amerasia Journal* 34, 3 (2008): 127–50.

Park, Peter, Mary Brydon-Miller, Bud Hall, and Ted Jackson, eds. 1993. *Voices of Change: Participatory Research in the United States and Canada*. Westport, CT: Bergin and Garvey.

Park, Robert E. 1936. "Succession: An Ecological Concept," *American Sociological Review* 1 (April): 171–79.

Park, Robert E. and Ernest W. Burgess, eds. 1925. *The City*. Chicago: Chicago University Press.

Parks, Arva Moore. 1991. *Miami: The Magic City*. Miami, FL: Centennial Press.

Parson, Don. 1993. "The Search for a Centre: The Recomposition of Race, Class and Space in Los Angeles," *International Journal of Urban and Regional Research* 17, 2 (June): 232–40.

———. 2005. *Making a Better World: Public Housing, the Red Scare, and the Direction of Modern Los Angeles*. Minneapolis: University of Minnesota Press.

Pearlstone, Z. 1990. *Ethnic Los Angeles*. Los Angeles: Hillcrest.

Perea, Juan F. 1997. "The Statue of Liberty: Notes from Behind the Gilded Door." In *Immigrants Out! The New Nativism and the Anti-Immigrant Impulse in the United States*, edited by Juan F. Perea. New York: New York University Press, pp. 44–60.

Pessar, P. R. 1995. *A Visa for a Dream: Dominicans in the United States*. Needham Heights, MA: Allyn & Bacon.

Phillips Preiss Shapiro Associates. 2004. *America's Chinatown: A Community Plan*. New York: Asian Americans for Equality.

Pogrebin, Robin. 2005. "Downtown Arts Plan Remains Uncertain," *New York Times*, March 15, p. E1.

Poole, Jean Bruce and Tevvy Ball. 2002. *El Pueblo: The Historic Heart of Los Angeles*. Los Angeles: Getty Publications.

Portes, A. 1996. "Global Villagers: The Rise of Transnational Communities," *American Prospect* 25 (March/April): 74–77.

Portes, A. and Robert Bach. 1985. *Latin Journey: Cuban and Mexican Immigrants in the United States*. Berkeley, CA: University of California Press.

Portes, A. and R. D. Manning. 1986. "The Immigrant Enclave: Theory and Empirical Examples." In *Competitive Ethnic Relations*, edited by S. Olzak and J. Nagel. Orlando, FL: Academic Press, pp. 442–58.

Portes, A. and A. Stepick. 1993. *City on the Edge: The Transformation of Miami*. Berkeley: University of California Press.

Putnam, Robert. 2000. *Bowling Alone: The Collapse and Revival of American Community*. New York: Simon and Schuster.

Rieff, D. 1987. *Going to Miami: Exiles, Tourists, and Refugees in the New America*. Boston: Little, Brown.

———. 1991. *Los Angeles: Capital of the Third World*. New York: Simon & Schuster.

Riis, Jacob. 1890. *How the Other Half Lives: Studies Among the Tenements of New York*. New York: Charles Scribner's Sons.

Ritzer, George. [1993] 2008. *The McDonaldization of Society* (5th edition). Pine Forge Press.

Roberts, Sam and Jim Rutenberg. 2005. "With More Private Giving, Bloomberg Forges Ties," *New York Times*, May 23, p. A1.

Robertson, Roland. 1992. *Globalization: Social Theory and Global Culture*. London: Sage Publications.

Rodriguez, Nestor. 1995. "The Real 'New World Order': The Globalization of Racial and Ethnic Relations in the Late Twentieth Century." In *The Bubbling Cauldron: Race, Ethnicity and the Urban Crisis*, edited by M. P. Smith and J. R. Feagin. Minneapolis: University of Minnesota Press, pp. 211–25.

Rosenau, Pauline Marie. 1992. *Post-Modernism and the Social Sciences: Insights, Inroads, and Intrusions*. Princeton: Princeton University Press.

Ross, Andrew. 2000. *The Celebration Chronicles: Life, Liberty and the Pursuit of Property Value in Disney's New Town*. New York: Ballantine Books.

Rouse, Roger. 1991. "Mexican Migration and the Social Space of Postmodernism," *Diaspora* 1, 1: 8–19.

Rydell, Robert W. 1984. *All the World's a Fair: Visions of Empire at American International Expositions, 1876–1916*. Chicago: University of Chicago Press.

——. 1993. *World of Fairs: The Century-of-Progress Expositions*. Chicago: University of Chicago Press.

Sanders, Jimy M. and Victor Nee. 1987. "Limits of Ethnic Solidarity in the Ethnic Enclave," *American Sociological Review* 52, 6 (December): 745–67.

Sandrow, Nahma. 2001. "The Actors Who Make History Live," *New York Times*, December 30, Section 2, p. 2.

Sassen, Saskia. 1988. *The Mobility of Labor and Capital*. Cambridge: Cambridge University Press.

Sassen, Saskia and Alejandro Portes. 1993. "Miami: A New Global City?" *Contemporary Sociology* 22, 4 (July): 471–77.

Schmidt, Yolita. 1978. *The Moderne Style in Architecture: A Houston Guide*. Houston: Houston Public Library.

Schwartz, Benjamin and Christina. 1999. "Going All Out for Chinese," *Atlantic Monthly* 283, 1: 28–35.

See, Lisa. 1995. *On Gold Mountain: The One-Hundred-Year Odyssey of My Chinese-American Family*. New York: Vintage Books.

Shelton, Beth Anne, Nestor P. Rodriguez, Joe R. Feagin, Robert D. Bullard, and Robert D. Thomas. 1989. *Houston: Growth and Decline in a Sunbelt Boomtown*. Philadelphia: Temple University Press.

Simpson, Moira G. 2001. *Making Representations: Museums in the Post-colonial Era* (revised edition). New York: Routledge.

Smith, Michael Peter. 1992. "Postmodernism, Urban Ethnography, and the New Social Space of Ethnic Identity," *Theory and Society* 21, 4: 493–531.

Smith, Michael Peter and Joe R. Feagin. 1987. *The Capitalist City*. Cambridge, MA: Basil Blackwell.

Soja, Edward. 1990. *Postmodern Geographies: The Reassertion of Space in Critical Social Theories*. London: Verso.

Sorkin, Michael, ed. 1992. *Variations on a Theme Park*. New York: Hill and Wang.

Steinhauer, Jennifer. 2005. "The Arts Administration," *New York Times*, October 23, p. 1.

Stofik, M. Barron. 2005. *Saving South Beach*. Gainesville, FL: University Press of Florida.

Stoller, Paul. 2002. *Money Has No Smell: The Africanization of New York City*. Chicago: University of Chicago Press.

Suttles, Gerald. 1984. "The Cumulative Texture of Local Urban Culture," *American Journal of Sociology* 90, 2 (September): 283–304.

Taylor, Monique. 2002. *Harlem between Heaven and Hell*. Minneapolis: University of Minnesota Press.

Tönnies, Ferdinand. [1887] 1963. *Community and Society*. Translated and edited by C.P. Loomis. New York: Harper and Row.

Urry, John. 2002. *The Tourist Gaze* (revised edition). London: Sage Publications.

Van den Berghe, Pierre L. 1994. *The Quest for the Ethnic Other: Ethnic Tourism in San Cristobal, Mexico*. Seattle: University of Washington Press.

Venturi, Robert, Denise Scott Brown and Steven Izenour. 1972. *Learning from Las Vegas*. Cambridge, Mass.: M.I.T. Press.

Viglucci, Andres. 2006. "Conflict Slows Overtown Project: Two Years after the City of Miami Announced a Plan to Overhaul a Part of Overtown, the Project Lies Dormant," *Miami Herald*, August 7. Available online at http://www.floridacdc.org/articles/060807-1.html. Retrieved July 1, 2009.

Viglucci, Andres and William Yardley. 2003. "New Housing, Retail Space in Works for Overtown after Decades of Broken Promises," *Miami Herald*, July 27. Available online at http://www.floridacdc.org/articles/030803-1.htm. Retrieved July 1, 2009.

Villa, Raul. 2000. *Barrio-Logos: Space and Place in Urban Chicano Literature and Culture*. Austin, TX: University of Texas Press.

Waldinger, R. 1989. "Immigration and Urban Change," *Annual Review of Sociology* 15: 211–32.

Walton, John. 2001. *Storied Land: Community and Memory in Monterey*. Berkeley, CA: University of California Press.

Ward, David. 1989. *Poverty, Ethnicity, and the American City, 1840–1925: Changing Conceptions of the Slum and Ghetto*. Cambridge: Cambridge University Press.

Weaver, John D. 1973. *L.A.: El Pueblo Grande*. Pasadena: Ward Ritchie Press.

Weber, Max. [1905] 2003. *The Protestant Work Ethic and the Spirit of Capitalism*. Translated by Talcott Parsons. Mineola, NY: Dover Publications.

Wilson, Joe and Lee Udall. 1982. *Folk Festivals: A Handbook for Organization and Management*. Knoxville: University of Tennessee Press.

Wilson, Kenneth L. and Alejandro Portes. 1980. "Immigrant Enclaves: An Analysis of the Labor Market Experiences of Cubans in Miami," *American Journal of Sociology* 86, 2 (September): 295–319.

Wilson, Kenneth L. and W. Allen Martin. 1982. "Ethnic Enclaves: A Comparison of the Cuban and Black Economies in Miami," *American Journal of Sociology* 88, 1: 135–60.

Wohl, R. Richard and Anselm L. Strauss. 1958. "Symbolic Representation and the Urban Milieu," *American Journal of Sociology* 63 (March): 523–32.

Wong, Cy. 1988. "Chinatown Landmarks." In commemorative booklet *Los Angeles Chinatown: The Golden Years, 1938–1988*. Los Angeles: Chinese Chamber of Commerce, pp. 23–27.

Wong, Cynthia Sau-ling. 2005. "Denationalization Reconsidered: Asian American Cultural Criticism at a Theoretical Crossroads," *Amerasia Journal* 21, 1/2: 1–27.

World Urban Forum. 2004. *Dialogue on Urban Cultures: Globalization and Culture in an Urbanizing World*. Barcelona, Spain: UN-Habitat World Urban Forum.

Yancey, W. L., E. P. Ericksen, and R. N. Juliani. 1976. "Emergent Ethnicity: A Review and Reformulation," *American Sociological Review* 41, 3: 391–402.

Yeh, Chiou-Ling. 2005. "Celebrating Freedom and Ethnicity," *American Quarterly* 57, 1 (March): 279–88.

Yudice, George. 2005. "Miami: Images of a Latinopolis," *NACLA Report on the Americas*, 39, 3 (November/December): 35–40.

Zeiger, Mimi. 2003. "Lost in Chinatown," *Los Angeles Forum for Architecture and Urban Design* 4 (February 22). Available online at http://www.laforum.org/content/online-articles/lost-in-chinatown-by-mimi-zeiger. Retrieved July 1, 2009.

Zhou, Min. 1992. *Chinatown: The Socioeconomic Potential of an Urban Enclave*. Philadelphia: Temple University Press.

Zhou, Min and John R. Logan. 1989. "Returns on Human Capital in Ethnic Enclaves: New York City's Chinatown," *American Sociological Review* 54 (October): 809–20.

Zorbaugh, Harvey W. 1926. "The Natural Areas of the City." In *The Urban Community*, edited by Ernest W. Burgess. Chicago: University of Chicago Press, pp. 219–29.

Zukin, Sharon. 1980. "A Decade of the New Urban Sociology," *Theory and Society* 9: 539–74.

——. 1982. *Loft Living: Culture and Capital in Urban Change*. Baltimore: Johns Hopkins University Press.

——. 1988. "The Postmodern Debate over Urban Form," *Theory, Culture and Society* 5: 431–46.

——. 1990. *Landscapes of Power: From Detroit to Disney World*. Berkeley: University of California Press.

——. 1995. *The Cultures of Cities*. Cambridge, MA: Blackwell Publishers.

INDEX

Civic Partnership and Design Center
(CPDC) 134
Civil Rights Act (1964) 187
class polarization 204
Cleveland, Grover 74
Cola Nip Bottling Company 130
collective memory 49–50
collective sentiment 240–1
Collins Center for Public Policy 134–9
Columbia (personification of the US) 73
Columbus Park 210, 241
commercialization of folk art 260
Committee to Revitalize and Enrich the
Arts in Tomorrow's Economy in
Chinatown (CREATE) 233, 235, 249
community activism 51–3, 244–5; Los
Angeles 6–8; New York Chinatown
206–7
community development: ethnic heritage,
art and 9–13; ethnic social capital and
53–6; place-based and ethnic-based
238–9, 241–2
community power structures 248–50
Community Redevelopment Agency
(CRA): Los Angeles 41, 186, 202;
Miami 134–5
comparative sociology 20
competition, cutthroat 229
condominium towers 109, 118–21, 123,
124, 158
Consolidated Chinese Benevolent
Association (CCBA) 54, 176, 189, 206
construction boom, Miami 118–21
consumption 58–9
crime: Los Angeles 179; Miami 113–15,
158
Crist, Charlie 120
Cross-Bronx Expressway 78, 88
cross patterns in streets 104
Crosswinds Overtown project 135–9, 250
Crumbley, Sharmin 141
Cruz, Celia 125, 150
Cuban American Freedom Tower 39,
123–6
Cuban American National Foundation 125
Cubans in Miami 36–7, 110, 113, 115–16,
117–18; see also Little Havana
Cullen Center 99
cultural authenticity 234–7, 256–62

cultural center initiative 233–4, 235, 242
cultural heritage 16–17, 23–56; ethnic
place preservation and public history
24–6; ethnic preservation movements
37–42; ethnic social capital and
community development 53–6;
globalization and renewal of ethnic
places 32–7; glocalization and
global–local dynamics 46–50; local
culture and ethnic history 50–3;
removal and renewal of ethnic
communities 27–31; transnational
capitalism and postindustrial growth
machines 42–6
cultural ownership 234–7
culture 32–3, 46; Houston 84–7; local see
local culture; Los Angeles Chinatown
192–8; Miami 108–9, 110, 142–5,
152–8, 161, 162, 163, 164; New York
229–34
Czolgosz, Leon 69

decentralization 90–1
decline 48–9
deflected immigration 227–9, 246–7
deindustrialization 34, 42–3, 48–9
Delano grape fields 7–8
Denkler, Joan 99
Department of Housing and Urban
Development (HUD) 100, 122
diaspora, Chinese 212–14
Diaz, Manny 117, 121
disinvestment 55, 245–8
'Division of the Barrios' mural 79, 186
Dodger Stadium 79, 186
Dorsey House 130, 131, 132
'Downtown Overtown' project 135–6
dragon, Chinese 177–8
drive-to-maturity period of capitalism
57–8, 61, 61–72, 80; Los Angeles
Chinatown 167–8, 169, 170–9
Duany Plater-Zyberk (DPZ) 121–2, 126,
133, 139, 253, 256, 267
Durkheim, Emile 9

early modernism 83–4
East Coast 1–4
East End Area Chamber of Commerce
93